The Voyage to Excellence

The Ascent of 21 Women Leaders of India Inc.

The Voyage to Excellence

The Ascent of 21 Women Leaders of India Inc.

Conceptualized
Written
&
Promoted by

Nischinta Amarnath

Debashish Ghosh

PUSTAK MAHAL®
Delhi • Bangalore • Mumbai • Patna • Hyderabad

Publishers
Pustak Mahal, Delhi-110006

Sales Centres
- 6686, Khari Baoli, Delhi-110006, *Ph:* 23944314, 23911979
- 10-B, Netaji Subhash Marg, Daryaganj, New Delhi-110002
  Ph: 23268292, 23268293, 23279900 • *Fax:* 011-23280567
  E-mail: rapidexdelhi@indiatimes.com

Administrative Office
J-3/16 (Opp. Happy School), Daryaganj, New Delhi-110002
Ph: 23276539, 23272783, 23272784 • *Fax:* 011-23260518
E-mail: info@pustakmahal.com • *Website:* www.pustakmahal.com

Branch Offices

BANGALORE: 22/2, Mission Road (Shama Rao's Compound), Bangalore-560027, *Ph:* 22234025 • *Fax:* 080-22240209
E-mail: pmblr@sancharnet.in • pustak@sancharnet.in

MUMBAI: 23-25, Zaoba Wadi (Opp. VIP Showroom), Thakurdwar, Mumbai-400002
Ph: 22010941 • *Fax:* 022-22053387
E-mail: rapidex@bom5.vsnl.net.in

PATNA: Khemka House, 1st Floor (Opp. Women's Hospital), Ashok Rajpath, Patna-800004
Ph: 3094193 • *Telefax:* 0612-2302719
E-mail: rapidexptn@rediffmail.com

HYDERABAD: 5-1-707/1, Brij Bhawan, Bank Street, Koti, Hyderabad-500095, *Telefax:* 040-24737290
E-mail: pustakmahalhyd@yahoo.co.in

I.S.B.N.: 81-223-0904-6

Edition : April 2005

Printed at : Param Offsetters, Okhla-I, New Delhi-20

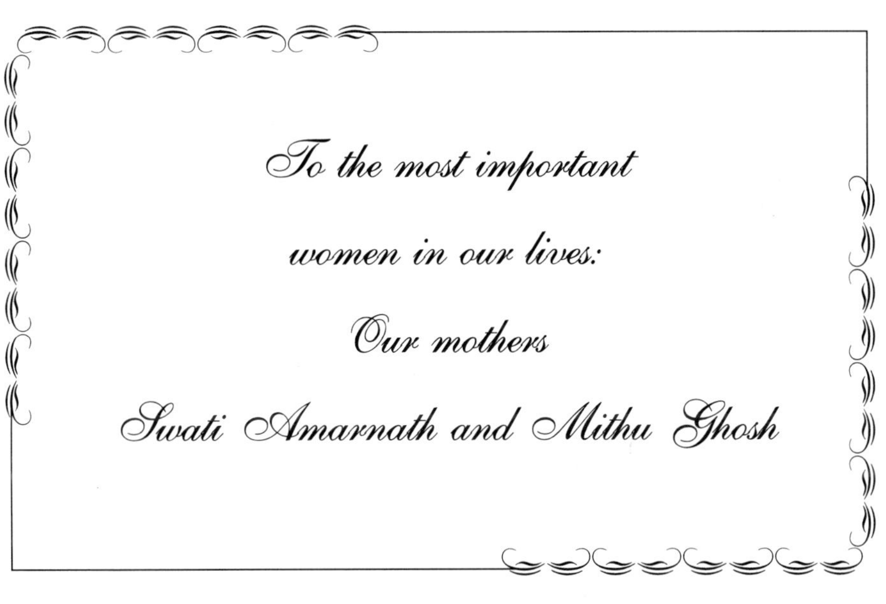

To the most important

women in our lives:

Our mothers

Swati Amarnath and Mithu Ghosh

Acknowledgments

We owe the successful completion of this project to the love, strength and support we derived from our families and contributors.

Many 'Thanks' to Mrs. Gita and Mr. Ashok Nambissan for their wholehearted involvement in our dream venture and a wonderful stay in Mumbai. We enjoyed many lighter moments with Sweta and Ujjwal Nambissan, who not only helped us unwind and de-stress but considered themselves a part of our team too.

Thanks are in order to Mr. Vijay Kumar, who coordinated our activities in Delhi with great gusto even amidst his pressing business commitments and hectic travel. Every time we received a call from him, we could imagine him smiling at the other end, notwithstanding our hardest efforts to jerk him into action!

We are grateful to Mr. Brian Caszo (Former Principal) and Mrs. Geeta Rajan (Teacher of Economics) of the Sishya School, whose inspiration forms a core ingredient of the book. To Mrs. Geeta Rajan, who reviewed our concepts for the book as well as Mr. K.T. Jaganathan (Senior Assistant Editor, The Hindu) and Dr. Rita Jacob Cherian (Principal, Women's Christian College, Chennai) who critically evaluated certain portions of our manuscript, thanks.

A project of this magnitude could never have been completed without the help of the business and corporate heads, who spared their valuable time for the interviews and validated our work (even amidst unimaginably tight work timetable and travel programmes), with the executive assistants and corporate communications managers pitching in to streamline the progress.

A special mention about the friends and professors at the Department of Management Studies, IIT, Madras whose support and inspiration lay with us, right through.

Furthermore, words cannot describe the sacrifices our families have made for us to make this project possible. Our gratitude to Mr. R. Amarnath, who helped us in the execution of the project and shared his profound knowledge and expertise with us right through.

Mr. Rohit Gupta and his team from Pustak Mahal have played an indispensable role in the making of the book.

Our sincerest thanks to all of you.

Finally, we won't forget to thank each other. *Hey buddy that's a cool job done*! We would consider ourselves successful, if the stories of these leaders can inspire you to soar to greater heights.

–The Authors

interviewees could not keep up their commitment due to lack of time. But we had the satisfaction of having contacted all the leading businesswomen in the country.

In the twenty-one stories that follow, each woman (or group of women) has achieved an extraordinary feat, which makes her stand apart. The list is not exhaustive by any means; nevertheless, it is an embodiment of the resurgent face of Indian women.

Women in business have begun to exert a greater influence at the workplace. As more such icons are created, newer breeds of women leaders are springing up at different levels of various organizations. Yet, statistics claim that the percentage of women who hold senior positions in the corporate world across the country is far from significant. Recruiters and women career contenders must reflect on what action can and should be taken to effect a change. In the face of the disintegration of joint families today and the fast-paced expansion of nuclear families, women of the progressive future generations may have to scour for a closer substitute for the joint family.

Moving on to the issue of gender disparity, we believe that success does not support gender; the traits required for success are not gender-sensitive. While the age-old term 'proprietress' was long since abolished, lady film celebrities are being referred to as 'actors' today. Yet, lady business heads continue to be addressed as 'chairpersons'. In the book, we have chosen to refrain from employing the term 'chairperson' for our lady CEOs, resorting to the use of 'chairman' instead.

As against their foreign counterparts, Indian women pride themselves on certain intrinsic strengths. However, they are bound by specific limitations of social infrastructures and the non-availability of such support systems as crèches at workplaces, attributable to our poor social systems, which adversely affect the development of the career women.

Each story carries a glimpse into certain traits, which have made these ladies the best in their chosen fields. This, we believe, would inspire women to ward off social barriers and shatter the glass ceiling, both of which are so very desirable to achieve the national objective of balanced growth. Though no particular quality has been found to emerge as the elixir of all ailments, there is a unity in the diversity of their leadership traits.

We have covered ladies who head a diverse range of business sectors – right from traditional fields like banks and the sugar and engineering industries to modern businesses like hospitality management, fashion, art, media and

Preface

The Voyage to Excellence is the product of a partnership and competition between two students from the streams of economics and business management. Given our academic backgrounds, business was a natural source of attraction for us.

Our book is a compendium of the stories of an exclusive galaxy of women industry leaders who have redefined the standards of the industries they lead, contributing substantially to the social, economic and entrepreneurial growth and development of India.

Today, the economic scenario is much conducive to the growth and development of entrepreneurship on the national and global scales. And the world is throwing up myriad opportunities for young achievers who seek to carve a niche for themselves in the international arena of business. Through this book, we seek to encourage women to draw inspiration from the successes and achievements of some of the best ladies in Indian business, each of whom has not only won global repute but also turned in sterling performances in the most challenging of circumstances, conquered the odds and influenced changes at every level by their diligence and sheer dint of merit.

Besides, the book would draw the attention of menfolk to the challenges these women have conquered (notwithstanding numerous obstacles on both the home and career fronts) and motivate students who are on the threshold of choosing their career paths. The language is not wholly technical. We have been careful to present an appropriate combination of light reading and information on various aspects of business.

Our work spanned across a year. Our 'Lady Biz Barons' venture not only put our writing skills to test, but also served as a full-fledged project management exercise, which taught us to deliver with precision. We had a wonderful time touring across India (Mumbai, Delhi, Bangalore, Pune and Coimbatore to name a few) at split-second notices. We transcribed tapes, wrote and rustled up more ideas even during the course of our train journeys – as students, we never had the luxury of flights.

Appointments were cancelled and an interview was discontinued mid-way, while many others were re-scheduled. We surmised that our potential

❖❄❖

Contents

entertainment, including the globally competitive biotech barons and rural entrepreneurs, who carry the unique flavour of India.

Neither education nor geography is a barrier if one truly aspires to be successful. These women have proven this fact with their stupendous success. They were hardly conscious of their gender as they immersed themselves in their work. A handful of them have weathered personal crises in their lives. These crises probably strengthened them from within and developed in them a desire to achieve the best not only in their quest for academic excellence during their halcyon school days but also in terms of the early recognition of merit during the course of their careers. Some other women contend that age is no barrier in business. They earned their success after considerable struggle, establishing the best-quality enterprises. Perhaps, their experience worked as an asset.

Here is a glimpse into the core values each of these ladies radiates, carving a distinctive identity for herself.

Effective People Managers

These successful businesswomen were found to be very sensitive to the needs of their employees. They have created a well-proportioned blend of care and discipline to build strong, likeminded teams, whose strength has made these seemingly ordinary ladies extraordinary and powerful leaders.

Creativity Arousers

They dare to think differently, each of them boldly straining away from the usual mould. They do not view work as 'work'. For them, work is all about forging dreams and realizing them. They are also wilful risk-takers who create opportunities and excel in their attempts. It was their desire to be and do something different that translated their thoughts and dreams into world-class organizations.

Goal Seekers and 'Change' Masters

Every successful leader continuously fixes targets, setting progressively higher ones each time to leave her imprint in every project that she had undertaken. All women feel that one should enjoy one's work in order to be the best at it. Also, they have operated successfully in environments that have brought forth a barrage of instabilities. It is their power and status that enabled them to induce change at various levels of society and impact many lives.

Multi-tasking Specialists and Efficient Time Managers

Women business heads are often more successful in multi-tasking their activities compared to male counterparts. Most of them have an astute sense of time. While many firmly believe in prioritising their tasks to achieve equilibrium in their quest to find harmony between their personal and professional lives, some others have attained this balance by integrating their homes and careers. In striking contrast, a few others chose to compartmentalize the two. Even in the midst of immense pressures, they have never defaulted on their balancing act.

Socially Sensitive Leaders

These tycoons unequivocally view that corporate entities should shoulder social responsibilities, without which their existence would have little meaning. Women who have seen long-standing success received unconditional love and support from their husbands and families. Some of them didn't have the support right through. However, they tactfully transformed the initial opposition into wholehearted support through sheer persistence and commitment.

The content and style of the stories have been influenced by the time that was available with the business leaders as well as their degree of eloquence and extroversion. With a view to providing more variety to our readers, we have conceptualised the text in accordance with the nature of the ladies' domains of business. We have presented various facts and figures on the basis of statements made by the interviewees and/or their authorized staff, as well as information sources available in the public domain. The book is not about defining business and entrepreneurship but about celebrating the spirit.

In the pages that follow, we have attempted to capture the insights from some of the best-run corporations, worldwide. We have not adhered to any particular order in which the stories must be read – that is entirely at our readers' discretion. You can even start with the appendix and quiz your abilities to manage the real-life situations and challenges of business! Our stories are not only reflections of the triumphs and tribulations of Indian lady business leaders, but also bring to light their sound strategies and the meticulous execution of their plans and tasks.

For us, this venture is nothing less than a pilgrimage into the minds and spirits of the successful thought leaders of the present century. Here is our tribute to the women who dared to make their mark against all odds. It is a celebration of 'Indian Women at Work'.

–The Authors

In Her Eyes

Many women today, in the corporate world and in other fields, are being recognised for their contributions in the economic and social sphere. This new wave is fairly recent and a welcome development in a country like ours. I must congratulate the young authors of this collection of bio-sketches of Indian women business leaders for bringing to life their vision, passions and determination to make a difference. The 21 successful women profiled here – some of whom I know personally – make excellent role models for other women to emulate and for men to better understand the changing aspirations and priorities of women in today's times.

I think this is probably the first time that two students have undertaken an ambitious project like this. What I found noteworthy is that they have approached the subject with sensitivity and a sense of objectivity. Their effort will no doubt inspire other young authors to delve into business and social issues and bring them to wider audiences.

Being young and enthusiastic, the authors have focused on the success stories of women. The reality is that for every successful woman there are many women who face serious hurdles in their voyage of becoming 'complete' and realising their dreams.

Perhaps, when it comes to women, very few societies swing between such extremes as ours. In public, women are accepted and venerated, but in private they are subjugated and dominated by men. On one hand, we have had Indira Gandhi as the Prime Minister and Sonia Gandhi is the President of the Indian National Congress, but on the other hand the right to survival is denied to the female child in many parts of India. In many families a lower priority is given to the education of the girl child. If financial investment has to be made for higher education, a male child would be favoured rather than a bright female sibling.

I have no concrete data, but talking to people in the education field reveals that women are toppers in schools and colleges, and yet this is not reflected when it comes to the number of women holding high positions in organisations. Is this because women are not equipped to take up higher responsibilities or is there something coming in their way? Besides the external hurdles I mentioned earlier, women create some of the pitfalls themselves. For example, many women, unlike men, don't take work very seriously and give up working after some time. Having said that, gender discrimination and harassment at the workplace are live issues and need to be addressed.

In our society a man is still considered the breadwinner. In large parts of India, women are allowed to work only to supplement the family income. But what is heartening is that there is a growing number of women who work for self-fulfilment, as this book demonstrates.

What are the qualities needed to be successful in the business world, especially at higher levels? The ability to scan the environment, take risks, to be decisive and assertive, and a willingness to be mentally engaged with work for long hours are some of them. On top of this, married women with demanding careers have to find a balance between work and family life. This can take a toll, unless they have supportive husbands and parents who can make things easier for them. It is at times true that many women succeed at work in spite of their husbands!

We tend to judge women and their success or failure using the corporate world as a yardstick. However, women have excelled as homemakers, which is a very demanding 'job' and in the fields of art, music, entertainment, teaching and counselling – to name a few. In the corporate world also we do see several talented, confident women making strides and several forward-looking organisations are creating opportunities for that to happen. There is certainly a change but we have to accelerate the pace.

To end on a lighter vein, I quote Charlotte Whitten, who said, "Whatever women must do, they must do twice as well as men to be thought half as good. Luckily, this is not difficult." ...As all the women in this book have demonstrated.

–Anu Aga
Former Chairman, Thermax India

Akhila Srinivasan (Managing Director of Shriram Investments Limited) has impacted several thousands of lives like Arjun's. Social service isn't the only area that displays her altruism. She took the reins of corporate India with a decisiveness that catapulted her to the peak of the finance world, earning her the status of a hardcore finance professional.

The Perfectionist

As a child, Akhila always strove to be the best in whatever she did and yearned to be the first at it, regardless of the activity she indulged in. She excelled in academics, extracurricular activities and sports. "My mother taught me the value of patience," Akhila asserts. "She vested all her hopes and faith in me and ensured that I received the best exposure."

She studied at the RSK Higher Secondary School in Trichy. Even at school, economics was her favourite subject in which she obtained an undergraduate and post-graduate degree from Seethalakshmi Ramaswamy College (Trichy), bagging the Best Outgoing Student award on both occasions. She is also an M-Phil in Economics from Madras University and is currently working on a PhD in Micro Credit from Madras University.

Her striking combination of candidness and diplomacy stems from her stint as an active debater during the five-year course of her undergraduate and post-graduate career. Her talent in classical music saw her participating and winning in music competitions and presenting music programmes too. On the strength of her multi-faceted endeavours, she was adjudged the most outstanding student in school.

Unplanned Occurrence

Joining the Indian Administrative Services (IAS) was Akhila's dream. However, her marriage to qualified chartered accountant H. Srinivasan, soon after her first year of post-graduation, changed her life. Her husband founded a stock-broking business with his company Bluechip Portfolios Private Limited. Their son was born during the second year of marriage. During the initial phase of motherhood, Akhila divided time between tending to her child and preparing for the preliminary examination of the Civil Services. After quite a bit of juggling, she gave up the idea. Instead, she thought she would work on a PhD and foray into the stream of teaching.

One morning in 1986, an unusual ad caught Akhila's eye while she sifted through the newspaper over her morning coffee. The *Shriram* Group had

1.

The Leading Light

Very few believed that he would survive for more than a few years. He was a poor, mentally challenged three-year-old child who was brought to an orphan care centre in Chennai from the Government's Children Hospital. Aiming to promote his welfare, the orphanage sent him to a special home in Maayavaram, a small town in Tamil Nadu. While every other orphanage and foster home refused to shoulder the responsibility of nurturing a child like Arjun, this Ashram had provided him a dignified life, shielding him from a torturous fate he would have otherwise succumbed to. By supporting numerous such causes she has proved that business is the best form of charity.

Akhila Srinivasan
Managing Director, Shriram Investments Limited

In His Eyes

I am happy to note the impressive progress made by women entrepreneurs since the 1980s. The women entrepreneurs who have emerged in the past two decades in India have successfully shattered the glass ceiling to grow into vital, dynamic leaders.

Nischinta Amarnath and Debashish Ghosh have interviewed twenty-one of these remarkable businesswomen in this book, *The Voyage to Excellence*. The book charts the challenges and successes of women industry leaders in India. From Ritu Nanda of Escolife, to Lalita Gupte of ICICI Bank, to Akhila Srinivasan of Shriram Investments, they come from vastly different backgrounds, but have a similar dynamism, and an overriding drive to excel.

Each of the women in this book has overcome significant odds, social or economic, to achieve success in her business. Jaswantiben Popat and six other women borrowed Rs. 80 to start the Lijjat Papad venture, a company that has grown to over Rs. 300 crore today. Kiran Mazumdar-Shaw established Biocon, today a Rs. 5,000 crore company, at the age of 25, without experience, business contacts, and with a starting budget of Rs.10,000. Naina Lal Kidwai, who was the first Indian woman to graduate from Harvard Business School, is today the Vice-Chairman and MD of HSBC Securities and Capital Markets, and has been listed among the world's 50 top corporate women by *Fortune Magazine*.

What is interesting is that these businesswomen – from rich families or poor, from college backgrounds or otherwise – were all women who drove change within, and outside the business. They were unwilling to back down from each challenge thrown at them, and shouldered the multiple responsibilities of their company and their family with courage.

Nischinta and Debashish have narrated the stories of these leaders with skill and empathy. Each story is an insight into a fascinating journey – as the book puts it, a voyage. *The Voyage to Excellence* serves as an important inspiration for women today. Women in India still constitute a small percentage of the workforce, and businesswomen comprise 20% of Indian entrepreneurs. Stories like these are essential to inspire more women to challenge the status quo, and to motivate them towards courage, awareness, and independence.

–Narayana N R Murthy

Chairman of the Board, Infosys Technologies Limited

placed the ad, calling for executive trainees. She promptly applied. Shortly thereafter, she attempted the entrance test series, following which she was selected among twelve persons who were short-listed; she was one of the few lady executive trainees in the group.

Once she joined *Shriram* in 1986, she discovered that the organization was charged with a dynamism that granted immeasurable scope for every person to exercise his talents and realize his potential. She began her stint as the marketing manager in 1987 subsequent to her executive traineeship. With her expeditions to every nook and corner of the country, sometimes travelling with more than a few of her male colleagues, she created massive public awareness about the *Shriram* Group. She was promoted to the post of General Manager of Marketing in 1993 and the President in 1994, before she took *Shriram* under her wing as the Managing Director in 2000. "I always had the satisfaction of contributing to the growth of the company and society. We were able to record this growth immediately and reap the results," Akhila unveils with a smile.

The company's dividend records were sound, its levels of profitability soared and the share it held in the financial services market enlarged even further, bringing in a wide lattice of investors. Nurturing her company's ambitions, Akhila evolved Shriram Investments Limited from a tiny corporate entity to a large empire. One of the star performers of Shriram, she captured the Best Executive tag for three consecutive years.

Outfoxing the Challenge

When a repugnant financial crisis struck India in 1998-99, fly-by-night operators and entrepreneurs who had floated partnership firms faced a deplorable plight. The closure of finance companies was a reflection of the prevailing mismanagement. Panic-stricken people queued up outside every office to withdraw their money. In the midst of this distasteful scenario, Shriram surged forward with conviction with Akhila at the forefront, struggling to survive in an environment where every client, bank and financial institution distrusted NBFCs (non-banking finance companies) to the core.

Sustaining public confidence and endeavouring to build and expand the business further in the wake of the gloomy climate proved to be the greatest challenges in Akhila's professional life. It was only during this hour of crisis that the management realized how well its people had done. As customers stood staunchly by Shriram, Akhila realized that it was the depth of the foundation the company had laid for itself that was keeping it in good stead.

Truckload of Success

The Shriram Group's Truck Financing Entities came into vogue in 1979 to promote greater social advantage, which used trucks were believed to generate. It won the loyalty of many such customers by supplying them with finances for the purchase of old vehicles. Today, the truck-finance companies have the best Internal Rate of Return (IRR) in the industry and a huge spread and margin in the used vehicle business.

> *"Truck financing has always been safe and profitable in more ways than one. Furthermore, we must assume a proactive role in financing the transportation requirements of the country. In spite of a limited volume of funds, the demand for trucks has been increasing incessantly over the last few years. We can scour for new avenues only when we have exhausted every other opportunity in this realm of business."*

Citicorp (a subsidiary of Citibank) and UTI Bank reposed their faith on *Shriram*'s expertise in the truck-finance business and began to bank on Shriram to manage their portfolios. Today, Shriram manages a large portion of their funds. While Citicorp and UTI became *Shriram*'s strategic partners with equity participation, Reliance and FMO (a development financial institution from Netherlands) became *Shriram*'s financial partners.

Besides appointing a head for each activity, Shriram Investments Ltd has also incorporated an immaculately sound reporting system with regular audits and accountability at all levels. Shriram Investments Ltd prides itself on collection efficiency (certified by PricewaterhouseCoopers), viewed as one of the best in the country.

The company's next target is to lend Rs.2000 crores to the trucking sector and diversify into other financial services like life insurance. Shriram is working towards becoming the first ranker in retail product distribution too. Year after year, the company shall continue to set targets and grow aggressively by leaps and bounds. Offering its investors various products under one umbrella, Shriram is now positioning itself as a 'financial services super-bazaar'.

Passion for a Cause

Akhila's yearning to involve herself wholeheartedly in corporate philanthropy and social work motivated her to set up the Shriram Social Welfare Trust in 1993. Over a span of the last ten years, she pioneered innumerable programmes and events for marginalized women and children as an integral part of the Shriram Group's corporate social responsibility scheme.

The Trust has adopted a proactive role in the following areas:

- Orphan and destitute care (the company runs an orphan care centre and a destitute home in Chennai).
- Free primary education for the rural poor.
- Enabling rural women to attain self-reliance through micro-credit finance.

Aside from these activities, the company has been instrumental in rehabilitating several street children and co-managing a home for juvenile delinquents along with the Juvenile Welfare Board to place distressed children on the path of normalcy.

Under Akhila's direction, the company currently runs four schools in villages, where considerable focus is laid on primary education for the rural poor. She also undertook several measures to provide education to children of poor widows. One of these measures included initiating a specific programme to grant educational scholarships to more than 1000 poor children in an attempt to encourage them to continue their education. She plans to set up many more schools in Tamil Nadu and Andhra Pradesh in the future.

She has encouraged dozens of women from Below the Poverty Line (BPL) families to establish a self-help group mechanism, extending credit facilities, loans and grants to each woman and trained them to engage in gainful economic activities. These enterprising small-scale entrepreneurs are then extended useful linkages to the market to propel the sale of their products. Numerous women who emerged from the self-help groups with greater conviction and confidence have ignited sparks in their localities by setting up small business units of all sorts – ranging from setting up tea stalls and grocery shops to making *agarbathis.*

Her team is currently working in 122 villages across the expanses of Tamil Nadu, Karnataka and Andhra Pradesh. In the coming year, she hopes to enlarge the scope of this activity to seven other states, tailing this activity on a more aggressive note.

In the next three years, Shriram plans to lend finances to 300,000 women from the BPL rungs. Akhila is involving herself hands-on in this project, visiting villages and interacting with many women. She adroitly introduced the yardsticks of review, transparency and accountability in enabling her company to champion the cause of social services. Constant performance appraisals follow suit.

"Akhila appreciates people and the performances of her employees regularly," smiles Subhasri Sriram, Vice President (Finance), Shriram Investments Limited. "When I perform well, she doesn't hesitate to phone me and congratulate me. Many a time, she even calls me over to her office and chats with me over a cup of coffee. Before I leave, she gifts me a box of chocolates and asks me to take it home to my family. When I don't handle something well enough, she doesn't hesitate to tell me that she is not very happy with what I've done. Her frankness makes all the difference."

Ticket to Excellence

Honours and accolades have never shunned Akhila. The services she rendered in the areas of social welfare and rural development made her one of the three prize-winners in the *Compaq* contest, which lured the participation of 70 top-notch corporate entities, nationwide. Along with TISCO and Forbes Marshall (Pune), Shriram was adjudged a winner of the *Social Responsiveness Award* (instituted by *Businessworld* under the auspices of FICCI, Delhi), which she received from Kishan Kant, the Honourable Vice President of India in 1999.

In 2000-01, Akhila won the *Outstanding Woman Professional Award* instituted by the *FICCI Ladies Organization*. In May 2002, she received the award from Sheila Dixit, Chief Minister of Delhi.

In 2002, Shriram Investments Limited got the *Mother Teresa Award* [instituted by Loyola Institute of Business Administration, Chennai] for corporate citizenship in acknowledgement of its unwavering social commitment to downtrodden and underprivileged children. While Shriram Investments was declared the winner, Tata Tea Limited (of the Tata Group) emerged a runner-up. Renowned agricultural scientist *Prof. M.S. Swaminathan* gave away the award at a function held in Chennai in 2003.

"The awards served as a reputation-enhancing mechanism for the company," Akhila states. "Were it not for my company, I wouldn't be what I am today."

> *"Any award that acknowledges one's excellence or contribution to society is immensely important. Moreover, extending a forum for recognition and hitting the spotlight on greatly accomplished sports persons, musicians and achievers in virtually every other segment inspires other aspirants to achieve and emulate them too."*

Akhila believes in hiring the services of the best persons, enhancing their managerial abilities and empowering them. The training she received in the corporate ambience gave her a professional approach, which made her refrain from adopting any other strategy for building a proper and efficient management system. She has given Shriram Investments Limited a crystal-clear focus, bringing the company closer to its goals and objectives.

"Akhila is very fair in her dealings with people. A great team-builder, she is good at picking up the right people and empowering them, giving them total freedom and free play to their creativity," agrees Umesh G. Revankar, President, Shriram Investments Limited. "She drives us all to perfection and sets high goals and standards, enabling us to think big and achieve even bigger targets."

Holding the Bridle

On looking back, Akhila recollects several occasions when her children have fallen ill while she was away on tours. Dispelling the strong urge she had to rush back to them, she willed herself to pull on. "Today, after travelling for years on end, I do not experience any regret because I don't think I have neglected my children ever," she says. During her son's tenth and twelfth grade years, she restricted her travel to be with him. "Pressing domestic situations arise all the time. The quality time you invest in each role you play is what matters most," voices Akhila. She has performed the duty that would be expected of every role that she played.

Most of Akhila's colleagues are males. "No problems have arisen on grounds of my gender," she is quick to assure us. "I am one of the most accepted persons in the group. Working with them, I have experienced wonderful feelings of fraternity, friendship, respect and warmth."

> *"What matters is the person you are. I would like to be viewed as a human being first. While at work, I am hardly conscious of the fact that I'm a woman."*

Akhila was determined to make the best of herself. "Getting to the right spot at the right time can really do wonders," she points out, glad that she had discerned well and joined the right company. "If you are fortunate and you believe in your ability to perform and excel, you must just do it," she urges. "Else, you miss a golden opportunity in life."

To be or Not to be

Akhila defines the image of an ideal woman as, "One who makes the right choices, has her priorities intact, puts her intelligence to constructive use and gives full expression to her talents, still managing to retain her grace and femininity in her aggressive quest for distinction during the course of her career."

She is not a woman who can easily get into the stress mode. She exercises strenuously and practices yoga and meditation, which she diligently incorporates into her regimen. She has built various activities of interest into her lifestyle. A believer of holistic living, she gives free play to the lyrical self in her, pampering her zeal for music, literature, cinema and good friends and associations.

The child in her comes to the fore as she discloses that she loves South Indian food and enjoys cooking traditional varieties of *Paayasam.* A family person at heart, Akhila would ideally like to maintain the equilibrium between her professional and personal life. "Even today, that's how it works," she maintains. "My family occupies the highest position on my list of priorities. The company follows next."

Akhila shares a compatible relationship with her husband. "My husband has guided and supported me right through," she says. Broadminded in vision, astute in business and compassionate at heart, he firmly believes that every woman should exercise her talents and skills to the fullest extent possible.

Akhila's children have imbibed their industrious nature from her. While her son Hari is pursuing his final year in Engineering, her 13-year-old daughter Janani is mid-way through her ninth grade. Akhila never tells them much about what she does. Her children do come across several write-ups on her company and read snitches about her in interview excerpts. They take the fame and repute she wields very casually, though. "But they have understood my aspirations too," she divulges with pride.

On a goodbye note, she happily declares, "Indeed, *destiny* has given me all support. I surrender myself to the will of God."

> "True success is getting beyond real life challenges, coming to terms with inevitable adversities and maintaining your equanimity. Material acquisitions do not portray success. Corporate and personal successes are both determined by the quality of relationships we share with the surrounding people and stimuli as well as our ability to give back to society in large measure. Our desire to achieve higher goals, which are of use to society, should propel our actions. And the fruits of our actions should not bind us. For me, successful actions are those that promote the betterment of people around me."

Chanda Kocchar
Executive Director, ICICI Bank

2.

Better Than the Best

Armed with an MBA degree, she joined ICICI Bank as a trainee and conscientiously climbed up the higher boughs of the corporate ladder, only to take the chair as an Executive Director. A strong believer of women power, her credentials belie her docile next-door image.

Chanda Kocchar symbolizes the aspirations of the Indian youth, giving a new face to resurgent India. Her clarity and commitment to goals define her approach to life. She is not one who minces words. She succinctly states, "You may be able to take on certain activities, while you may not be able to indulge in certain others. You should develop a clear idea of what you aim to do."

Budding Financier

Born in Jodhpur and raised in the pink city of Jaipur, Chanda was determined to prove her mettle, right from the early years of her childhood. She emerged from a liberal-minded family of high-calibre professionals. Her father was the principal of the Jaipur Engineering College, which he set up himself. Chanda enjoyed an amiable ambience at home. As the youngest of two sisters and one brother, her siblings pampered her. "Our parents always treated us equally," she informs. "No one at home believed that hunting for a career was more important to my brother than it was to me and my sister." Becoming an IAS officer was her most recurrent childhood dream. The banker in her only evolved much later.

Unfortunately, Chanda lost her father at the young age of 13. Soon after she finished her schooling, she and her family moved to Mumbai, where most of her relatives resided. Her father's death was a shock for her and it took the family a long time to tide over the trauma. Nevertheless, the city's magical charms played their role in grooming her into a confident young woman. Chanda graduated from Jai Hind College and then went on to acquire a management degree from Jamnalal Bajaj Institute of Management Studies (JBIMS), Mumbai. At college, she was an active player of badminton and an enthusiastic participant in numerous elocution contests, oratorical events and dramatics shows.

In 1984, ICICI recruited Chanda Kocchar as a management trainee, soon after she emerged from JBIMS, with a fine brand name to her credit and a wide trail of laurels behind her. She began her career in Project Finance – an area that was ICICI's bread and butter back then. When ICICI decided to establish a commercial bank as a separate entity, Chanda moved fluidly into a team that was instrumental in conceptualising the bank's operations.

Following this large venture, ICICI introduced two other pioneering initiatives. An infrastructure industry group arose from the portals of ICICI for the first time in India with a view to funding an extensive series of 'infrastructure development projects'. A major clients' group sprung up, thereafter. This group was the product of a radically new concept of dealing with large corporate bodies through client relationship banking – an area that flaunts Chanda's invaluable contributions to its growth and evolution.

Biting the Bullet

Chanda currently heads the retail banking division at ICICI Bank. The newfound confidence that she acquired from the enriching experiences and expertise, which she garnered through her stints with various departments in ICICI, comes to the fore as she declares with a sprightly smile, "My work has not only stimulated me with its challenging wings, but speeded my progress on the learning curve too."

She has continuously faced up to challenges in taking on newer jobs, creating ideas and policies and initiating them. Her switch to the distinctive realm of retail finance was the turning point of her fifteen-year corporate banking career. "Apart from gaining a profound insight into the ins and outs of the retail banking industry, I learned to create a team too," she reveals.

ICICI Bank's cross-selling and up-selling initiatives have seen phenomenal success under Chanda's efficient rein. The bank quickly rolled out her retail business products, while simultaneously advancing credit cards, car loans and home loans. The bank set up a distribution network and numerous customers began to pour in. Chanda realized that selling more than one ICICI product to the same set of customers made good business sense. Doing so was again a challenge as she was compelled to manage these areas and motivate her colleagues to continue remaining focused in their respective activities to sustain the growth of the business.

In an attempt to provide her team-mates an incentive to multi-task their activities, Chanda created mindsets, fixed measurement targets and introduced back-up systems and processes to smoothen the flow of cross-selling without throwing up procedural hassles and catch-22 situations. As a result, over 30% of ICICI's housing loans rose from cross-selling to existing customers. Chanda has meticulously been tracking the current developments of international banks, keeping herself abreast of every venture. "Most banks often talk about cross-selling," Chanda opines. "Since it is a big challenge, most of them aren't able to see the results."

ICICI began the concept of putting an add-on limit to one's second cardholder. If a card were issued to you, you could create a limit for your daughter so that she could spend a certain portion of it. ICICI also introduced co-branded cards (including ICICI and HPCL cards), which customers could use to buy petrol. Chanda Kocchar has constantly sprung up with new variants of existing products, increasing their utility value and luring larger numbers of customers.

> *"Excellence is my seat of passion. In my view, success is excellence. Success essentially lies in excelling in what you do and performing better than your best."*

Tricks of the Trade

Chanda's initiatives at ICICI Bank have not only contributed to a sea change in the bank's fortunes but also brought forth a new era in the Indian banking sector. We journey through an entrancing conversation, which revolves around the ideas that shaped the future of banking at ICICI. *Excerpts from an exclusive interview...*

- *How would you say you made a dent in the overcrowded business of credit cards?*

  Before you roll out your strategy and create the right team, you need to ensure that every bit of your strategy is right. Making product propositions that wield a higher quality than those that are on offer in the market is really the secret behind it all. Creating a distribution network wide enough to improve reach to the public would be a shot in the arm too. Prompt customer-servicing and efficient back-up systems and operations are essential to expand sales and accelerate the pace of growth in the industry.

- *What responses did your innovations elicit from competitors?*

  In many a customer's mind, questions initially arose in connection with whether our initiatives would function effectively and be of use to him. We ourselves mulled over various aspects such as finding vendors to develop products with them, analysing the cost advantage and investing in cutting-edge technology. The belief that we had in our dreams augured well for us, propelling our efforts to fruition. Today, our policies and schemes have given rise to a big change in the industry by influencing the conduct of transactions too. Online transactions are growing in popularity and use. To this end, we have tied up with Indian Railways and other such organizations.

- *Can you provide us an update on your e-business strategy and city-specific portals?*

  Well, we view the e-business as part of the main business itself. Every business has the 'e' aspect to it! (*Laughs*) If we are to find a niche for ourselves as leaders in any business, we should besides considering physical factors, rope in distribution, technology and back-office operations too. First things first, e-business provides us a podium to differentiate ourselves. Secondly, technology plays a powerful role in cost control. Any new e-business venture is an extension of our physical business. All we really do is drive the e-business.

- *Besides lending activities, what other course of action have you taken for the expansion of investment marketing?*

  We created new trends in transaction banking in India, with the spunky measures we introduced in our deposit gathering endeavours. Only below 30% of the transactions are carried on through the branches, today. The remainder is done through other e-channels like ATMs, Phone Banking, Internet Banking and Mobile Banking. We have also embarked on the business of distributing investments and service products. We distribute RBI bonds, insurance policies and mutual funds of various companies. We clearly hope to lead the sector with our strong customer base and large distribution network.

The Positive Reinforcer

When we are through firing our volley of curiosity-aroused questions, Chanda grins almost mysteriously at us and rises from her seat. Informing us that she is attending the party she and her team had thrown to celebrate the success of the housing loans department, she disappears through an inner door to join the celebrators in the adjacent room.

> *"As a team leader, you are required to show your team-mates the route they can take by giving them a proper strategic direction and empowering them. A manager who follows these guidelines can become an excellent motivator. Finally, you have to express a certain fairness and justice in rewarding and penalizing people."*

On returning from the soiree, she proudly reveals that the market share of ICICI's housing loans division surpassed that of the traditional market leader by a significant margin, garnering huge economies of scale to cover all its operating costs. (The distribution and operating costs are divided over a much larger portfolio.) Celebrations of victory are believed to stretch targets too. And ICICI has always espoused a culture of working and celebrating.

A Sound Shield

A plethora of women have performed exceedingly well in the banking sector. "The art of banking calls for an intense and accurate understanding of money and the minds of people. Inherently versatile in personality, women fit well into the multifaceted business of banking," Chanda concurs.

If more women are taking on leadership positions today, they aren't doing so because special preference is given to them. "I recollect that a company representative once approached us seeking advice to increase the strength of women personnel in his organization," Chanda narrates. "I promptly told him that we were the wrong people to provide any suggestions as we had never taken particular effort to follow any such model ourselves."

Chanda moves on to cite the underlying reasons for the capacity of the Indian woman to outshine her foreign counterparts in managing workplace situations. "People tend to listen when a woman shows fortitude and asserts her point of view," she expresses. "A resource of Indian ethnicity, the joint family culture serves as a backbone and an additional support system to help women tackle their domestic responsibilities – one which women from other corners of the world cannot readily avail of."

The most perceptive and intelligent of women is often reckoned to have ridden through coarse terrains as she darts between her home and office. It wasn't any better for Chanda. Nevertheless, women would achieve excellence on the personal and professional fronts alike if they believed they were good wives and mothers. Furthermore, taking that extra mile always sees them through their lives and careers. Chanda has excelled in both spheres. "Prioritising one's tasks is the key to effective management in any domain," she avers. She plans her day and organizes her activities meticulously. Little wonder then that she accomplishes twice as much as one usually could, even within a period of twenty-four hours.

Constituting a strong support system, her family always found pleasure and pride in her personal and professional growth. A caring husband made all the difference to her. "Well, my children *have* sometimes complained," Chanda admits. "Nevertheless, they radiate a sense of pride in my achievements, and value the quality of time that I spend with them rather than the quantity."

Chanda revels in the time she enjoys with her children, while taking a leisure break. She is fond of Thai and Mughlai food and loves music. She can be found listening to any form of music at any time, in any corner – be it at home, in the car, in the office or even in an elevator. "Music is my stress-buster," she confesses, laughing. So intense an impact has it cast on her that she has never felt the need to attend a stress management programme.

Chanda Kocchar represents an entire ethos of women who are becoming equal partners in marriage as well as decision-making in both the domestic and corporate sectors. The new icon of women professionals is indeed well on her way to becoming 'better than the best!'

Ekta Kapoor
Creative Director, Balaji Telefilms

3.

The Story-teller

She is known for her fiery temper. Yet, the volcano of creativity that reposes within her continues to fan the flames of success. She dramatized real life, brought her characters and creations to life in the living room of every urban Indian and held critics spell-bound through the ingenuity with which she spawned different ideas, revolutionizing the soap opera scene of Indian television. Indeed, her success has silenced detractors.

No one has made it bigger on the small screen than ***Ekta Kapoor*** (Creative Director of Balaji Telefilms, Mumbai). Today, Balaji Telefilms has become the biggest content provider and stationed itself as a public limited company. Plunging into the business of television serial production even before she completed her college degree, Ekta Kapoor has blossomed into a perceptive entrepreneur today. TV artistes have come to accept that starring in an Ekta Kapoor serial spells sure-fire success, even if it means enduring the young lady's temper tantrums.

Clad in a simple kurta and an old pair of trousers with a dab of divine *kum-kum* on her fair forehead, she looks no older than fifteen. Her purposefulness raised her status to that of the largest and youngest single producer of television software ever chronicled in the archives of India's entertainment industry.

When the Going Gets Tough, the Tough Get Going

Films and business aren't unfamiliar to Ekta. Her grandfather traded in artificial jewellery. Born in the line of movie connoisseurs, Ekta was always fascinated by films. One of the handsomest and most illustrious hoydens of Indian cinema, Ekta's father Jeetendra Kapoor married Shobha, an ex-airlines professional, whose financial adeptness saw her turn entrepreneur soon after her alliance with him.

Ekta is a product of the Bombay Scottish School and Mithibai College, Mumbai. Ekta recalls bunking classes often and landing in hilarious soups, time and again, while at school! The excitement and adventure of a journalistic career drew her interest as a child. She always felt great pride in telling a story. "I found that adding drama to reality made good fiction," she laughs. As she stepped over the threshold of adolescence, she found that she didn't believe in laying any platform by which she could develop tough ambitions and chase lofty dreams. She was a far cry from her brother Tusshar, who wept even on securing an exceptional 96 per cent in an exam because he had lost four marks to a silly error. Excellence in academics did not receive the highest ranking on her priority list.

"I just wanted to be myself," she recalls. Well, did her dream become a reality? "My reality rather became a dream!" she exclaims jovially.

Ekta forayed into the film factory at the impressionable age of eighteen. Her enterprise took its birth with an initial capital of rupees sixty lakhs. The path to success was a particularly rough one for her. When she began production, she made six pilots, consisting of three episodes each and ran up a bill of a whopping figure of Rs.5 million. Her stories were rejected. While she did feel despondent at times, she never lost heart.

She received no returns for her investments. No other challenge of such enormity had she been confronted with than retracing her steps to square one and beginning meticulously from scratch. No sooner did she make up the loss than she zoomed upwards decisively. Her steadfastness and creativity in conceptualising and problem solving drove her on the road to much-coveted success. Her father was a fine teacher and she learnt well from him. "The Adhikari brothers cast a significant impact on me too," Ekta acknowledges. "At a time when my knowledge of television was zilch, they patiently taught me how to play the game."

The Rising Star

Ekta took the right step in embarking on her first big venture. She conjured up an interesting musical game show titled *Hungama*, which unfailingly struck a chord among the audiences, winning her much acclaim. The losses she had earlier incurred induced her to introduce concepts that were specifically cost-effective. *Hungama* conveniently met these criteria.

Hum Paanch catapulted Ekta into the gallery of longstanding success and fame. The serial struck the right balance of depth and humour and stirred strong sentiments among its viewers. The comedy series stayed on the air for more than five years. At an age when many would just begin their careers, the willowy teenager became the youth icon of the media.

Since Ekta produced her first blockbuster television programme, she has rewritten the script on TV entertainment for the masses, creating over twenty soaps on ten major Indian networks. While *Kyunki Saas Bhi Kabhi Bahu Thi* and *Kahaani Ghar Ghar Ki* were particularly well-known serials in the popular K-series, which she established as her trade name, *Kahin Kissi Roz* held TV-watchers in a grand mall of suspense.

On the floor are two new films – *Koi Aap Sa* and *Kitne Kool Hain Hum.* While *Koi Aap Sa* is a love story that caters exclusively to women and college students, *Kitne Kool...* aims at increasing mass appeal with its witty dialogues and comical scenes.

The 28-year-old is now just as busy as ever before, fashioning arrestingly new concepts of casting, styling, shooting, scheduling and marketing. Today, she has corporatized the media and established innovative benchmarking practices for selecting her technicians and personnel.

Finding a Rhythm

Unravelling the pulse of the Indian audience with practiced competence and insight, Ekta discovered a tempo in her life and work with the powerful beliefs and traditions she imbibed and set for herself. These composite traditions, which she soundly projects in each of her stories, are attributable to her unusual storylines, sky-high TRP ratings and runaway success.

"I have found the concept of the family a topic of timeless interest among Indians," she tells us. Indeed, innumerable traditions, festivals, social occasions and celebrations of success with family, friends and relatives, occupy the place of pride in Indian clans and families. Weaving together these insights, Ekta created a wide array of characters, each characterized by certain beliefs and habits, asserting his distinctness from the others.

Ekta's belief that each culture requires its own space to breathe, grow and develop further, led her to infuse shows with a wise combination of modern thinking and Indian traditionalism. "Why should there be a balance between Indian and western culture?" she queries. Right from her halcyon days, she always gleaned the positive facets of both Indian and western cultures and attempted to incorporate them into her own life and career.

Over time, Ekta obtained a sharp understanding of the needs of global television. According to her, entertainment is more important to the viewers than intellectual fodder.

"The international arena looks for a significant entertainment quotient," she maintains. "However, preserving the taste of the international audiences is crucial to capture their interest and improve the acceptability of Indian television standards, abroad." Her well-articulated views precisely explain why TV shows that lack thought-provoking ideas continue to keep viewers relaxed, happy and boredom-free.

With the progress of generations and the worldwide impact of the momentous achievements of headstrong young women like Ekta, women are securing impressive posts in the media. The domain of on-screen television is especially believed to open expansive shores to enthusiastic young media entrants. Ekta explains that the exploitation of women by men is not known to take place on TV since it is a woman who is chosen to be the protagonist as well as the antagonist in many a case. "In light of the present scenario, the question of on-screen exploitation does not arise. The exploitation that does exist is what is meted out by one women to another," Ekta contends in the lilting tone that has become her distinguishing feature.

"A slim degree of male domination and gender bias does persist," she concurs. Nevertheless, she takes little slights in her stride. She has always sought to perform to the best of her intellect, letting her work speak for itself. "It is your work that brings you respect, rather than your age or gender," she points out.

> *"We should not differentiate Indian women by labelling them 'Indian women'. We are categorizing them by placing this tag on them. It is futile to categorize people. Strengths and weaknesses are predominantly personal for every man or woman. We should each discover our strengths, identify our forte and rectify our weaknesses. Women take pride on their strength of character and the power of their minds. Constraints do plague them in a country like ours. But perceiving them as disadvantages is the biggest disadvantage in itself."*

Reel Vs Real

Ekta Kapoor's serials intend to propagate perpetual middle-class values. The 'Queen of Soaps' believes in acquiring a host of new skills to stay ahead of competition. She enlightens us on the minutiae of her work and the social value of her stories. *Excerpts from the exclusive interview...*

❑ *Violence and unrealism in the visual media are thought to have invaded numerous living rooms via serials, increasing the susceptibility of impressionable young minds to negative stimuli. What are your comments in this regard?*

Unrealism is a part of the visual media. What catches the eye and keeps you glued to the screen is the drama the story revolves around. It is perhaps a necessary evil. Most of the serials show that the outcome of violence and unrealism is usually negative. However, the extent of unrealism leaves the viewers pondering over how similar instances can hold true in real life too. This reduces the susceptibility of the impregnation that impressionable young minds may otherwise be prone to.

❑ *Criticisms have come to pass in connection with the social irrelevance of your characters. What is your response to critiques?*

Arguments revolving around the societal significance of issues that carry a negative tone to the audiences are purely uni-dimensional.

Every show is replete with positive and negative characters. Vamps and villains are cast in a faintly darker light than the other characters; the aura of good characters offsets the evil influences of bad characters.

- ❑ *What is the significance of the K-factor in your serials?*

  Well, I must admit that the K-factor is a kind of quirk. But I like to keep K titles as they hold good promise for me.

- ❑ *Have you considered the option of making short tele-films to replace the endless serials that continue to drag on today? How receptive do you think the viewers will be to short tele-films?*

  Short films would be well accepted in the market. However, serials would attract a greater percentage of viewers to the idiot box, facilitating a long-term bond between people and the characters of the show. Serials aren't about concrete storylines. One yearns to know more about other people with the passing of each day. And this curiosity of the viewers is what serials cash in on.

- ❑ *If you were to select the best of your serials, which one would it be?*

  Even today, I would promptly say *K-3* and *Ek Aasha*. Both shows have presented their themes and characters subtly. And that appeals to me.

- ❑ *Given your beauty and commanding presence, you could appear on the silver screen too. Haven't you given acting a thought?*

  (*Laughs*) I must thank you for the compliment. But acting just isn't my cup of tea. My talents and interests lie behind the camera. It takes an enormous volume of effort to emote and play a role which you haven't conceived yourself!

The Midas Touch

Harnessing the energies of youth would further expand the latent talent resource pool in the country. Ekta has done just that. Proving her point, she plunged headlong into a talent scout earlier in 2004 to scour for fresh, young faces for an upcoming programme for M-TV. "Fresh faces make our shows look pretty and young, as they are synonymous with fresh energy, fresher passion and even fresher zeal as well as the desire to make it big in life. While established television actors carry the baggage of the earlier characters they have played, the fresh ones are more mouldable," she contends, punctuating her words with her disarming mega-watt smile. She has moulded and groomed them exceptionally well indeed.

Ekta's accomplishments won her much tribute in a very short span of time. In 2001, *Asiaweek* magazine adjudged her one of the fifty most influential communicators in Asia. A proud recipient of a series of *Indian Telly Awards* over the last two years, Ekta was labelled India's *Ernst & Young Entrepreneur of the Year.* She also bagged the coveted titles of *Society Achiever* and *Best Entrepreneur of the Year,* 2001. She was recently chosen to head the entertainment committee of the Confederation of Indian Industries (CII).

Geared for the Future

"To me, my mother is what balance is all about," Ekta acknowledges, recalling the numerous instances her mother shuttled between home and work, producing exemplary results with her balancing act. "Extreme success or obsession with goal orientation can become expensive. It is eventually a balanced life that counts."

Does Ekta Kapoor see herself as an artist or a business baron? "I choose to call myself a creative person in a commercial line," she replies fittingly.

As the Indian showbiz skims through every move of hers, she continues to produce absorbing dramas that enthral viewers across the subcontinent – be it a story that centres on an ambitious tycoon or a beautiful yet conniving wife who cunningly schemes and conspires the downfall of her anathemas or even a seventy-year-old grandma who is on a hunt for a job!

Exploring different routes and bringing to the fore one core theme that 70% of the viewers would remember is the strategy that Ekta Kapoor plans to adopt to manoeuvre her future course of action. She is directing her energies on boosting her company's brand equity in conjunction with success and quality, either through television or films.

The clear focus Ekta laid on her goal has enabled her to achieve newfound heights with every novel venture. In her own words, "Success for me is entirely subjective. Working and staying happy are my personal missions. It would be foolish on my part to switch to a completely different track and let my competitors perform a dance of victory on an empty field."

> *"Just be yourself and do what you are good at. The moment you discover yourself, you won't have to live through another dreary workday. You would perceive each day as yet another opportunity to grow and fulfil your dreams. So, just go for it!"*

Jyoti Naik
President, Lijjat Papad

4.
Rolling Out a Bright Future

It was a hot day in the summer of March 15, 1959. Most of the women inhabitants of a large, old residential building in Girgaum (a thickly populated area in south Mumbai) bustled around, busily attending to their usual domestic chores.

As the sun shone brightly in the cloudless sky one morning, a brilliant idea evolved among seven women who together thought they should make papads for themselves, as much as their families thought they should attain self-sufficiency. It is a story of more than 42,000 heroines who have grown valiantly, proving that the simple principles of Sarvodaya make great business sense.

The world applauds as ***Lijjat*** (meaning 'tasty') becomes a generic name for papads, weaving its way into local Indian homes and abroad.

The Gandhian Girl

An active founder-member involved with the phenomenal spirit, Jaswantiben Popat represents the entire ethos of rural women across India. It was her determination which broke the myth that 'Entrepreneurs should have high academic qualifications and financial prowess', showing the world that a corporation could be built even when you had neither. *The Economic Times* described Jaswantiben as a 'feisty traditionalist who heads the Rs.315 crore Lijjat Papad co-operative, continuing to rise at 4.30 a.m. to ensure that the masala passes muster'. ET honoured her many a time. But her outstanding achievements do not hold a candle to the smiles she has brought to the faces of thousands of poor and illiterate women, countrywide.

The institution began from scratch on a borrowed sum of Rs.80. This money was lent on the condition that Rs.200 should be returned within a stipulated period of time. In the earlier days, the path wasn't easy. The faith and patience of the members were put to test on several occasions as the institution had to stomach its own trials and tribulations.

To begin with, they had no money. Donations were not accepted, even on a voluntary basis. A reservoir of steadfastness grew slowly and expanded boldly over time against all odds, meeting the dynamic women with a smile.

The Rare Triad

Shri Mahila Griha Udyog Lijjat Papad has progressed exemplarily over the last forty years of its existence. The institution is a synthesis of three different concepts: (i) Business (ii) Family and (iii) Devotion.

This synthesis gave rise to an extraordinary Lijjat way of thinking. The institution adopted the concept of *business* right from birth. Lijjat has always believed in producing quality goods and selling them at quality prices and carried out its commercial dealings in a sound and pragmatic manner. It has never accepted any donations, gifts or grants from any charitable quarter. Contrarily, the Lijjat members are known to collectively donate their resources for noble causes, time and again.

An idée fixe of the members, the notion of mutual family trust, concern and affection entails tackling all commercial and corporate affairs of Lijjat on precisely the same pattern as that of families, which perform their own household chores everyday.

Resting on a firm belief that 'work is worship', the concept of devotion is the most important of the three. Lijjat isn't merely a place where one earns one's livelihood. Members, employees and well-wishers view Lijjat as a place of worship, where each person devotes her energies not for her own benefit, but for the benefit of all. Besides the basic principles of self-reliance, co-ownership and faith in the dignity of labour, the institution has also fashioned three Golden Rules.

- All the rights of the institution must solely belong to the institution.
- The quality of Lijjat should be maintained at any cost.
- The accounting system must be clean and time-bound.

Over the years, Lijjat has paved the way for women to gain self-reliance and self-confidence, providing them the right platform to improve their status in society. While hordes of cooperative societies across the country have been creaking hopelessly under the shackles of mismanagement and political interference, Lijjat stands as a breed apart and proves its prowess in business with its firm foundation of ethics.

A Walk Around

The market teems with papads of all types, forms and sizes – but there is only one Lijjat papad. You are stumped; even academically unqualified sisters can tell you what goes on behind the papad-making process.

The day begins early for every sister. The branch offices officially work from 6:00 a.m. to 10:30 a.m. during which time the dough is distributed and papads made during the course of the previous day are collected.

One kilogram of atta is given, after which the number of papads to be rolled is specified. Every sister is required to take a minimum of 3 kilograms of atta per day. For every kilogram of atta that is provided, the women are required to bring back 800 grams the following day while the remainder of the flour is offered to them as an allowance. The shape and size of the papads are fixed too.

"We personally visit the site and conduct surprise checks to assure the highest quality standards," informs Jyoti Naik, President of Lijjat. "The women workers in our Polymer division package the products in our factory premises themselves."

The payments for the rolling (referred to as '*vanai*') are made daily; accounts are never kept pending. The women receive Rs.17 per kg of the atta that they roll. Some portion of the dues is reduced if proper arithmetic records are not maintained. Age does not figure in Lijjat's reward list. All women, the young and the old alike, receive the same rates. Every sister who works for six hours from home can make about Rs.2000 – Rs.3000 every month. Profits are distributed in the form of additional *vanai* charges to working sisters.

"Anyone can rise to the top at Lijjat," Jyoti beams with a smile. "The only qualification one needs to acquire to reach the high rungs of the Lijjat ladder is the skill of rolling papads."

> *"Lijjat is a place for all women, educated or uneducated. Since most women bring their young daughters along, there is a strong attachment to our institution, which ensures that our network continues expanding. Although many are not aware of it, rolling papads calls for tremendous hard work. Any woman can learn to roll papads at the age of fifteen if she so desires. We have learnt it the hard way too."*

Swift Progress

The institution began to regulate its activities from 1966. One of the important events was a formal constitution by its members on 25 July 1966. Lijjat was then registered as a 'society' under the *Provision of Societies Registration Act, 1860*, and a 'public trust' under the *Provision of Bombay Public Trust Act, 1950*. In the same year, Lijjat was also recognized by U N Dhebar from the Khadi and Village Industries Commission (KVIC).

The institution's miniscule sales figure of Rs.6196 in 1959 has now magnified to Rs.315 crores. The membership, formerly just seven women, has now extended its hands in welcome to 42,000 women across the rural topography of India. Today, Lijjat has evolved into a vast and prestigious organization with its own fleet of vehicles to facilitate the smooth transport of goods from one destination to another at all levels. The vehicles are well equipped with various facilities to conduct an entire gamut of day-to-day operations. Jyoti Naik proudly asserts, "This organization shall remain indebted to the late Shri Chhaganbapa who showed us the correct *marga* (path) to the institution and continued to guide the activities till he breathed his last in 1968."

That Special Something

Right from the beginning, self-reliance and self-growth have been core components of Lijjat's culture. In accordance with the principles of Sarvodaya, all the sister members of the institution are its owners. The members jointly share the profits and losses of the institution. Each member is permitted to exercise her authority in deciding the manner in which this profit or loss can be apportioned among themselves.

No male can become a member of Lijjat and any male employee who works on a salary or honorary basis has no right to the institution. Of an executive committee comprising twenty-one members (who manage the affairs of the institution), six are elected as the office bearers, which encompass the posts of the President and Vice President as well two secretaries and treasurers, each.

Sanchalikas are chosen to supervise the day-to-day operations of their concerned departments. The daughter of Lijjat's founder-member Jaswantiben is a *sanchalika* herself! While each and every member of the institution can take any initiative or decision, she also has a considerable degree of power to veto. Every decision, major or minor, is based on general consensus among members. A single member can however raise an objection, which may nullify a decision. While the women discharge their duties, they have full freedom to fight for their rights too. Today, every woman in Lijjat can proudly declare that the organization is her own.

Tradition of Glory

Every family prides itself on certain traditions exclusive to that family. A family of 42,000 sisters, Lijjat prides itself on a system of strong traditional values, which have been closely developed over the years. *A brief insight*:

- ❑ Largely a public institution, Lijjat is no place for private affairs. People are encouraged to voice their opinions boldly.
- ❑ No one can direct any sister to leave the organization. However, the sisters can dismiss any employee (paid or honorary) without citing any reasons.
- ❑ Sisters who are affectionately referred to as *ben* are not required to provide any reasons for acquiring loans.
- ❑ Members in the vicinity are the ones who take the decisions; those who are not present at the crucial moment simply miss the opportunity of partaking of the decision-making process.

Anyone who has the enthusiasm to take the responsibility to execute various tasks is entirely free to do so. But there shall be no excuses; promises are to be kept. Moreover, anyone can check the accounts, which are entered into the records everyday. Women may not bring anything from home or take anything back either. Faultfinding finds no place in Lijjat. Women are encouraged to go with the flow of the institution and own up to their mistakes.

With top quality as Lijjat's recipe for success and products being well received in the market, many people are beginning to wonder about ready consumer acceptance. "We have no trade secrets. Our manufacturing is open for inspection," Jyoti Naik says.

Sensitive to the fact that she deals with food products, Jyoti ensures absolute hygiene conditions. From the variety of products that the women have, they can only take the papads home for rolling. They are flooded with hundreds of applications requesting for franchisees. But they refrain from allocating their units to anyone before evaluating the basic hygiene and water facilities.

Jyoti's instructions are strictly adhered to. Only raw materials and ingredients of the best quality are used during the papad-making process and members continue to check the quality at every stage of production. "We just crush inferior papad varieties to crumbs or throw them in water; we never pass them on to anyone," Jyoti reveals.

The sisters hire the administration staff solely for operational purposes; they have no decision-making powers. Lijjat appoints a large number of salesmen and distributors to market and distribute its products. If distributors fail to reach the customers, *sanchalikas* step in themselves! As one sister points out, "We even send the papads directly from our office in case the distributors fail to deliver the products. We are then compelled to change them if they don't adopt corrective measures, even after they are given due notice."

To maintain its standards, Lijjat opts for a central purchase system, ensuring that substandard ingredients are precluded. The materials are then distributed to various locations across the country. "We never use machines. We are entirely manual. If any error occurs on this account, the entire bunch of papads is rejected," informs Irene Almeida, who has been working with Lijjat for over two decades. No substandard papad has ever reached a consumer in the history of Lijjat.

All that Glitters is not Gold

Even in today's world of corporate glitter and outstanding MBA graduates, Lijjat has consistently made its presence felt at different forums. The Khadi and Village Industries Commission conferred the *Best Village Industry* award on Lijjat from the period 1998-99 to 2000-01 at the national convention on Rural Industrialization. The programme was featured in BCC World in the show *Business Bizarre.* Jaswantiben Popat expressed her only grief that none of the other co-founders was present to receive the award from the *Economic Times.*

Jyoti received the Economic Times Award of *Businesswomen of the Year* in 2001-02 for corporate excellence. What followed was a standing ovation from the CEOs of India Inc. as she addressed the crowds in chaste Marathi.

"I got emotional when the ladies went up to the stage to receive their awards. Goose pimples prickled my arm; I wanted to cry!" ad filmmaker Prasoon Pandey disclosed passionately.

In Her Epistle

At the conference room we had a lively chat with the leaders of the rural women mass movement and their deputies. Led gently by Jyoti Naik, the women have upheld the true tradition of Lijjat. Jyoti narrates the story of the triumphs and tribulations of her life and Lijjat. *Excerpts from an exclusive interview...*

- *When did you join Lijjat? How has your journey been till now?*

  I joined Lijjat 23 years ago. I used to first roll papads with my mother. As I continued coming over by myself even after she retired, I learnt and grew gradually. I kept this trend after I married too. In short, I wormed my way through the ladders of Lijjat – I worked in stores, distribution outlets and every other field. I was then chosen as a committee member before I was sworn in as the President five years ago. Perhaps, people liked my work. (*Laughs*) Little did I know that I would rise up to such lofty heights when I came here at the age of fifteen in 1971.

- *Have your products been competed away by rival players in the food industry? How did you tackle such instances?*

  Over the years, the philosophy we developed was so robust that we didn't ever need to change that. People buy our papads solely because of their quality. We have no competition in terms of quality. Of course, there have been instances of rivals who have attempted to copy our techniques of packaging even. But you can't be a leader by copying others.

Driven by glamour and fanfare, many MNCs are springing up in the fields of atta. You can taste our papads and differentiate them from the rest – the only fluctuation is evident in the raw material prices of our papads. But the taste of our atta is genuine. Our customers have reposed tremendous faith in us.

- *What approach do you follow to manage your home and career with equal efficiency?*

  Well, we manage our families first. I have three kids – two boys and a girl. My husband and children lend infinite support. They handle the domestic affairs when I am out on tour. My husband even took a VRS to shoulder some of my responsibilities at home.

Other members of the organization support Jyotiben fiercely. "Thirty years ago, my husband earned only Rs.80," reveals Vice Chairman, Kamalben Dandore.

"A secondary source of income became necessary. I started rolling papads to supplement the family earnings; I struggled to make papads on the terrace of my neighbour's house for the first three months prior to joining Lijjat."

> *"We take care of our sisters in every possible way. We have a doctor in every branch. We have also made arrangements to educate the illiterate women at our branch. Moreover, we grant educational scholarships for meritorious students who are pursuing their higher secondary education. It isn't long before women come back to us to tell us that they are earning much higher pay packets than their husbands and can afford to send their kids to good schools."*

Once Kamal joined, she invested hour after hour of labour in rolling papads in the nights, many a time working till 2 a.m. or even beyond. "Everybody who rose up the ladder worked really hard to achieve her position," she concludes, grinning. On being asked how Lijjat has made a difference, she gently replies, "Here, we treat everyone equally – be it Jaswantiben or any other sister. We believe that girls should be provided the opportunity to educate themselves. In addition, they should take up a professional or vocational course." Her voice rings with newfound pride as she adds, "We taught the children of our sister members the brass tacks of computers; they are currently working and are economically and financially secure and independent."

The Road Ahead

Lijjat never hesitates to diversify into areas where large numbers of ladies can work. From Kashmir to Kanyakumari, Lijjat had its presence in some of the remotest of villages. Where there was no scope for papad, it diversified into products that were most suitable for each region. Lijjat has phased in Khari, Bakery and Kakhri in Gujarat, detergents in Mumbai, Pune and Hyderabad and banana chips in Chennai.

Lijjat has not only earned an impeccable reputation in India, but also created a brand name for itself in numerous other parts of the world. The global demand for the crisp Lijjat papads continues to grow more. Lijjat has done what many of our conventional industries could not do – it has exported roughly 30-35% of its production, garnering a host of consumer countries like the USA, Singapore, Hong Kong, Japan, the Middle East and the UK.

Lijjat has now set up a Flour Division in Navi Mumbai (at Vashi) and Nasik, where flour is milled from Urad Dal and Moong Dal. Another Masala division stands bravely at Cotton Green. Here, different kinds of spice powders are carefully prepared and packaged in consumer packets. Turmeric, chillies, coriander and tea masala are only a few to mention. In addition to these, Lijjat has established a Khakhra division too.

Lijjat is also exploring different avenues to manufacture detergent powder and cakes, which are popularly known as SASA or 'Symbol of Women's Power'. The Chapatti division in Mumbai is another promising endeavour. This unit seeks to secure the distribution of readymade Lijjat chapattis in retail markets, which cater to the fast-paced lifestyles of customers who do not have sufficient time to prepare their own food. Indeed, Lijjat has flexed its marketing muscles to penetrate niche market segments, where small groups of women meet a large local market demand. 'Mass women empowerment' is the guiding principle behind Lijjat's expansion to many related product areas.

"We want to continue expanding at a good pace," Jyoti reveals. And Lijjat's expansions shall follow the tenents of sarvodaya.

> *"Even during natural calamities, we haven't hesitated to contribute to society. When the dreadful earthquake struck Gujarat in 2001, we immediately called for a meeting with our sisters at Rajkot and distributed food to some of the more obscure villages in Gujarat, especially those that did not have surfaced roads or proper transport links to towns and cities. Our sisters walked several miles till they reached their destination. We also adopted a village called Bujkar, which we entirely built ourselves. We mobilized funds from every other branch to support this cause."*

Dignity of the Papad Roller – A Temple called Lijjat

The Lijjat system isn't aimed at creating millionaires. It has nevertheless defined its success over the years by helping innumerable women realize their dream of employing themselves in a dignified fashion. During the initial years of Lijjat's growth, a few genuinely expressed their apprehension that Lijjat would collapse like a house of cards under the umbrella of the growing numbers of women.

In striking contrast, the institution has only gathered momentum as it sped along, skilfully drawing its reserves from the simple Gandhian principle of trusteeship. The increase in Lijjat's strength is largely attributable to the vision and mission of the late Chhaganlal Karamshi Parekh and Damodar Dattani – the prophets who resolutely stood behind the cause of 'social entrepreneurship'.

> *"We aspire to double the number of women who are working with us to 80,000 in the next five years. We could have achieved this target even now. But we want to ensure that our women are entirely independent financially. This can make a visible difference in their lives."*

Lijjat's phenomenal expansion into a multi-product "women's-only" institution, which dispenses all forms of competition or mechanization, banking instead on the philosophies of labour and love that will spawn greater employment opportunities for the sister-members and provide a new dimension of home-based trades in the face of typically stressful work environments, especially given the fact that family members would continue to help the women in their work on the home front, further boosting the rate of productivity of women workers.

As an experiment, Lijjat is a very simple model. Many NGOs seek to develop small models along the lines of Lijjat, which has a vast potential to empower the female population in the country. This system generates just sufficient money for its workers and nothing more. In the near future, it would be difficult to see a large-scale emulation of the Lijjat concept.

Today, Lijjat continues to serve as a catalyst for the chain reaction of 'mass women empowerment' and numerous small self-help groups shall continue to draw their inspiration from the story of Lijjat.

> "Do not be afraid of working hard. Nothing is impossible. Women (especially those who hail from rural areas) should aspire to join together to initiate a small-scale business of their own. They can generate fantastic results if they pool their resources and strengthen their bonds with one another."

Kiran Mazumdar-Shaw
Chairman and Managing Director, BIOCON

5.
The Tale of the Tigress

A lone silver bubble flitted through the air in the golden, early morning sunshine. As the bubble soared through the trees of a sun-kissed, flowery garden, a gaggle of children gathered by the scramble of bushes below and looked up at it in wonder. "That frail little bubble is going to burst soon!" one of the boys cackled mockingly, as the bubble neared a particularly thorny rosebush. "Yes, it will," another agreed. That frail little bubble never burst. Instead, it delicately skirted the prickly shrubs, rose higher up in the air, gathered momentum and soared through the azure skies, flying far and wide as it garnered large motleys of golden and silver-tinted bubbles along the way. Over time, the bubbles combined to form an expansive ocean. Great flagons of fish and whales swim in the empyrean waters, today. And the younger fish are learning to swim and sustain themselves, discovering newer paths and bigger frontiers like their big brothers and sisters. She has made the young fish to taste the global waters.

BIOCON, India is a skylight to the inspiring story of a woman who built an invaluable organization and created enormous value and wealth from nought. Many know the company's dramatic evolution from that tiny bubble to the limitless ocean of genes and enzymes that it has become today.

Kiran Mazumdar-Shaw (Chairman and Managing Director, BIOCON, India) is a classic example of an ambitious young woman who began pursuing an entrepreneurial career in a society and era when women merely took up jobs or stayed at home. She established BIOCON at the age of twenty-five in 1978, promising herself that she would one day become a poster-girl for Indian women entrepreneurs. She wove a team of likeminded people who had the vision to excel and take the company to global environs. When she built BIOCON, she had no money, business qualifications, experience, political clout or contacts with industrial and business houses.

The company was set up in a rented garage on a shoestring budget of Rs.10,000. With BIOCON, she succeeded in dispelling the prevailing myth that biotechnology was a poor cousin of Information Technology. Today, she has transformed her enterprise into a global patents-driven kingdom where a multitude of novel, proprietary products and advanced systems of technologies are being granted PCT and US patents. For Kiran, the initial public offer (IPO) marks a high point in a 26-year journey, which transformed BIOCON from a small enzyme-maker into a drug firm, even challenging global insulin makers like Eli Lily and Novo Nordisk.

Kiran secured the highest civilian honour of Padmashri, as early as 1989. Apart from awards conferred by *The Economic Times* and *Financial Express*, she won several mentions from *Forbes*. In 2004, ET conferred the '*Businesswoman of the Year Award*' on her and declared BIOCON as '*The Emerging Enterprise*'. In the Johnny Walker Business Case Studies survey conducted by Corporate Dossier (*The Times of India*) in December 2004, Kiran emerged as one of the top ten most powerful CEOs in India.

The Guidepost

Kiran dotes on her supportive, close-knit family, consisting of her parents and two elder brothers. The daughter of a master-brewer at a leading liquor-manufacturing company *United Breweries*, Kiran proudly says that her father can almost be referred to as the inventor of the *Kingfisher* beer. A man who was unconventional in his thinking and encouraging in his measures, Kiran's father was the driving force behind every movement of hers.

"Dad always told me I should pursue a career," Kiran reveals in a deferential tone. She gazes wistfully through her office window at the robust almond tree, under which her father's ashes lie today. "If Dad were alive, he could have seen me the way I am today," she whispers serenely. As though remembering, her eyes abruptly brighten as she proclaims, "From that tree, Dad watches me every moment of my life."

A silent catalyst for BIOCON's stupendous success, Kiran's mother was a constant source of strength and guidance. Mrs Mazumdar proved to be a good anchor for her daughter, especially after the tragic demise of her husband.

It normally so happens that children draw inspiration from their mothers but in Kiran's case, it was entirely the opposite. With the undying support and encouragement she derived from her daughter, Mrs Mazumdar invested in two businesses – the *Mazumdar Farm* and *Jeeves*, a dry cleaning and laundry service agency, both of which have blossomed into successful enterprises today.

The *Mazumdar Farm* produces a large range of vegetables typically difficult to cultivate. Carving a niche for herself in the ambit of organic vegetables, Mrs Mazumdar raised a business that entails supplying her produce to five-star hotels and expatriate communities in Bangalore. Kiran recalls that it all began when the representatives of a catering institute, 'The Christ College', approached Mrs Mazumdar one day and asked her to teach them to grow asparagus.

Jeeves specializes in rendering dry-cleaning and laundry services for airlines like Lufthansa and Jet Airways, giant companies like Infosys and BIOCON and all the hotels in the city. "At BIOCON, all of us give our laundry to her," Kiran confesses.

With this venture, Mrs Mazumdar obtained so phenomenal a success that she is now purchasing an industrial shed. "She's doing a really great job," Kiran reflects proudly. "I believe I have inherited my business-acumen genes from her."

Igniting the Spark

As a child, Kiran's aptitude for colour and insatiable thirst for adventure heightened her yearning to explore the intricacies of life and people. During most of her spare time, she would experiment with colours and paint with even, nimble strokes.

At school, Kiran was very studious, categorically committing herself to every endeavour she took on. She loved teachers who voiced radical views, taught different concepts and generated new ideas.

Kiran always had good English teachers. She recalls the love she received from Anne Warrior, one of her English teachers at school. "She sowed in me the seeds of unconventionality," Kiran recounts with heartfelt reverence. "She would dole out interesting projects to her students, eliciting creativity and imagination from each of us. She encouraged us to think innovatively."

The mysteries and colours of the sciences had always mesmerized Kiran. Genetics and molecular biology began to captivate her during her undergraduate career at college. "I drew a lot of inspiration from my science professors who made an excellent faculty there," she beams.

Kiran's larger-than-life carriage won her the loyalty of numerous friends in college. When Kiran didn't get a seat in medicine, which she had earlier tried for, she shoved her disappointment aside and unperturbedly equipped herself with a BSc degree in Zoology, in which she stood first in the university. She then travelled to Australia to pursue her post-graduate studies in Brewing and Fermentation Sciences from Monash University.

She was the only female student in her batch and the youngest in class. "At twenty-one, I was also the most inexperienced as I had barely received exposure to the industrial and corporate environments," she admits ruefully. "In contrast, all my colleagues in Australia were not only either in their late twenties or early thirties but had acquired solid work experience too."

The all-round girls' college, which Kiran had graduated from, gave her few opportunities to interact with men. In Australia, she gradually learned to equate with men. Her steadfastness won her the admiration of male colleagues, most of whom established sturdy friendships with her and sat with her to work out several papers, helping her quicken her progress on the learning curve. Unsurprisingly, Kiran topped the class.

On returning to India, a peeved Kiran found that her gender did not permit her to make a dent in the brewing industry in spite of her high qualifications. It was her ingenious thinking in the face of adversity that laid the foundations of BIOCON.

A Test of Time

The 80-acre BIOCON premises, which stands majestically amidst the most elite of electronic hotspot centres on Hosur Road today, constituted a remote, jungle area twenty-one years ago, when the company had no telephone.

Kiran manufactured simple enzymes, extracted from sources as diverse as raw papaya and tropical fish. The firm initially supplied simple enzymes to an Irish company, which also bore the name BIOCON. In due course, the Anglo-Dutch conglomerate Unilever bought over BIOCON India's Irish partner. As a partner of Unilever's empire, Kiran observed that global giants outsourced research extensively, which her company could leverage. Thus began her journey.

Kiran travelled extensively from the apex of Kashmir to the base of Kanyakumari to build her business. During those times, trains and buses were her best allies; she couldn't afford the lavish comforts of flying. "The train was my most preferred mode of transport even when I took trips to Delhi," Kiran grins.

She had an age and gender credibility to contend with too. In Kiran's times, you had to be over forty to head a company in India and be taken seriously. Kiran had no credible investment bankers to back her; they perceived her as a gullible young child. Her gender did not help her either. "It was extremely difficult to find people who were willing to work for me too," Kiran recollects. She finally succeeded in impressing investors with her intellect and '*I will succeed*' attitude.

Acquiring her first bank loan was only the tip of the frosty iceberg. Raising money to build her factory and adopt new R&D technologies was a Herculean task, especially in light of the fact that R&D was an up-and-coming area for industries and was virtually unheard of. Furthermore, R&D outcomes were so uncertain that applying normal investment criteria was rather difficult. Undaunted by the lukewarm response her ideas evoked, Kiran launched *Syngene*, a contract research company in 1994. She gathered sufficiently large volumes of venture capital with the intention of honing India's outsourcing skills and enhancing her potential for contract research. BIOCON's initial public offering (IPO) was oversubscribed a record 33 times in spite of the presence and clout of the oil-refining giant ONGC. As the Indian biotech sector grew exponentially, the industry was flooded with a surge of new biotech entrants, which began to embrace Kiran's self-coined concept of 'research process outsourcing'.

Kiran believed in generating employment for the poor and unskilled labour force. When she began BIOCON, she hired fifty unskilled workers, vowing that she would permit no differentiation between the labour force and the management. It didn't work. Education – or the lack of it – became a big divide.

A problem arose in 1986-87 when the labourers decided to form a union. Although momentarily startled by their announcement, Kiran calmly attempted to reason with them. "How can you address the management on a one-to-one level if you organize a union?" she queried. The frustrated workers saw no logic in Kiran's argument.

"What are your problems? Please discuss them with me," Kiran requested.

"We are perfectly fine. We have no problems," the workers assured her. "We are happy with the work ambience. Nevertheless, we would like to belong to a union."

Kiran couldn't understand their motive. "Why should you belong to a union, then?" she mused, baffled. The workers didn't take her question in the right spirit. The wide gaps in communication bred a lot of ill will and animosity. Workers would squat on the floors, brandish pickets and effigies and call her all kinds of names.

Kiran began to find their attitude an encumbrance to the company. She took a bold decision. Jettisoning the workers, she shut down the company's operations. After many weeks, an automated BIOCON was established.

With this move, she incurred the wrath of the workers. Back then she lived alone. In the middle of the night and wee hours of the morning, she would receive phone calls from the union leader, who said that she would be done for, if she didn't give in soon. The union even threatened to fling acid on her.

"As a man, you cannot make such threats," Kiran retorted. "If you want to fight me, fight me on a different plane." Refusing to buckle down from the sheer exhaustion of it all, she gathered her wits to sustain herself.

On another occasion, one of Kiran's R&D colleagues reminded her that he wanted to purchase a computer for the company. As Kiran had to meet several other financial commitments, she couldn't afford a computer that cost Rs.30,000. She told him as much. "If you desperately need a computer, find the money for it," she added, unequivocally. And find the money, he did. He took a loan from his grandfather. The company acquired the computer and later repaid the loan to his grandfather.

Kiran and her colleagues had the slenderest pay packets in comparison with industry standards. "My first salary hovered around Rs.50. The salary of the President of the R&D department was not more than Rs.1200 when he joined the company. We took the same salary ever since," she reports. Another ingenious young man joined BIOCON India as the marketing manager for a monthly pay of Rs.2500. When the Head of Operations came along in 1990, he obtained Rs.4500. The deplorable plight they faced then is a far cry from the whopping turnover of around Rs.5000 million BIOCON has achieved today.

Kiran's expression is one of tranquillity as she looks back at the company she built patiently. "We were able to build the company only because the team accepted the low-salary scenario and held on patiently," she acknowledges with satisfaction.

Into the Fray

With a view to launch anti-cancer drugs, BIOCON plans to build Asia's largest anti-body facility in concert with CIMAB, a renowned Cuban research institute, which has received recognition for its meticulous research in antibodies and immuno-therapies, particularly in the field of oncology. The first product, an anti-EGFR (Epidermal Growth Factor Receptor), targets antibody h-R3 and is due to undergo clinical trials in Bangalore. "We expect to launch the product into the Indian market by the end of 2005," Kiran informs with an upbeat smile. "This will be followed by two more antibodies, anti-CD3, (an immuno-suppressant for transplants) and anti-CD6 (which would work against rheumatoid arthritis and T-Cell lynphoma)." Also in the offing are three cancer vaccines: EGF, TGF-alpha and Her1.

BIOCON has discovered a plethora of medium-term opportunities in the area of insulin production. The company has also launched the world's first recombinant human insulin (r-DNA) 'Insugen' with the objective of capturing a share of 20% over a span of the next two years in the fast growing Rs.2.2 billion (USD 48.74 million) human insulin market. Besides manufacturing enzymes and drugs to fight diabetes, cancer and cholesterol, BIOCON has separate units, which offer contract research and clinical trial services for global clients in a bid to cash in on relatively inexpensive scientists. BIOCON aims to grow at the rate of 30% per year – a percentage which carries the potential to make it a billion-dollar company by the end of the decade.

BIOCON intends to make a foray into the US market and is waiting for the US Food and Drug Administration (USFDA) to spell out its regulatory policy on the generic version of insulin. Kiran has already submitted a drug master file to the USFDA, becoming the first Indian insulin producer to do so. "The US and European markets are our long-term targets in view of the regulatory barriers," Kiran discloses.

BIOCON India has also become a major global player in statin technology. "Statins, however, provide us only a short-term opportunity," Kiran informs clearly. "We believe we can discover long-term opportunities in antibodies and proprietary molecules." Statins, insulins, antibodies and immuno-suppressants are now major areas of focus for BIOCON.

An Ocean of Wealth

Sporting a fancy scarf, a trendy haircut and a friendly smile, Kiran hardly looks like a scientist who heads a 1,200-strong team of technical experts and a company with more than 130 patents to its credit.

If she is the richest woman in the country today, she always attached a strong value for money. Every product or service BIOCON was charged for was handpicked. "Even today, we negotiate the price when I purchase machinery and equipment for BIOCON," Kiran professes. She never spent money for extravagant purposes. Wherever she went, she bought the cheapest train tickets and made sure she stayed in the cheapest of hotels. It is no wonder that she hasn't been able to attune herself to 'The Richest Woman of India' title.

> *"The word 'rich' gives a connotation that money has not been obtained in the kind of way I would like it to be perceived. Richness can be inborn, inherited or usurped. The tag name 'rich' should throw light on the impediments we have fought against to climb to this position. The BIOCON story is all about wealth creation. Anyone who is committed enough to the cause of creating wealth can achieve it."*

The words 'ennui' and 'status quo' do not exist in Kiran's dictionary. She believes she can influence change at different levels, particularly by encouraging women to think differently about themselves. She has been active in motivating women to speak up for themselves and retaliate when they are treated subserviently or accused for 'not doing things right'. Kiran set up BIOCON Foundation as an exclusive CSR (Corporate Social Responsibility) body, which would focus on bringing about a social change in the areas of health care and education.

On power and influence, she rightly says: "Being powerful doesn't mean throwing your weight around and ordering people. Power grants us the ability to induce social change."

The Dialogue Box

Numerous parents have sought advice from Kiran, asking her to suggest some of the finer biotechnology institutes in India where they could enrol their children. Touched by their earnestness, Kiran longed to help them. As the President of ABLE (*Association of Biotech-Led Enterprises*), she has decided to rate the biotech courses offered in India to provide potential students a clear idea of the premier schools of biotechnology in India, hoping to ward off any form of complacence in the institutes and promote their development to engender healthy competition among them.

Kiran's eyes take on a faraway look as she prepares to plunge into a legion of changes, which galvanized the biotech boom in India.

Excerpts from an exclusive interview with Kiran Mazumdar-Shaw...

- *What are the crucial ingredients of the National Biotech policy?*

  What is extremely important is the regulatory framework of the Government. We need to strongly address the funding requirements of the biotech sector. Today, hosts of innovative programmes are on the cards to facilitate industry-academia interactions, which play as imperative a role as the factors. Sponsored by CSIR, the New Millennium Initiative on Technology Leadership is a funding programme, which aims at promoting joint research and development. Furthermore, the creation of essential infrastructures and human resource development should receive prime focus too.

- *Is the Indian Government supportive of entrepreneurial ventures? What policy changes are you looking for?*

  Well, the Government must provide many more seed funds for entrepreneurship. Young entrepreneurs, who have no means of raising capital, should receive access to seed capital. Creating soft funds would be a shot in the arm too. Such benefits would enable aspiring entrepreneurs to lucidly explain the objectives of their programmes and give them an encouraging push to set themselves in motion. Directing a focused initiative in every stream of activity is the need of the hour. Akin to venture capitalism, a growth model of this sort would fetch us monumental returns.

- *In the sphere of corporate governance, where does India rank on the world index?*

  New companies are practising good governance. Older companies will, however, have to strive to arrive at higher levels of corporate governance as their exposure to the stringent *Licence Raj* has modified their stance, making them believe that the corporate environment continues to be very corrupt, when it is not so. With the Government offering to serve as a *facilitator* rather than imposing its authority as a controller, the old mindset must change.

- *What impact do you feel inhaled insulin manufactured by BIOCON would cast on the public demand for insulin?*

  There is a large market potential for inhaled insulin. The emergence of inhaled insulin in the market will increase the quantity and requirement of insulin, countrywide. This gives us a global edge over other countries. Our product meets the highest global standards and Bristol Myers-Squibb has endorsed it. We are currently exploring various avenues to develop oral insulin in alliance with the US-based Nobex Corporation.

- *You have been associated with initiatives like BATF and 'Keep Koramangala Clean'. Are they intended to serve as elitist campaigns?*

  Well, it is our duty to educate the illiterate masses and these initiatives, which I have been involved in, endeavour to instil in them the need to maintain a clean environment. So, to a certain extent, they are elitist campaigns, since the regular slum dweller doesn't possess an awareness of the fact that unhygienic conditions and garbage-strewn areas can cause deadly diseases and epidemics. It is largely a question of civic mindedness.

- *If there were one thing you could change about BIOCON, what would it be?*

  I am satisfied with the way we built BIOCON. And I haven't led a more fulfilling life. (*Laughs*) I would, however, like to be involved in writing a book on BIOCON. The book must bring to light the life and soul of BIOCON, capturing the travails behind the sweat and blood which have been invested in the making of BIOCON. Now, that would make a great story.

The Vision Beyond

BIOCON aims at standing as one of the top ten corporate biotech conglomerates, worldwide. Kiran fervently hopes to see a BIOCON molecule in the world market in the next five years, placing India in the coveted league of rare and vibrant biotech forerunners. "India is one of the biggest centres for biotechnology in the areas of healthcare and pharmaceuticals," she asserts.

Her vision was ratified when the Karnataka Government founded a Biotechnology Vision Group, with Kiran as its Chairman. Kiran advises the Government on the policy initiatives it should introduce in the field of biotechnology.

Kiran has also been selected as the honorary Consul of Ireland for pharma-biotech ventures between India and Ireland. The $350 billion pharmaceutical industry revolves around 400 drugs, which fight ailments that are known to wreck human health.

The functional genomics should explode the universe to an ambit of 10,000 targets or more. In short, trillions of dollars of business have been set to explode globally – a potential that had Microsoft's Bill Gates subscribing to it too. Kiran has identified such an opportunity and skilfully developed it to place India in the global map of biotechnology. "A position as one of the top ten G-7 or G-10 countries in the world is what India should aim for," Kiran states with passion.

In the Same League

Kiran's expertise in the realm of biotechnology has won her a high opinion from the best of corporate heads. The phone buzzes amidst our pleasant chat with her. Kiran's eyebrows shoot up with amusement as she picks up the receiver. The caller is none other than Azim Premji (Chairman of Wipro). She laughs, listens for a while and then laughs some more before rendering her expert advice. Azim Premji has immense respect for Kiran's interests and appreciates her phenomenal success in the biotech industry. In fact, we caught him seeking advice from Kiran for his new biotech venture.

Over the years, Kiran established an enduring friendship with Azim Premji (Chairman, Wipro), Narayana Murthy (Chief Mentor, Infosys Technologies) and Dr Devi Shetty (Chairman, Narayana Hrudalaya). While Azim Premji developed a terrific brand image for India in the métier of software services, Narayana Murthy gave shape to his model company, Infosys, creating it from zilch – just like Kiran did with BIOCON.

To date, Azim and Kiran never fail to joke with one other. "Few people know the lighter, funnier side of Azim. So, don't be fooled by him," Kiran warns us with an impish grin. "Many believe that Azim is a very serious person who hardly knows what humour is. But that is what he does all the time as soon as he picks up his phone to talk to me." Her statement gives us scope to speculate that Azim has amused Kiran with one of his wily jokes over the phone! Once again, the lavishly adorned office fills up with her gregarious laughter as we hit the record button and resume our conversation.

"Dr Devi Shetty is one of the greatest inspirational forces in my life today," Kiran continues. "To me, he represents every facet of the modern Gandhi. His mind constantly teems with unique ideas for new measures, which he can introduce to induce social change." Kiran is proud of the fact that Dr Devi Shetty ensured that the poorest of men would be able to avail of the best of healthcare services.

The Receptive Employer

Trust in every employee and the full freedom that each member of the staff has at his disposal to work to his fullest potential are some of the best features of BIOCON. "The question of gender never arises with Kiran. Such is her personality," the employees state in happy unison.

Kiran candidly expresses her standpoint on workplace gender concerns: "Being a thoughtful manager has nothing to do with being a man or woman. You have to be very fair and just. People shouldn't perceive you as a bigoted, self-opinionated person who favours certain kinds and classes of people. What's more, you have to be approachable and communicate clearly to your folks. Perhaps, the only difference I discern between a man and a woman is the historical belief that men belong to the more powerful sex. A woman is more aware of the sensitivities of people than a man is. If one of my employees requested me to listen to a personal problem, I might at the least be able to understand an iota of the turmoil they are going through. But men don't have the time for that. In all likelihood, employees (and female employees in particular) would not openly discuss their problems with a male CEO simply because they would not be quite so comfortable doing so. A woman whose husband physically abuses her at home would feel more at ease when she talks about her horrid experiences to the woman in me."

Symmetry of Life

Kiran married John Shaw at the age of forty-five. A tall Scotsman, John was forty-nine and the Managing Director of Madura Coats, when he met Kiran. Her family appreciated the certitude with which she married John. "My family declared that they would be happy as long as I was happy with the man of my dreams," Kiran says.

John left Madura Coats to join BIOCON and work in concert with Kiran. He felt that his financial finesse and Kiran's scientific acumen would provide a good complementary fit for BIOCON. John never had a complex that he wasn't quite so high-profile a personality as his wife. "There has been no insecurity in our relationship," Kiran divulges, her husky voice tinged with pride.

Kiran hasn't given much thought to raising a family of her own; she and her husband spend most of their time at work. "Women lay claim to excellent multi-tasking skills," she adds. "They can establish stability between their personal and professional lives with more ease than men, if they desire to do so."

Kiran spends a lot of quality time with her mother. When her brothers' families visit Bangalore, she leaves the office early to play with her niece and nephew. "But I tend to work late when they're not here," she admits sheepishly. She mentions that sister-in-law Catherine, a French professor at a university abroad and a mother of two teenaged children has achieved a strong equilibrium between her home life and work life. Catherine's husband (Kiran's brother) heartily cooks dinner for the family when his wife is compelled to work late.

"Men are required to understand their wives' needs and constraints," Kiran declares staunchly. "Women would find it difficult to strike a good balance if their husbands tell them that household work is *their* job." With Kiran's husband shouldering an equal burden of domestic responsibilities, she shares a happy and successful marital life with him.

> *"As long as women themselves don't have the drive in them to initiate an attitudinal change in the mindsets of people, change will not occur. It is very simple, really. Isn't it easier staying at home and sporting the 'I'm a homemaker' sash? Women account for 30% of employees in Biocon. Women head many departments too. If they can work, why can't the others?"*

Although a firm believer in God, Kiran doesn't remember being a devout Hindu; she never thought one religion was better than the other. Religious nuts just aren't Kiran's cup of tea. Reposing immense faith in the fruits of tradition, Kiran performs religious activities that hold the importance and charm of Indian culture and tradition. "For instance, I don't associate 'Bhoomi Puja' with the austerity of a Hindu custom," Kiran substantiates. "Instead, I perceive it as an integral component of India's rich, composite culture and tradition."

"The essence of the Gita is very profound," she reveals, her face caked with a philosophical expression. The principles of Buddhism and various facets of the Bible enchant her too. Inside that impervious exterior lies a compassionate soul and an altruistic heart.

"When I asked Kiran ma'am to give me just one month to decide whether I would take up the job of serving as her driver, I was touched to hear her say that she would wait for one year to hire me," avows Edward, who has been Kiran's chauffeur for eighteen years.

Kiran's faith in youth power has led her to believe that the energies of the youth should be harnessed and their talents encouraged, if the intellectual resource pool in our country is to expand further. When a group of students approached Kiran for her support in their new shaadi.com venture, she heartily agreed.

Jest like Kiran

Kiran's childhood penchant for art paved the way for her zest for artefacts of varied styles and antiquities, which she personally hunts for. Her best art collections are displayed in the office and her Spanish-style villa in Glenmore. "The first piece of artworks that I bought were priced nominally compared to the whopping rates people are charged with for similar works, today," she recalls. She paid Yusuf Arakkal Rs.3000 in three instalments for the first work of art she bought.

Her involvement with art is confined to merely buying exquisite art pieces, today. She also loves sauntering over to hosts of art exhibitions and updating her knowledge on the latest trends in the art business. One piece of art, which particularly touched her the most, was a colour-pencil drawing by her 11-year-old nephew, Eric. It read: "If I found a pot of gold, I would give it to my Aunt for her to make new medicine to fight very bad diseases."

A multi-faceted woman, Kiran is also a fabulous singer. She likes reading and listening to Indian classical music.

Kiran is notorious for making her folks the biggest April fools imaginable. Once she fooled one of her friends by posing as an NDTV director who was keen on interviewing the lady. This carried on for a long time. On the spur of the moment, she cancelled the interview. "Imagine my friend's reaction then. Boy, was it so comical!" Kiran laughs.

On another occasion, she adorned herself as a bride and invited her folks and friends for a mock engagement ceremony, managing to fool everyone.

"Kiran is a leader who is wide-awake, when everyone is fast asleep. There is an exciting pulse in her," reveals Neelima Roshven, Consultant and Director, Wadhwani Foundation, Bangalore. "We have visited a lot of wonderful holiday spots together. I especially remember the fun we had when we did the Caribbean dance!"

"I would have more time to pursue my hobbies if I were less busier than I am now," laughs Kiran. After a strenuous day, she delights in chilling out with a goblet of warm wine in her hand, Pavarotti in the background and the doting husband by her side.

A saviour for many, biotechnology has become a way of life, an absorbing philosophy, and an enthralling culture for all. With the industry clocking the highest growth rate in India, which is poised to cash in on the global boom, biotech is no longer deemed unconventional. Branded as 'the unconventional woman', Kiran has come to serve as an epitome of the new ethos of free enterprise and entrepreneurship in the Indian trellis of managed capitalism.

> *"A true entrepreneur is one who embarks on an unusual journey and creates a team of people who believe in that journey. The self-made entrepreneur is a fearless risk-taker, who possesses the courage, perseverance and will power to succeed."*

Lalita D. Gupte
Joint Managing Director, ICICI Bank

6.

Sporting the Leader's Badge

A large army marched behind her. The band of women who comprised this army marched for the cause of leadership. Wielding the flag majestically, the lady at the forefront steers the leaders. Even as the small number of women managers in corporate boardrooms continues to hog the newsprint, a few have effectively shattered the glass ceiling in the male bastion.

A key figure behind the successful diversification of ICICI's international banking activities, the soft-spoken and self-effacing ***Lalita D. Gupte*** (Joint Managing Director, ICICI Bank), symbolizes the increasing role of the enlarging army of women in the corporate vista. She has over three decades of expertise in the financial services industry, today.

Three years ago, the *Fortune* list selected her as one of the fifty most powerful women in international business. "I attribute my credentials to ICICI Group. This recognition motivated me to work harder than ever before. We have so much more to achieve," she stated modestly, on being felicitated. She played a pioneering role in building the erstwhile ICICI Limited into a full-fledged universal banking corporation, which sprouted from the roots of a one-time development financial institution. The efforts of the ICICI management team culminated with a successful merger of ICICI Limited and ICICI Bank Limited.

Under Lalita's stewardship, ICICI was the first Indian enterprise and the second bank in Asia to be listed in the New York Stock Exchange (NYSE). She shaped a battalion of women leaders including Kalpana Morparia, Shikha Sharma, Renuka Ramnath and Madhabi Puri Buch as the divisional heads and CEOs in the ICICI Group.

The Keystones

Lalita was born into a family that comprised a confluence of enlightened minds. Her father joined the Indian Civil Service and later rose to the position of a Cabinet Secretary, while her mother belonged to a business family. Her father's industrious nature and her mother's social and philanthropic outlook cast a profound impact on little Lalita. Her mother was the president of the Maharashtra State Women's Council in the 1950s and worked in Mumbai at Asha Sadan, the social service organization, which she helped set up to assist women and children.

Lalita and her siblings held brilliant academic records. Her eldest sister, Vijaya Anand, who specialized in gynaecology, became the Chief Medical Officer in the State Bank of India. Her second sister Sharda Dwivedi grew to be a renowned historian, while her brother was effective in creating the super-computer Param.

Lalita and her siblings were raised in an atmosphere that was very accommodative and conducive to their personal growth and development. "Ours was a very happy, close-knit and gregarious family," Lalita informs. "We had a large circle of friends and cousins."

Lalita did her schooling from Mumbai and New Delhi. Till she completed her seventh grade, she studied in Queen Mary's, following which she enrolled in the Convent of Jesus and Mary, which she passed out from. She then proceeded to Miranda House (Delhi) to pursue her undergraduate course in Economics Honours before joining Jamnalal Bajaj Institute of Management Studies (JBIMS) to acquire an MBA degree. She performed exceptionally well. Thereafter, she could take her pick from a wide range of choices that lay at her disposal. "ICICI Limited was an easy option," Lalita mentions with a smile. She promptly began her career with ICICI in 1971 as a trainee in the Project Appraisal department.

Lalita married an Indian Naval officer, Dileep, who gave as much importance to her career as his own, at a time when there were very few officers' wives who pursued careers themselves. Lalita and her husband had to maintain two homes very often, flying to meet each other at least once a month. They took transfers in their stride. Every time Lalita shifted her residence during the thirty-year span of her marriage, they created a home together, adamantly insisting on choosing for their new house a getup similar to the one that had prevailed earlier!

"We cannot afford to let guilt consume us," Lalita counsels. "Managing and planning one's time efficiently can go a long way in helping one discover the right mix of home and work." Many a year, Lalita has been away on business tours for long periods. However, as the day faded imperceptibly into the night, her children's lunchboxes have been as important to her as any merger and acquisition (M&A) deal.

Milking the Market

Lalita seeks to try the untried and know the unknown. Right through her career, she has exploited emerging marketing opportunities and searched constantly for new ideas and concepts. When opportunity struck the retail finance sector, she and the management team at ICICI placed the company on the path of retail banking after a careful study of the prevailing opportunities with a view to diversifying and de-risking the activities of the ICICI Group.

When opportunities flooded the ICICI Group in the insurance stream, the team decided that the group should enter the insurance sector. The decision Lalita took to diversify the bank's portfolio and product mix propelled the organization to newfound heights of success, credibility and profitability. Her tasks lay not only in moving strategic directions but also in choosing leadership at various levels along with K V Kamath, CEO and Managing Director of ICICI Bank.

In 2000-01, the Board gave Lalita a new challenge, which involved leading the ICICI Group's international initiatives. Under Lalita's supervision, her colleagues carefully examined the opportunities for the bank in the international arena, looking at areas of Business Processing and International Banking, both corporate and retail.

With the boom in the BPO sector, ICICI Bank began to pay more attention to processing and setting up a centralized processing hub. *ICICI Onesource*, the BPO company with a separate identity, has already done very well with Anand Mukherji as the CEO. "We realized the importance of service-level agreements only when we worked on the BPO project," says Lalita. What followed the emergence of *ICICI Onesource* was a purposeful attempt to make a dent in the field of international banking.

Before long, ICICI Bank secured an exalted international image in the market. Every phase has seen many and varied challenges. "We worked in concert as a team to build these initiatives," Lalita informs. "We view international banking as an area which is an extension of what we do and how well we do, both in both corporate and retail banking in India," she adds. In the same breadth, she continues to explain the bank's global ambitions in USA, Canada, Sri Lanka, Bahrain, Dubai, Singapore, China, Bangladesh and South Africa with a practiced precision, which is characteristic only of her. Lalita hopes that International Business will contribute over 15% of the bank's total revenues in the next five years.

ICICI Bank was the first Indian bank to earn an investment-grade international credit rating award. Also the first to popularise the ATM culture in India, the organization built widespread ATM networks, which forever changed the methods of banking in India, introducing the benefits of technology to serve Indian customers. Right from banking and asset management to pension and insurance, the financial services industry has begun to extend significant opportunities in every field.

ICICI Bank continuously implements several quality initiatives. Lalita improved the company's systems and processes and revised the bank's quality initiatives, bringing in higher levels of income and profitability. The bank internationally serves the NRI communities and Indian corporate bodies in overseas markets. Under Lalita's stewardship, ICICI Bank will provide trade, corporate banking, and retail banking services internationally.

Various combinations of factors have influenced Lalita's success over a series of years. A woman who welcomes change and difference with open arms, she constantly adopts measures to improve her management style.

"Achieving the goals that you set out to achieve within the parameters you have laid down gives you a feeling of confidence and success," she opines with a smile. She spotted the right opportunity to raise equity and built strong management teams. Clearly, Lalita is playing a pivotal role in steering the business meticulously in the direction of a new vista for growth.

> *"At ICICI Bank, you are an individual in your own right and a member of TEAM ICICI. The ICICI Group's undying team spirit is one of its greatest assets."*

Circuit

Lalita takes us on a heart-warming tour through various aspects of her life, career and society. *Excerpts from an exclusive interview…*

- *The percentage of women who hold key leadership positions in the banking sector and ICICI, in particular, has risen creditably. Is the banking sector more amenable to ladies?*

  In a study that we conducted for CII, we discovered that a lot of women opt for a career in the tertiary sector. Perhaps, the services industry is more amenable to women than the manufacturing sector. Women who work on the shop floor are fewer in number. The banking and financial services industries, besides posing interesting challenges, provide an extended scope for variety in one's career.

- *Would you say that the company's HR policy carries special provisions to encourage larger numbers of female employees in the workplace?*

  ICICI Bank is an organization driven by meritocracy. We view merit and performance as the core criteria for promotions; they are the rationale behind the underlying success of several young professionals in our organization. Gender and background have no role to play in this regard. Contoured by a sensitive and uplifting spirit that lies within its façade, ICICI has been neutral to both males and females alike, in its treatment of employees over its time frame of fifty years. ICICI Group has been the single employer for many of our employees. Our employees and managers express enthusiasm to stay with us and work in ICICI; those who wish to leave will always remain our goodwill Ambassadors. The positive energy that we generate augurs well for the congenial ambience we provide here.

- *Personally speaking, would you have cut better deals abroad?*

  Well, I did get offers from many international banks. Nevertheless, I was presented with numerous challenges and opportunities in ICICI itself. (*Laughs*) The level of interest my work generated was sufficient to hold me here. As is true of most of us though, I wasn't certain which direction my course of action would lead me to. But then again, you can't plan what you're going to do ten years from now.

Hallmark of Achievement

Lalita is not a woman who confines herself to the territory of strong ethics alone. She has garnered tremendous admiration for the impeccable governance standards she set for ICICI over the years.

> *"Indian companies are no less than their foreign counterparts in the sphere of corporate governance. In particular, those companies which are maturing are taking painstaking effort to put in place the best corporate governance and corporate philanthropy standards. For years, Indian corporate entities have created vast opportunities for the public and proactively spearheaded educational and philanthropic activities in towns and villages."*

The bank has also segregated the tasks of the executive management team from those of the Chairman. "We are a part of an organization which has a sound belief in our role as corporate citizens," Lalita declares proudly. A special group has been set up to propagate social and humanitarian causes. To this end, ICICI has worked actively in several areas. "In particular, we work on three core platforms – education, healthcare and micro-credit," Lalita informs.

In her eyes, education and learning have always been components of a continuous learning process. One of Lalita's last exercises involved grasping the nitty-gritty of the six-sigma concept in a classroom. "The capacity to perform is directly linked to one's ability to learn," she views. "One has to continue to learn at every stage of life."

ICICI introduced a multitude of social initiatives to promote the cause of education. In the healthcare segment, ICICI has enthusiastically been involved in several UNICEF campaigns for oral dehydration and AIDS Awareness.

Lalita's thirst for action, education and welfare of women have had her chair select expert groups and enrol as a member in many others. Earlier a member of the Board of Governors of the Indian Institute of Technology (IIT), Mumbai and The Expert Group on Foreign Exchange Markets in India, (constituted by the RBI in November 1994) and the member-secretary of The Expert Group of Commercialisation of Infrastructure (set up by the Government of India in 1995), she was also the Chairman of the Confederation of Indian Industry – National Committee of E-commerce and the first CII Women Empowerment Committees.

Never one to pivot on a single source of inspiration, Lalita picked the best qualities from a wide and diverse range of people. And her knowledge has been handed down to her team at ICICI. During her career, she received numerous awards for her novel ideas and efforts in various domains, including *The Twenty-first Century for Finance and Banking Award* instituted by the Ladies' Wing of the Indian Merchants' Chamber in 1997, the *Women Achievers' Award* from the Women Graduates Union in 2001 and the *Woman of the Year Award*, presented by the International Women's Association in 2002 (in acknowledgement of her achievements in the corporate world). "The awards serve as a recognition of the institution we work for," Lalita opines, her tone ringing with modesty. "They result from a volume of collective efforts. There are many who are more deserving of the awards than I am."

The Powerful Netting

Several issues crop up during the course of every phase in one's life. Lalita strongly abides by the policy of taking things as they come. Life would get pretty difficult when her husband took off on official tours, every so often. Invariably that was the time when Lalita would have to contend with meeting numerous deadlines at work and attend her children's PTA meetings and functions at school. Lalita mentions that her husband did exactly the same when she was away. "Dileep has been a wonderful father and husband," she smiles. However, these are situations all working couples face. Working couples must share not only the fun which parenting involves but the responsibilities that follow too.

"I dare say I have been fortunate though," Lalita confesses with a grin. "My children are level-headed, well-balanced individuals, today. Perhaps, Dileep and I just let them grow – we didn't place any pressures on them." Even during their childhood, they learnt to adjust to the fact that both their parents were working.

> *"Women work enthusiastically soon after they graduate from B-schools or complete their education in other disciplines. Once married though, they don't get adequate support to help them unearth the right balance between their homes and careers. They need to find the right people to whom they can entrust the responsibility of looking after their children. Organizations must pitch in to help women by granting extended leave to new mothers and introducing flexi-time options for them."*

Cushioned within the veneer of the strong business baron is a gentle heart, which confides that one has to take every experience in one's stride. In the earlier years, weekends entailed spending time with her children, experimenting with new recipes in the kitchen and watching inane soaps on TV. Now that her children are away, she misses them a lot. She rises in the wee hours of dawn and is promptly in the office by 8.30 a.m. Her punctuality speaks volumes about the importance of discipline in her life.

Eager for dramatic growth, she continues pushing the limits once again with her swift pace and neat style. Since the days Lalita D. Gupte joined ICICI, she has treaded a long path to achieve the status she enjoys today.

"Decide what you want to do in life. No one can decide for you."

Naina Lal Kidwai
Deputy Chief Executive Officer, HSBC

7.
The Master Strategist

The horse gallops at full speed through the fertile meadows, as her silvery silhouette contrasts strikingly with the background of the setting sun in the twilight horizons. On its sturdy back sits a prim young woman, her proud chin pointing upwards in the air. As the horse approaches, looming larger with every majestic step, the lady clutches the bridle with newfound vigour. With the progress of each measured step, the magnitude of her successes becomes larger too.

The young woman on horseback has evolved into one of the most discerning master strategists in the field of Indian banking. ***Naina Lal Kidwai*** (Deputy Chief Executive Officer, HSBC, India) is a woman of purpose and direction who has time and again revealed her ability to anticipate new areas of growth in the retail and investment-banking sectors, spotting the right opportunities at the right time.

"Horse-riding was once a favourite sport of mine. But I haven't pursued it since I broke my shoulder and ribs in a riding accident eight years ago," Naina welcomes us as she breezes into her spacious office, which is well known for its magnificent views of the turrets and domes of Bombay's 19th century buildings.

Time magazine listed her as one of the fifteen emerging 'Globally Influential' icons in 2002 while the *Fortune* magazine picked her for her outstanding achievements in the corporate sector, naming her 'The World's Top 50 Corporate Women', every year since they began the listing in 2001. She is the only Indian woman who is on the *Fortune* list, every year. Her status as one of the most powerful and influential global banking ladies worldwide hasn't made her the slightest bit arrogant. She is a plain *dal-roti* person with a penchant for different varieties of tea. Every endeavour of hers is fuelled with a conviction that the future of India is embedded in her grassroots.

The Wannabe Manager

Surendra Lal was a lucky man. And why not! A top executive of an insurance company, finance and golfing were two of his greatest passions in life. Every daughter of his inherited each of his passions and honed her talents further. Sports weren't alien to Naina. Her sister Nonita Lal Qureshi emerged as a leading golfer. Nonita was a recipient of the Arjuna Award and credited to be India's highest-ranking golfer, nine times over. Naina's visual acuity and astute mind also made her a wunderkind in games. "I played basketball and badminton for my school and the State of Himachal Pradesh," she recalls, harking back to her carefree years of childhood.

Naina acquired her extraordinary financial finesse from her father. As a child, the swirling office chair and the large oak desk in her father's office mystified her. The professional ambience openly spelled respect, value and appreciation. She experienced an overwhelming desire to be the boss in such an office one day. "One can stretch to the vantage point of success in life only when both parents support and stand by you," she reckons.

Religious by nature, Naina's mother was a woman of strong values. Naina imbibed her mother's ceaseless thirst for knowledge and her father's yearning for perfection. She grows sober as she mentions, "My father passed away when I was thirty-three." As we probe into her antecedents, she reveals, "I was born in Kolkata and grew up in Mumbai, Shimla and Delhi. My father's family hailed from U P (Mussoorie) while my mother's family belonged to Punjab (Ludhiana). Born a Hindu, with a Sikh stream running through one of our forefathers, I was educated in a Christian boarding school. I am now married to a Muslim. I regard myself as a true amalgam of all that is India. This is not the era of caste or creed or religion. I am proud to be quintessentially Indian."

Skyward Bound

The positions of leadership Naina held during her school years culminated with the post of Head Girl in her final year. During the course of her stint in Lady Shriram College, Delhi, where she pursued her undergraduate course in Economics Honours, she proved her leadership mettle with the first-ever inter-collegiate cultural extravaganza, which she organized as the Secretary of the College. She later became the President.

A graduate at the tender age of 19, Naina aspired to travel abroad to earn a post-graduate degree in business management. She was not disheartened when told she was too young to sign up for a management programme. Instead, she boldly decided to try her hand in Chartered Accountancy. She was one of the first three women who joined Price Waterhouse in 1977.

Naina Lal Kidwai did travel abroad to chase her dream of studying business management. Graduating in Strategy and Finance from the Harvard Business School in 1982, she was the first Indian woman on their rolls to do so. While most management aspirants who enrolled in this Ivy-League institution were twenty-six years of age or above, Naina was only twenty-three.

Harvard's impressive faculty, state-of-the-art computer laboratories, well-stocked library and intellectual charms won her over, making her two-year course at Harvard a rewarding experience. Naina recalls the exhilaration that pulsed through her veins, when she worked for hours on end on her case studies and research papers. "Executives from top-notch companies and corporate bodies would come over and discuss the cases with us," she informs.

Naina even worked on a consulting assignment under well-known professor and management guru Michael Porter. Today, she has not only pioneered innovative stratagems in the corporate realm but charted out a tactical approach for a fulfilling life too.

Post-Harvard, Naina Kidwai was offered several lucrative assignments on foreign shores. Despite the insistence of the recruiting firms, she did not take the campus route to make her first career move. A fierce patriot, she politely declined their offers to return to her motherland in an era when many aspired to work abroad.

She secured two impressive offers for jobs in India while still abroad. "One of them came from Citibank," she recollects. On setting foot in India, she talked to several banks before opting for Grindlays, the largest foreign investment bank at the time in the country. She was only 32, when she headed the western region in less than three years. She took charge of the investment banking operations across the country and became the youngest-ever head of the largest foreign investment bank in 1989. In 1991, she switched to retail banking for a 'fresh challenge' even while ANZ began grooming her for bigger jobs. Her activities entailed dealing with a thousand-plus workforce across the nation. During her tenure, she almost tripled the NRI deposits from Rs.633 crores in 1991 to Rs.1748 crores in 1992.

She shot into the limelight in 1994 when she was headhunted by Morgan Stanley and later initiated a joint venture with J M Financial. Grindlays and Morgan Stanley persuaded her to set her sights on greener pastures abroad. Their attempts were futile; the wilful young woman was stubbornly firm on her decision.

During Naina's time, the Grindlays premises held few women although the numbers continued to grow. During the entire span of her career though, her age played a more inhibitive role than her gender. When one's age and experience in the organization counted more than one's inherent competence or level of commitment, it was quite natural for fresh young blood to make a beeline for foreign banks, eager to acquire due value for their merit and enhance their prospects of promotions in the future.

"Foreign banks provide ample scope for personal and professional growth and development," Naina points out. "They are known to value professionalism and invest in training." Being recognized irrespective of her age remained one of Naina's primary concerns during the tough initial phase of her career. Every branch of the tree she climbed with an urge to reach the apex regularly had another person – a potential rival – who was older than her by five to ten years.

If Naina had decided otherwise and settled abroad permanently, would she have been as renowned as she is today? "I would have probably brokered bigger deals," she admits. However, it was not money that provided any impetus for her. "I don't regret my decision," Naina smiles. "Sometimes though, I can't help but wonder if the decision I had taken had been the right one – especially when India's growth slowed down and the country became more insular. As I look back now, I realize that the decision I made was the right one."

"Understanding a country and being a part of it is vastly beneficial," she reflects. "The challenge of setting trends in one's own country is indeed a stimulating, one-of-its-kind experience. If you are the first person to strike a $ 200 million deal in India, you may be the 101st person to do the same abroad."

This lady has broken new ground and galvanized policy changes in the country. She belongs to a large number of committees that believe in the same cause. "Had I chosen to stay abroad, I would not have gained such experiences during the course of similar assignments," she states.

The Top Job

Naina proceeded to head the HSBC Securities and Capital Markets Company in 2002. In 2004, she was assigned the role of the Deputy CEO of HSBC in India in addition to her existing responsibilities as the head of the Equities Research and Investment Banking operations. With that, she also has direct responsibility in taking charge of the bank's corporate interfacing jobs, institutional banking functions and custodial services. In a nutshell, she has taken every other domain under her wing, aside from retailing.

"I wish to see HSBC achieve a leadership position in every sphere of activity," she aspires. "That is the vision I hold for my company." She also hopes to attract more financial resources from the group abroad and channel them effectively into India. "The inflow of financial capital into China is much greater; our challenge lies in attracting sizeable volumes into India too," she lets in. We nod in agreement. India indeed has to reposition herself; and that calls for a joint responsibility.

Naina firmly believes HSBC's current focus lies in recognizing merit and talent in evolving a merit-based corporate enterprise. She believes in a team-based ethos, which she has actively propagated through her career. She is also establishing strong mentoring systems. Her team is now working on nurturing a certain number of women in the organization. While Naina keeps a steady eye on the ratio, she doesn't compromise on the quality. The pay packets are more variable and the implementation of functions is more performance-driven today; each member has to deliver.

Naina also chairs the Diversity Committee of the bank. "Diversity is not as big an issue in India as it is abroad," she opines. "Here, we are already culturally diverse in the workplace. People heartily celebrate every festival together." However, she is working on inducing a more disability-friendly environment and enabling economically challenged individuals to enter the workplace too. As an integral component of HSBC's corporate social responsibility initiatives, she has lent ample support to global NGO bodies, which are engaged in India and the smaller local ones functioning at grass-root levels in India.

> ***The World's 'Local Bank' Culture of HSBC in India***
> *"HSBC has a presence in the locality of many countries. Whichever country we operate in, the policy of integration will receive the highest preference."*

The Five-Point Success Formula

Following her intuition and shrewd business insight, Naina aggressively chased information technology opportunities. She worked on Wipro's New York Stock Exchange listing, smoothened the progress of Tata's acquisition of VSNL and delivered some of the country's most path-breaking IPOs. (Bharti Telecom, Maruti Udyog, GAIL and Biocon are some of these.) For Naina, each deal presents a different discipline, and a unique challenge.

"Besides that, just working for the right company at the right time and tapping opportunities and investing in high-quality companies which hold a lot of promise in the future and convincing them to perform the right action for themselves can do a lot of wonders," she smiles. Egg her on further and she gives you her five-point potion to clinch successful deals:

- "Forging a solid relationship is the need of the hour. It is essential to understand the clients' desires and expectations."
- "Privatisation can serve as an instrument, which would enable the Government to accept and understand the process. Dealing with people who do not understand the mechanism and even those who are unfamiliar with the term 'finance' poses the biggest challenge. No

matter how bright and smart bureaucratic circles are, they have little or no knowledge of the Indian capital market structures."

(The fact that they change constantly, keeps Naina's team-mates constantly on their toes, as they are compelled to educate a fresh group of IAS officers, once in two years.)

- "We need to apprise the Government of the working of the price mechanism. On working in concert with companies, we also need to identify the right decision-making process and help them achieve."
- "In an M&A deal, convincing the selling party about the real worth of the company takes precedence at all times. When the seller is also the founder of the company, assuring him that its actual worth is much lower than he believes can be particularly testing. Unless you bring him down to reality, making a sale will remain a castle in the sky."
- "Making MNCs appreciate the true value of India would be a shot in the arm too. As a country, we excel in concealing our best and revealing our worst. We must work untiringly to position India and infuse in her people the desire to excel, if our country is to be a quality and value provider. A regulatory process can throw up contradictory regulations. And firms like HSBC are required to handhold investors through this maze."

The Indian Vista

Indian companies have heroically proved that they can compete with the best. They are inspired to compete on a global scale too. This league of companies is nevertheless a small one. Naina outlines the strengths and weaknesses of India Inc. and offers her suggestions to rectify prevailing weaknesses:

"With the lapse of ten years since the Indian economy opened up to foreign influences, a fresh breed of spirited young entrepreneurs has surfaced from the relics of the License Raj era; with the good grasp that these dynamic individuals have on the rules of the game, they have arrived at a stage which would take them on a cruise to global competitiveness. HSBC is instrumental in backing them, and supplying them with capital and helping them acquire companies as they mushroom further. Many crucial deals including Tata's purchase of Daewoo, Birla's acquisition of mines in Australia and Reliance's acquirement of Trevira in Germany evince the enormity of the trends, which HSBC has set industriously over the last year. In the1990s, companies flailed their arms and struggled to shape up in an attempt to brace themselves for the stiff competition, which was an inevitable offshoot of liberalisation and globalisation.

"Over ten years ago, only two types of cars (the Fiat and Ambassador) dominated the market. Twenty sleek models are on the cards in the automobile showrooms today. When Fiat and Ambassador were the only models, the manufacturers were given two plausible options: they could either change to keep pace with their competitors, even outstripping them many a time or adopt a complacent status quo approach and fade away into obscurity. It was like Gandhiji's do-or-die concept. While some companies faced a tragic demise, the cleverer ones boldly reinvented themselves. The Indica (by Tata Motors) and the Scorpio (by M&M) are classic examples of such productions of human intellect. In the truck market, we don't see much of the Volvo. Indian companies are just managing to hold on and compete. In the midst of it all, some succeed and strengthen their staying power, cutting down on their costs and introducing new, innovative products. They have geared up to tackle competition from foreign players and challenges the international market hurls at them. They are warmly welcomed into foreign markets.

"To begin with, Indian companies must continue to reinvent themselves. Fast thinking and swiftness in action would determine the degree of their success. Crowing over our victory and resting on laurels with every little success we've had won't urge us to achieve further. In today's turbulently fast-paced era, companies should prepare themselves for the challenges they would have to shoulder tomorrow; the services sector in particular will see this even more. The Information Technology-enabled Services (ITeS) sector is witnessing perpetual change. Ironically, the same company that declared it wouldn't swell the ranks of call centre conglomerates did just that. It went right ahead and acquired them in a few years. Wipro's acquisition of Spectramind is an example. Companies should endeavour to revisit their strategy and continuously engineer newer models. This high-speed process of change enables us to learn from our past experiences. One should keep one's eyes peeled for new ways of doing old things. Industry biggies require a ready access to international capital markets and banks to count on for their offshore ventures; they will soon outgrow the Indian banking system."

Expecting the Unexpected

"I am very bullish about the progress of the Indian economy. India is really a place to be in. Apparently, many people are acknowledging this fact and coming back to their motherland. The biotechnology and pharmaceutical industry, the ITeS and BPO segments, R&D and genetics are clearly the sectors to watch for. Auto-ancillaries make up another area of potential growth and expansion. India's global competitiveness in these sectors will attract foreign investment and expand the magnitude of our foreign exchange reserves. The garment sector is an industry where we can be naturally competent too. As the global textile market has carried India as a dominant player for a long span of time, we stand a good chance of excelling in this field. And jobs such as those that command skills in data analytics are being outsourced on a vast scale to India. Competitors like Glaxo and Ranbaxy have struck a joint venture with each other, each purporting to leverage the research skills of the other. So, the probability of unexpected occurrences is in itself an indication of economic growth and development in our country."

'T' for Transparency

Naina emphasizes the need to inject more transparency in the Indian capital market and suggests different measures that can be adopted to make it more investor-friendly.

"With Infosys, Wipro and the Tata group companies as harbingers of transparency and good corporate governance, we have certainly come a long way from where we were before. But do we really have to look far beyond? We have the best standards in place here. The market reflects it all – the scrip rated at the highest multiple is essentially the one that carries the finest principles of corporate governance, communicates its ideas clearly and accurately to the market and follows first-rate standards of disclosure. Indian companies are known to have set the standard for their foreign counterparts in the sphere of corporate governance. When I worked on the foreign equity issues of ICICI and HDFC Bank, they were the first Asian banks to embrace total transparency in their reporting. There are many more Enrons and Worldcoms in the global scenario than in India.

"SEBI is implementing various programmes with a view to presenting a more inviting vista and enticing larger numbers of investors. While steps have been taken to radically improve corporate governance procedures, the number of companies listed in the stock exchange should be reduced."

> *"India is the only country that carries a list of more than 6000 companies, when not more than 2000 companies should figure in the stock exchange list. Small companies, which have established no credibility, only spell danger. Obviously, we wouldn't want the unsuspecting investors to be taken for a ride. However, venture capital should be encouraged, as lack of it would increase the vulnerability of our stock-markets."*

A Peek Inside Her Person

Naina may have a host of awards and honours to her credit, but achievements that have won her universal acclaim haven't moved her. When requested to comment on the numerous awards she has won, her voice rings with modesty: "Ask the deciding authorities. Perhaps, they merely see a handful of women in the business and occasionally select a few every year." Naina has continuously been catalogued in the repertoire of women who are viewed as the greatest influencers the world over.

> *"We influence the people we work with and the direction our company should move in. Only time will tell how much of an impact we have made. I would consider myself a failure if I don't exert influence in areas outside of my work. I shall feel very satisfied if I can touch a few lives during the course of my own."*

Naina has proven her influence in a wide range of activities. Apart from helping several NGOs in strategy, finance and marketing, she regularly meets people whom she can advice. She sets aside some portion of her time to work with grassroots organizations like SEWA. She has also been involved with NGOs who work with ICT (Information, Communication and Technology) to bridge the digital divide. ICT has answered many questions that arise in connection with what technologies can be adopted for the benefit of the rural poor and how they can be galvanized to integrate with mainstream organizations on a much healthier note.

Naina likes nothing better than to spend time with fresh, enthusiastic young people through numerous forums she addresses, time and again. "They are our future," she affirms solemnly. Once again, we observe an unstinting synchronicity between HSBC's temper and Naina's personal qualities. The accuracy of our judgment becomes apparently clear when she says: "We sponsor a lot of projects. Environmental and educational sciences, particularly those revolving around women are areas close to my heart."

> *"Education is particularly a great enabler. Through it, you can influence health concerns and enable empowerment, stimulating vocational independence."*

People who work under Naina do not view being a male or female as an impending issue they have to thrash out. For Naina too, that is hardly a concern.

> "Male or female, every boss presents a different skill set. A man can have an impeccable character, but he may be a lousy manager. In such circumstances, I would not be the only person to dislike him. I would define a good boss as one who is pleasant to interact with, one who can deal effectively with people and most importantly, one who knows what he's talking about. He should have adequate knowledge of the business that he is involved in. Different people enjoy strengths in different areas. But some like you and some just don't. So, each of us obviously isn't everyone's cup of tea. People tend to grope for the same connecting cord with a statement like: "*This man is easy to work with.*" Likewise, the remark, "*This woman is a lousy boss*" isn't meant to target her gender but is rather directed to reflect on the quality of her performance. Unfortunately, we tend to brood too much over the man-woman issue. Even if one extends the scenario from a lady boss to her subordinate, it is only a question of one's unique strengths and weaknesses. Perhaps, the myth that women do not cooperate with one another stems from the movie industry. In a mature organizational environment, however, women extend a lot of support to one another."

Companies like General Electric organise small gatherings, intended to serve as forums for women who can join hands together to seek advice from one another and strengthen the bond between them. While they don't exclude men, women form a large chunk of the group. Naina recalls that she has often addressed similar groups.

Resolving the Gender Query

Naina provides us an insight into her intriguing perspectives on the status women hold in Indian society and prevailing gender issues, stressing the need to extend the scope for granting ample opportunities to women. *Excerpts from an exclusive interview...*

- *In your perception, how is our society changing to empower womankind in our country?*

  I take a lot of heart from parents of several bright, young women, who approach me and ask me, '*What does my daughter need to do to be able to join a bank?*' So, you see, society is moving towards a paradigm where young girls are being thought about. I would personally like to get there and talk to people. (*Smiles ruefully*) Often though, it isn't entirely possible for one to do that with a job like the one I am involved in.

- *How can we draw many more women into the ambit of mainstream economic activity?*

  We should make women understand that the doors aren't closed; we must make it known to them that we are equal-opportunity employers and create the right opportunities for people to stay on. A young woman came up to me at an airport recently; she heads GE's power equipment systems – a field largely dominated by male engineers. She sells her equipment in distant locations, often travelling to every corner of the country. I think her job is really much tougher than mine. Many other enterprising pioneers like her are instrumental in luring greater numbers of women into full-fledged mainstream careers.

- *Why do we find many women holding important posts in the banking sector as against other secondary/tertiary industries?*

  I feel the work environment is substantially more encouraging in the banking sector. Moreover, most banks are located in metros. Consequently, one doesn't have to travel much. Furthermore, for women it is easier to interact with educated and qualified men. Banking is a far cry from a marketing career or a job that warrants heavy travelling across the country. Also, where a few tread, others will soon follow. Back then we had a few leading women lawyers in our country. In a short span of time, many more women mushroomed as shrewd, intelligent and competent lawyers. When I joined Grindlays, few women reigned. When I left the organization, there were women in charge of many departments at every level. Of course, case histories are replete with instances of women quitting their jobs and the thinking and decision-making of the remainder is unduly affected. While there are still only a few women in the workplace their work shapes the destiny of other women.

- *How do you ensure that women are being treated fairly in your organization?* One can do that in many ways. However, we do it by just being fair. (*Laughs*) Besides keeping a watchful eye on how many women we hire, we need to actively monitor the percentage of women who get in and the percentage that continues to stay. To make certain they continue to stay, it is mandatory on our part to see that we don't make exceptions or create a community of favours. The core essence merely lies in being fair and just – with an eye on yourself, of course. It is necessary for us to question and criticize our own moves. If I send a group of my male colleagues to recruit new people, would they hire only men? Obviously not! Women who hold high posts in HSBC essentially constitute sterling examples of women empowerment.

The Reality Check

Naina Lal Kidwai seeks to compartmentalize her activities between life at home and life at work. The nature of her job, however, never really allowed her to adhere to that model. As home impinges on work and work impinges on home, one is impelled to manage both with equal care and efficiency. "I am so devoted to my work that this impingement is almost automatic," Naina expresses. "If your child is in trouble at school, you are compelled to attend to the impending problem at hand. Aren't you?" So she advises, "Deciding what is right for the moment can keep our lives in control."

Daughter Kemaya, and son Rumaan have always been Naina's reality check. She discloses that her daughter is neither wary about what she does, nor thrilled on glimpsing a newspaper write-up or a magazine article about her mother. "Sometimes, she even exclaims, 'You are so boring!' when she sees me being interviewed on TV," Naina discloses with a laugh. "Such instances keep me from being engulfed in my own sense of inflated pride and self-importance." At thirteen, Kemaya advises her mom to direct focus to her work rather than attempting to sort out her daughter's life.

"My presence is important when my children need me the most," Naina concurs. "But Kemaya is not used to having me sit around with her. A young filmmaker at 25, Rumaan exposes me to a whole wide world of young creative India, which works hard and plays hard. His eye for detail and appetite for good food make him a great consultant for the good qualities of life," Naina reveals.

Naina's husband, Rashid who tries to be around for Kemaya in her absence, dutifully partakes of parental responsibilities. Naina is all praises for her husband as she declares, "I would not have achieved but for my husband's support and encouragement." A steady mentor and her strongest critic, he accurately guides her on the strategies she should adopt to counter numerous situations. However, she admits that there are complaints of 'You're late again' or 'You are planning to spend the night at the office!'

"I truly appreciate his candidness though," she states. As the head of an NGO, Rashid's work in the non-profit sector brings Naina closer to the other India – the India she doesn't get to see while at work.

A balancing factor, the family has helped her tune off from work and unwind. "Were it not for them, I would in all probability breathe work," Naina confesses. To this, Rashid comments, "Kemeya is on a much higher rung in Naina's priority list than me."

Naina agrees, "One doesn't give up one's family for a career. What one really sacrifices are hobbies and interests, which one may not have much time to pursue."

In Lighter Vein

She recommends *Ignited Minds* by the Hon'ble President of India Dr Abdul Kalam as an absolute must-read for all. A music-lover, Naina appreciates both western and classical styles, which she aptly listens to as much as she possibly can, whether at home or in a car.

The composite Indian culture has constantly provided nectar to her soul. The numerous architectural styles and patterns she has encountered during the course of her extensive travel, appeal to her more quixotic senses. "I particularly like old buildings, South Indian temples and Mughal architecture," she reveals. She also loves handloom fabrics and cotton and silk varieties. "Our Indian weavers are exemplary in style, pattern and colour," she declares with pride.

She avows that India is an incredible tourist destination. "The more I travel and see the world, the more I grow to recognize what we have here. The tourism industry in India can dial a higher rate of growth if we get our act right," she sums up. "Just look at the scale and history of places like Hampi – or the forts and deserts of Rajasthan or the wilds of Corbett." Wildlife and reading are other interests of hers. Orchids are her favourite flowers and Corbett her much beloved tourist spot.

> "Do what you like to do. Don't allow yourself to be compelled to engage in a job you might regret taking up, later on. Half-heartedness won't get us anywhere. We can engineer our own success if we put our life and soul into what we do. So, set your bar at a higher level each time; and dare to think big."

Preetha Reddy
Managing Director, Apollo Hospitals

8.
Touching Lives

Her swift feet cast magic upon the stage. When the ardent Bharat Natyam dancer concluded her Thilana, holding the audience in a trance, very few expected that she would touch millions of lives one day. Dancing upon the stage of life with the same grace and poise that defined her young-girl persona, she now directs a colossal medical empire, which encompasses a group of private hospitals spanning eight countries across South Asia, Africa and the Middle East.

Preetha Reddy, Managing Director of Apollo Hospitals, Chennai, has devoted her efforts to the cause of healthcare. Her untold compassion for people, further heightened by her attachment to children, has catapulted her to the summit of success in the efforts she initiated to bring Apollo Hospitals to pristine heights on the global health front.

The Creation

Dr Prathap C. Reddy started Apollo Hospitals in 1983. The hospital took its form as a modest five-storey building with 150 beds in the hub of Chennai.

Given the regulatory environment, Dr Reddy's economic sense in starting a profit-making hospital was questioned by many. Undaunted, he vowed to himself that he would make certain that India had world-class health facilities. Taking advantage of the bullish investment climate in the country, Dr Reddy listed his growing parent company in the Bombay Stock Exchange and raised money.

Today, the Apollo Group has 6400 beds and 16,500 employees. With its emergence as an integrated global healthcare provider, the Apollo Group has acquired the status of the leading private hospital chain in Asia and one among the largest in the world. Each of Dr Reddy's four daughters (Preetha, Shobana, Sangeeta and Suneeta) runs his medical conglomerate with judicious care and efficiency.

Preetha didn't have a choice in her career. She wished to pursue medicine. She reveals that her father wished to fulfil his responsibility of getting his daughters married and see each of them raise a healthy, happy family of their own. "So, Apollo Hospitals was not exactly planned," Preetha smiles. Seeing that her father needed more hands to support his dream and vision, she got into the fray in 1989. "And I have been working ever since," she says simply.

Learning the Ropes

Born in Hyderabad in 1957, Preetha spent her school and college years in Chennai. A student of Besant Arundale School, she graduated from Kalakshetra under Rukmini Devi Arundale. She revered all her teachers, particularly her dance guru.

"Many years ago, one of Mrs Sucharita Reddy's (Preetha's mother) close friends took dance classes for Preetha and me when we were both young," reveals Dr N. Uma, Consultant Physician, Apollo Hospitals, Chennai. "Till today, Preetha's respect for her guru knows no bounds."

Preetha was only nineteen when she got married to industrialist Vijaykumar Reddy soon after she graduated in Chemistry from Stella Maris College (Chennai).

During the initial phase of Preetha's career, she struggled to meet challenges – inevitable for Managing Directors of huge medical corporations. "It was quite tough in the beginning. My brief stint in an advertising agency didn't prepare me for what I was to take on at Apollo," Preetha admits. "While I acquired all my learning from my father, the knowledge that I gathered later on, especially in areas of operational excellence or business expertise, has been gradual."

Dr Reddy never carried the word 'No' in his dictionary. Preetha recalls the fun-filled yet scary moments she and her sisters had as children, when their father took them out to swim. "He would shove us into the deep end of the pool and say, '*Come on, you can do it,*'" she narrates. "There was no questioning him after that. He helped us cope with our fears."

Regardless of his rigorous schedules, Dr Reddy never failed to spend quality time with his daughters when they were young. Even today, he has time for all ten of his grandchildren. "Don't ask me how," Preetha laughs, before solemnly adding, "I acquired my endurance and people-handling skills from my mother Sucharita."

Preetha's parents instilled in their daughters the need to look after one another. Anyone who knew the Reddy sisters would exclaim, "They are uncompromisingly close and influence one another in every way possible."

The Reddy sisters had an unusual secret up their sleeves: If they squabbled, they never slept without first patching up. "We were afraid that something would happen to one of us during our sleep," Preetha confesses. Nevertheless, they wouldn't hesitate to resume the quarrel afresh, the following morning! They had never heard of ill will, animosity or sibling rivalry. "To date, I share a perfect relationship with my sisters," Preetha reveals proudly.

Healthy Foundations

Apollo Hospitals has always traced a path radically unique from that of most other hospitals. It welcomes the largest number of foreign patients in India. Committed to treating patients with professionalism and compassion, Apollo's international patient programme extends support to patients and their family members who are compelled to face new people, new environments and complex medical procedures when their homes are miles away. "What patients need are efficient information systems that work faster and are disseminated in a pleasant ambience," Preetha avers.

The Apollo Group has developed a wide range of benchmarking and quality practices. Working in concert with the Government, Preetha was instrumental in forming a consortium of Indian hospitals to conduct workshops and apprise people of the importance of quality assurance in hospitals. "As no licenses are granted to private nursing homes, there is no question of withdrawing a licence. These aspects are unorganised right now," Preetha says. "But we are continuing to work on establishing an organized pattern."

Preetha Reddy has adopted the mantra of TLC (Tender Loving Care), which she affectionately applies to every patient of hers. An interesting anecdote lies behind this empathetic approach, which she has implanted as one of the strongest foundations of the hospital. Preetha remembers partaking of humble home-cooked meals of curd-rice with her sisters. She believed that the meals were tastier because they carried her mother's loving touch. "The curd-rice was more delicious than any other dish that we ate outside," she reveals nostalgically. "My sisters and I declared that she had put TLC in it."

Preetha was motivated to assume the same principle in her professional life too. "The patients and staff comprehend this language better," she points out. Affirms Dr N. Uma, "Preetha treats a person whom she has known only for a few days just as she would treat a person whom she has known for years."

The Sunrise

The Apollo Group has many firsts and other feats to its credit. The group has performed a large number of heart surgeries in the world. The twenty-sixth hospital of the Apollo Group and the first to be established outside India in 2002, the Apollo Hospital in Colombo (Sri Lanka) performed a hundred cardiac surgeries within a span of four months since it came into being. "When the Cardiac team of the Colombo unit told me that a hundred cardiac surgeries had been completed successfully, I thought they were joking," Preetha recounts, her face etched with an expression of pride and joy.

Under Preetha's leadership, The Apollo Specialty Hospital has carved a niche for itself as a major oncology referral centre in Asia. This unit is one of the few centres in Asia to offer Bone Marrow Transplantation. Also the first to perform Cord Blood Transplantation in India, the unit seeks to offer sophisticated treatment and care for cancer patients.

The Apollo Specialty Hospital has been the harbinger of many health-related initiatives. A large sum of several crore rupees was invested in a PET-CT Scan project to enable the doctors to detect cancerous cells at an early stage. "The recurrence levels are very low if the patient seeks immediate treatment for cancer," Preetha explains.

Credited to be one of the first hospitals to set up a rural telemedicine centre in 1999, Apollo has emerged as the single largest telemedicine solution provider in India. In an attempt to spread the concept of telemedicine, the hospital has worked with multiple entities, including the Central and State Governments, medical bodies, private sector enterprises and public sector undertakings. The latest medical technologies (including a Telemedicine network, which facilitates electronic communication over long distances, connecting the Apollo team to the best medical professionals across the globe) and its stringent infection-control measures are the core ingredients of Apollo's success. Apollo's telemedicine network currently stretches over 33 locations in India and abroad.

Apollo holds the vision of providing a working model of telemedicine, which would self-propagate across India and the rest of the developing world. The telemedicine units are currently trying to impress upon the Government the need for toll-free lines and exploring various alternatives to reduce the communication costs. They would serve as centres for creating an awareness of AIDS and other health issues of primary concern.

The group has begun to explore the hitherto uncharted domain of health tourism too. Apollo recently opened a new clinic in Doha and plans to roll out 200 clinics in India and the neighbouring countries in the next five years.

"We also have family clinics in Chennai, where people can avail of treatment for minor ailments," Preetha says. "Women can get their regular gynaecological checkups done too. They will be referred to a hospital if the need arises."

> *"I have a professional management team to execute ideas and policies, as and when they are mooted. Once in three months, we make it mandatory for the CEOs of all our units to meet with the Chairman and delineate the strategies that we should adopt. It is always the first part that is the hardest. It gets easier once we have a blueprint of the plan and get the drift of how we are to set it in action."*

Snapshot

Preetha unravels her strategies and candidly expresses her views on crucial economic and socio-cultural issues that influence health concerns in our country. *Excerpts from the exclusive interview...*

- *In the face of globalisation and liberalisation, India invariably faces greater foreign competition. How do you handle these challenges?*

  India is performing remarkably well in the healthcare sector. To begin with, we have a cost advantage. While we manage to retain a high quality of drugs, consumables, infrastructures and equipment, our costs amount to roughly one-tenth of the cost for the same level of quality abroad. Moreover, we have a tremendous reservoir of manpower skills. Our people have handled enormous volumes. Even technically speaking, the expertise of a cardiac surgeon in India is on par with the standards of some of the best surgeons the world over. We also have the USPs of the warmth and hospitality of the east. Our nurses here are wonderful and simply much kinder. Just walk into a hospital in the UK or USA and you will notice the difference. The traditional system of medicine we have adopted to supplement the role of allopathic and Ayurvedic systems is yet another positive feature of ours. That is what gives us an edge over other countries.

- *How supportive or indifferent has the Government been in issuing industrial licences and policies?*

  Even today, the Government does not fully recognize the latent potential of the healthcare sector. As representatives of a leading healthcare concern, we consider it our responsibility to draw the Government's attention to pressing healthcare issues. When the Apollo Hospitals Group came into being, it was the first health corporate to get the Government to fund healthcare projects. We try to bring about changes in legislations concerning healthcare. To this end, the Chairman Dr Pratap Reddy approached the Government on several occasions. We have endeavoured to introduce the concept of cadaver transplants and give a fillip to the privatisation of insurance. Dr Reddy has been in talks with the Government for making health insurance mandatory. He worked on obtaining infrastructure for the health sector. Thus, we have to constantly initiate efforts to promote the development of the health segment, especially in light of the fact that it is a nascent industry. In fact, it has not yet gained full recognition as an exclusive industry in its own right.

- *How do you view the health-sector scenario in India today?*
  If you closely scrutinize the healthcare sector, it is quite mixed up. (*Laughs*) Some Government hospitals are performing relatively well, while others aren't. In addition, many charitable and trust-run organizations, private clinics and nursing homes do not figure under any benchmark of standardization. Little (if any) emphasis is laid on one's qualification and the quality of output. One easily opens a clinic and runs it in any manner he pleases; no one really questions whether he holds an MD or a basic MBBS degree. The Government has not imposed any law or regulation that insists on a fundamental eligibility criterion for such ventures. The healthcare industry needs to evolve into an organized sector.

- *How would you rate the health status of Indians in comparison with that of their foreign counterparts?*
  Indian society is a fairly strange one. Out of more than one billion people in our nation, one third can afford to invest in private health care. Two-thirds of the masses reside in rural regions. Fifty per cent of this segment of the population are plainly too poor to meet their fundamental requirements. Sadly, that is the current scenario of our country. The Government is channelling its revenues for purposes of improving the social welfare of the people in the arenas of primary, secondary and tertiary health.

- *What is the reason for the high incidence of communicable diseases in India?*
  People are not laying adequate focus on communicable diseases. The importance of sanitation, clean potable water and a hygienic environment does not receive much attention here. Unless people inculcate healthy and hygienic habits in their daily lives, our country will not be free from the spread of communicable diseases.

> *"If I were the Health Minister, I would induce a higher level of mass awareness and stress that communicable diseases have absolutely no business to plague our countrymen. I would improve the quality of drinking water, provide healthier nutrition and promote insurance to enable the poor man to avail of healthcare facilities. To begin with, India must focus on eradicating simple ailments and building the health of the masses. This is really where we should focus for the forthcoming ten years. Once the basic health of the average man is taken care of, we can make a dent in the arena of high-tech medical science.*

- *When the rich and the poor suffer the same pain and peril of dying (especially when the ailment can be fatal if left untreated), why should a poor man be left to bleed? Are good medical facilities the sole prerogative of the rich?*

  There has been an increase in the incidence of heart ailments, bone afflictions, cancers and diabetes. The poor cannot afford the exorbitant costs of treatment procedures for such ailments. It is disheartening to note that some lives are lost in spite of the heavy expenditure the patients' families incur. If only there were some form of mandatory insurance and cover for people, the rich-poor divide would be narrowed down. People could freely walk into any hospital for treatment. They wouldn't have to worry about paying heavy medical bills. We provide free treatment to about 10% of our in-patients and 40% of our outpatients. Yet, free-treatment measures extended by a few hospitals may not make much difference. It is therefore essential to ensure that everybody receives access to healthcare through insurance.

Wellness Vs Illness

The Apollo Group seeks to induce modifications in people's lifestyles. A pioneer of the Preventive Health Screening programme in India, the hospital offers a wide range of master health checkups to identify early symptoms of major illnesses and pinpoint potential areas of risk to ward off future health problems. With a view to focusing on the promotion of wellness in her patients, Preetha has adopted a radical approach of espousing alternative systems like Pranic healing and Ayurvedic treatments to supplement the role of regular streams of medicine.

Innovations aren't unfamiliar to Apollo. Circling around the belief that music possesses healing properties that are said to be scientifically effective, the hospital announced it would commence a course in Medical Music Therapy during its Twentieth Anniversary. The first of its kind in India, the Medical Music Therapy course provides enrollers an in-depth knowledge of the subject along with special emphasis on the effects of music on specific illnesses. "I don't have an adept knowledge of music though," Preetha laughs. "Sometimes, I even think I may be tone-deaf." Preetha's belief in the soothing effects of music on patients, however, induced her to purchase a large collection of music CDs for the hospital.

Preetha doesn't believe in projecting an image of healthcare corporate bodies as commercial enterprises; she wants people to stay well. And so, she has fervently been promoting the concept of wellness. The hospital takes up issues of anti-tobacco campaigns and healthy nutrition habits, to mention a few.

Preetha has personally contributed towards the creation of awareness, which entails addressing the slums and apprising them of the importance of hygiene.

As a family, the Reddys are known to be very religious. A temple has been erected in the hospital precincts too. "We believe that God will guide us and help us in the face of any untoward situation," Preetha states with conviction. It is this religious backbone that helps her sail through crises in more ways than one.

Social Conscience

The Apollo Group has established a reputation for itself as a health conglomerate with a social conscience. In 2003, Apollo screened the Hollywood blockbuster *Finding Nemo* as part of the TOUCH initiative, introduced solely for underprivileged children. The proceeds of the show were directed to the Save a Child's Heart (SACH) foundation, a charitable organization, which works towards rendering medical services to children who hail from the lower socio-economic strata of society and suffer from chronic heart ailments. TOUCH is an organization that collects money to garner materials for heart surgeries to be performed on children. During their stay, the children can avail of every other facility in the hospital. "Between Chennai and Hyderabad, we have done about seventy to eighty kids," Preetha reveals.

She is working continuously to implement several other programmes, which would ensure everyone's participation in the collection of funds towards saving a child's heart.

The Apollo Specialty Hospital introduced a scheme for cancer patients on Rose Day in September 2004. The hospital announced the launch of the 'Apollo Hope Foundation', an initiative that allowed cancer patients to 'make a wish to meet a celebrity' endeavouring to realize their dreams. The Apollo Hope Foundation also provides financial assistance for the treatment of impoverished children who suffer from leukaemia.

The Apollo Cancer Support Group (ACSG) was inaugurated to lend psychological and emotional support to patients and their relatives. The ACSG provides a forum for them to talk about their diseases without inhibition.

The Toy Bank is yet another initiative Preetha introduced to enable young patients to take their pick from a large variety of toys to play with. The idea sprung from the enthusiasm of the hospital's employees and the interest of well-wishers, each of whom came forward to donate new and old toys for cancer-afflicted children.

Apollo's trust takes care of patients whose affordability levels are very low. "A lot of people need to be made aware of it," Preetha confides. "While we do have money to tend to patients who are struggling to make both ends meet, we do not have enough money to create a very high level of awareness."

The Yin-and-Yang Model

The field of medicine and medical sciences has been a traditionally male-dominated one in India. Yet, Preetha has been able to create opportunities for the development of the new domain of healthcare and pave the way for further progress and advancement in the conventional field of medicine.

"The Yin-and-Yang factor is at play here," Preetha admits in a philosophical tone. Since time immemorial, men and women have been slotted to play certain roles. In the days of the early man, men were the lunch-chasers; women were the food-makers. Men tended to cattle; women tended to children. Men built homes; women kept houses.

"Historically speaking, male domination arose only because of the way things were," Preetha states. "We have evolved over the centuries. The scenario is changing more now and the gender bias is being dispensed with. Women have always played a strong role in every domain. Some have even fought against social evils like alcoholism. Their power can never be underplayed."

The 'man's world' syndrome isn't of much relevance, today. There is a very narrow line of distinction between a man and a woman. This disparity will in all likelihood fade into obscurity in the ensuing years. "Several women have made a brilliant foray into the healthcare industry," Preetha informs. "But to be perfectly honest, some areas of clinical medicine, like cardiac surgery, continue to remain men's turfs."

> *"If a female employee experiences problems, she goes to a lady CEO; if a man has an issue, he would prefer to discuss it with a male boss. What's important is being good buddies, first. A person with a problem needs to talk it out with someone who would hear him/her out."*

Women should keep their priorities intact and balance responsibilities well, Preetha opines. "When exigencies arise, their presence at home might be needed. Such pressures can be difficult for them to cope with. But we must accept it. Once we reconcile ourselves to the situation, we will be able to deal effectively with it."

Preetha takes prides in the extraordinary qualities she believes embellish the Indian woman. "The infinite patience she possesses stems from her rich cultural and religious background as well as her exposure to many people on various social occasions, right from the time she is young. The joint family system, predominant in earlier times, have trained women to live harmoniously with cousins, aunts and uncles, increasing their adjustability and flexibility. Indian women are consequently much more capable of managing people effectively and coping with workplace and career-related stressors than women in other parts of the world."

Preetha has disproved the myth that corporate heads and businesswomen have little compassion and regard for the softer sentiments of life. "Why should a woman have less of a heart because she is responsible for many people?" she explodes. "I am responsible for ten thousand employees; I have no business to be heartless. Being in the healthcare industry, I am frankly in the business of caring."

"Preetha has always treated us as constituents of a big family. The common goal that we share helps us strive to fulfil our quest for excellence," avers Dr Satyabhama, Director of Medical Services, Apollo Hospitals, Chennai. "I should also mention that Preetha is pleasantly tough," she continues. "Even if she does caution me, her tone is so gentle that I bask in the perceived glory of her words until I realize that she had actually meant otherwise! She hardly ever raises her voice in anger and she has motivated me to do the same too."

Home is Where the Heart is

Preetha lives in cheerful harmony with her in-laws, sister, brother-in-law and nephews. "All our children have grown up together," she says with a smile. On the home front, Preetha's husband and in-laws have extended unlimited support, especially whenever she has had to adhere to a rigorous travelling schedule. "My husband and father-in-law serve as strong sounding boards and play a good advisory role," Preetha acknowledges. Indeed, they do not expect from Preetha the role that would usually be expected of a traditional Indian daughter-in-law. "The house runs by itself," Preetha jokes. "We can't be around 24x7 at home for the simple reason that we are working. I have nevertheless been able to manage my home well as my folks are very understanding." Work also taught Preetha how she should spend quality time with her children. "If you manage your time well, you won't be a traditional nitpicking mother," she jokes.

The first thought that springs to her mind when she wakes up from her slumber is the hospital. But she firmly believes that children matter the most for a woman. She cites an example from her own life: "My son indicated that if I had been around more often during the course of his twelfth standard board examination, he could have scored higher. This got me thinking. After that, I took some time off to be with my children."

> *"I believe that a woman is responsible for her children's lives – much more than a man is. It is all very well to be the CEO of a company and enjoy the limelight and the adulation of the people and the media. But nothing can be sadder than a child's life being affected by the lack of support from the mother. She is the only person whom the child can depend on. On the other hand, another person can take over her post if she relinquishes it in favour of executing her family responsibilities."*

If one of her female staff members approached her with a personal problem and requested her to grant an exemption from a task at hand, Preetha would never hesitate to tell her, "If it is an issue with your children, please handle that first."

> *"I have encountered certain instances of managers grumbling about seemingly trivial issues. I don't blow my fuse with them. On one occasion, I calmly told one of them, 'Talk to the patient in Bed No. 64 in the general ward and then return.' He was quite perplexed because he could not comprehend what I meant. Nevertheless, he proceeded to Bed No. 64, only to find a poor little boy with an amputated leg and an empty wallet. While the boy was still scrambling desperately for the money that he was required to pay for his treatment, he had undergone the trouble of travelling all the way to the hospital with bright eyes and a cheerful smile just to say a gracious 'Thank You.' Now, what can be more heartrending than that? Such instances bring people down to reality."*

Interestingly, Preetha feels that she may have perhaps been a different person, if she were heading a manufacturing company rather than a healthcare conglomerate. "Being in the healthcare sector, my priorities are different," she explains. "If I have a social engagement and I am just not able to make it, I do not brood over it. Such things are not very significant, when people here are fighting for their lives."

Pet Passions

Preetha is an ardent booklover and a regular reader of Sidney Sheldon and Robin Cook novels. Dan Brown and Robert Ludwig are her favourites. Our eyes travel along the row of paperback novels that line her office shelves from top to bottom. She mentions that she has finished reading them all and intends to give them away to the hospital library being organized for the patients – another gesture of compassion. She dotes on Italian and Thai food and *The Last Samurai* is her best movie.

Usually clad in subtle hues of whites, off-whites and blues, Preetha has always been drawn towards nature, art and culture and sharply responsive to visually appealing stimuli. Goodwill is very important for Preetha. You can find her glowing in contentment in the midst of a neat, pleasant ambience and great company.

> "Look at the broader picture and develop conviction. You have something big to achieve in the future; you need to realize your goals to reach your ultimate end. Look ten steps ahead and foresee what the future would be like then, before you take a decision."

Priya Paul
Chairman, Apeejay Park Hotels

9.
Small is Beautiful

"This is a sector not to be in" was the comment repeated most often and circulated in hushed whispers among people when she took on established giants in the hotel industry. Undaunted by the remarks, she bustled around like a busybee, slowly and steadily expanding opportunities and pushing her imagination to the limits.

She drove across her point 'Small is beautiful' and stuck resolutely to the boutique hotel concept at a time when luxury hotels were equated with plush lobbies that had sleek bronze statutes, figurines and bars that resembled a rich man's alcove.

Priya Paul (Chairman, Apeejay Park Hotels) has redefined 'luxury' in the Indian hospitality industry and established the reputation of being innovative and adventurous in an industry usually slow in embracing change. With her unique blend of creativity and style, the 37-year-old hotelier has produced a collection of trendy, distinctive and art-friendly luxury boutique hotels as part of the powerful Park Hotels Group across the country. For Priya, life is indeed happening as she further expands her chain and unfolds a new saga.

The Years of Grooming

Born in Kolkata in 1966 into a traditional joint family, Priya spent her childhood drinking in the antiquated charms of the city. She was however a part of a very progressive family. Raised against the backdrop of a Punjabi upbringing, her father Surrendra was the youngest of seven brothers and sisters. He married a Sindhi girl Shirin and moved to the family house in Kolkata, where Priya recalls growing up with her uncles and cousins. Priya is the eldest of four children in her family. The togetherness Priya shared with her sister Priti and brothers Karan and Anand as a child strengthened the intimacy among them in the later years.

In Kolkata, she studied in Loreto House and the La Martinere School for girls. Her class teacher recognized her true potential when she began to top her class in the seventh grade. At school, she was many a times a proactive leader who took the initiative for every endeavour she handled. She left Loreto House after the tenth grade, with the bold stamp of 'Head Girl'.

"Shifting to La Martinere after the tenth grade helped me make lots of friends," Priya beams. At La Martinere, she received the Good Conduct medal for exemplary performance in the twelfth grade, leaving behind her imprints in the premises of a school where she had been for merely two years. Good grooming at home and the holism of a full-fledged ICSE/ISC academic environment laid the foundation for Priya's well-rounded personality.

When Priya finished school, her father aspired to send her to the USA, where she could pursue her undergraduate studies. She enrolled in the Wellesley College, Boston and opted for a course in Economics, when she began in 1984. "The college was staunchly pro-women," she laughs. "The four wonderful years I spent in the USA gave me a solid ground in thinking, managing and dealing with the more complex situations in life."

Priya briefly lived in France, where she learnt French in a liberal arts college. When Priya was eighteen, she chose an unusual combination of Astronomy,

Archaeology, Arts and French. Yet, she graduated in Economics. "At the time, there were no undergraduate courses in professional fields," she explains. "Education in liberal arts grants flexibility to select any combination of subjects. This leeway is very useful for an eighteen-year-old student who isn't entirely certain of which stream she would like to tread on for the rest of her life. It enhances one's exposure and broadens one's perspectives. That is what life is all about!"

Priya initially thought she would work in the USA, before returning to India. On her father's suggestion, however, she began working under his guidance in the family hotels in India from 1988. Surrendra Paul was deemed to be an excellent teacher. Priya was only twenty-two then.

Her parents shifted base to New Delhi in 1986 when The Park sprang up in the capital. The move was quite a transition for Priya who had a wide circle of friends in Kolkata. It was also a time when recession had hit the industry in light of the sluggish demand in the market. "On this score, I felt it was the toughest time to learn the nitty-gritty of sales and marketing," Priya confides. "I was especially reporting to my father."

Subsequent to working in the marketing division, Priya cottoned on the rudiments of hotel operations, which she began handling from 1989.

Conquering the Odds

In the midst of tragedy, they invariably work harder. The Surrendra family went through a most difficult phase when Priya's brother Anand succumbed to a car crash in 1989 at the tender age of seventeen. She had barely overcome the upheaval when the second shock struck in April 1990 – a terrorist in Assam murdered her dear father. There was little time for the traumatized family to grieve and tide over the trauma. Since her inherited family business had been separated in 1989 during her father's lifetime, her mother was obliged to take over the hotel group as the Chairman (with her uncle Jit Paul as an advisor) after her husband's demise.

At 24, assuming the responsibility as the de-facto head of three hotels was again an overnight transition for Priya. Brother Karan was still a collegian and sister Priti was busy managing the family's shipping business in London, soon after her graduation.

"My life took a dramatic turn – both from the personal and professional angle," Priya discloses. However heartrending the situation, she couldn't afford to break down. Handling multi-locational properties and different scales of operations was a tough challenge for Priya. To begin with, just consolidating the existing business took a few years. Priya meticulously tied up the loose ends and prepared a fresh ground to skyrocket her business.

Getting Strategy to Work

With her hands-on attitude, penchant for constant innovation and a predilection for working with teams, the hotelier is bullish on the Indian hospitality industry and holds the belief that the industry has a strong potential to grow and develop further. "The hotel industry is growing and evolving to suit the specific needs of the segment of travellers it is targeting," she asserts in an upbeat tone. "Customers constantly search for value-for-money products, which are fresh and inspiring too. This desire for variety pushes a large assortment of products into the market."

The world has moved on from the cookie-cutter concept of hotels. Globalisation, attention to detail and creation of individual experiences are crucial for the success of the hotel industry. Priya has consistently communicated clear positioning and branding ideas to her target groups to attract the right marketing mix for the services a hotel offers, proving her mettle in a very competitive marketplace.

> *"Tourism is the second largest contributor to the growth of the Indian economy. Indian skies are being opened up. The proposed dismantling of FIB is believed to induce a more investment-friendly climate. The Tourism Awareness Programme, launched by PATA in 1999, has given the industry much greater focus."*

Priya pioneered the concept of boutique hotels in India. Under her direction, The Park understood that the key to success lies in differentiating the product by being distinctive and relevant in approach, energizing people and generating a lot of fun. Travellers tire of predictable and routine ambiances.

"Unusual locations and concepts enhance the drama of travel, whether one is on an official tour or simply luxuriating. Distinctive elements of design, a focus on luxury in comfort and personalized services with a touch of intimacy are what we bring to our customers," Priya reveals. She has skilfully translated personal beliefs into her work. A lover of art, her hotels boast of a sleek, distinctive décor, which spells 're-invention'.

Continues Priya, "Our collection of luxury boutique hotels suggests style, sensuousness, opulence and intimacy." The specially designed environment she brings creates a wealth of experience for many.

With the foray of international entrants, who vie to compete aggressively with one other, the quality of service has improved manifold. This is a challenge Priya enjoys. She delights in bringing in new products and offerings for the locals to visit too.

Priya has a firm grasp on the bare bones of the business. She has honed her business acumen to react quickly to the market's requirement for exciting options at interesting price points.

Users of conventional hotels and the well-informed youth populations alike continue to find The Park a refreshing change. Although the group carries the tag of 'business hotels', it caters widely to leisure travellers too. To keep the interest and energy levels on a consistently high measure, Priya conceived an innovative marketing approach. She elaborates on her strategy: "For the local markets, we promote our products aggressively in F&B (Food & Beverages) outlets and host major events that revolve around art, fashion and book launches." Extensive advertising, direct mails and national and international media relations support her initiatives.

At The Park, sales and marketing teams located across the country take charge of executing various Relationship Management programmes like the *Preferred at the Park.* Team members personally monitor the changing preferences of each customer through rigorous market tests. The data thus obtained are compiled in a shared format. Thereafter, they are promptly acted upon. Regular direct mailers to customers keep them posted on the latest developments in this regard.

"*The Park* magazine, which is our quarterly, encapsulates the energy of the brand; it has become a much sought-after item," pipes up an enthusiastic Priya.

Hotelier Par Excellence

Priya's contributions to Indian hospitality and leisure over a short stretch of time have earned her numerous well-deserving awards. Based on membership, the *Preferred at the Park* programme is targeted at both corporate and individual travellers and is operational in all her properties. Recognizing this innovative step towards product enhancement, the Institute of Directors presented Priya Paul the prestigious *Golden Peacock Innovative Product/Service Award* in

1999-2000. Attracting over 3000 members from various cities in India, this unique loyalty programme extends benefits in F&B outlets and allows members to redeem points for an incredulous range of exclusive gifts they offer. The Park's radical approach changed customer perception. The marketing initiatives undertaken by The Park at Kolkata serve as the only case study in the category of hotel businesses in IIM, Ahmedabad.

On the international front, *Tatler Magazine*, UK rated The Park, Bangalore as one of the 101 best hotels worldwide in 2003. *Wallpaper* (August 2004), the contemporary magazine on world design, views *Fire* (the contemporary desi-flavour Indian restaurant) and *Agni* (the lounge bar) at The Park, New Delhi as invigorating chill-out zones on the strength of their funky motifs and patterns.

Priya Paul also secured the *Young Entrepreneur of the Year Award* in 1999-2000 presented by the Federation of Hotels and Restaurants Association of India and was nominated *Businessperson of the Year* by *Economic Times* in 2002-03 and 2003-04.

Priya also serves as the Vice President of the Hotel Association of India, a founder-member of the World Travel Tourism Council – India Initiative and an enthusiastic member of the Young President's Organization and the Advisory Board of Directors of the Indian Institute of Management (IIM), Lucknow.

In May 2003, The Park hotels in Kolkata, Bangalore and Chennai became members of the Design Hotels Inc., an association that represents and markets an international collection of design-oriented city hotels and exceptional leisure resorts under its own brand – Design Hotels™. The foregoing three properties are the only hotels in India to enjoy the benefits of this association. Each of these hotels distinguished itself from the others through innovative interior design and architecture, uncomplicated service and a sense of creativity and perfection in detail, all of which give it a very distinctive identity. Over 100 properties in 36 countries boast of the Design Hotels™ brand. Yet, they are deeply rooted in the local region and community, sharing an aesthetic dialogue with their environment. This marketing alliance enabled The Park to reach out globally. International travellers who are scouring for intimate luxurious experiences in India can now avail of them.

Menu for Success

Priya views situations as pictures at a macro-level as she continues to eat, drink and live business. In an enlightening, yet soul-searching tête-à-tête, she shares her beliefs, principles and practices, both personal and corporate. *Excerpts from an exclusive interview...*

- ❑ *How easy or difficult was it for you to be a part of a feted business house and make a mark in the legacy of your family business, in spite of having to contend with several crises during the earlier phase of your life?*

  When we are a part of a business family, we don't feel we are going through a major life-changing scheme. I received a lot of exposure from a young age. One gets much exposure, especially during holidays. I would visit my dad's office at the age of 15. Frequent discussions developed in me an instinctive understanding of various aspects of the company as it gave me a deeper insight into the business.

- ❑ *What role did your age and qualification play in the ups and downs of your life? Was your age an advantage or an obstacle to your ambitions?*

  My family connections helped. Without them, I would not be here. I had a role to perform and I desired to perform to the best of my ability. If there is something I cannot do, I take help from others. Age and gender are non-issues for me! (*Laughs*)

- ❑ *Can you apprise us of some of the unique people practices that you have incorporated in your hotel group?*

  We invest a large volume of our time and effort in providing training in systems and developing each person. And the essence of the initiative we have taken in this regard is evident in the sterling performances our people turn in. As a primary constituent of our corporate policy, we are transparent in all the issues we deal with. We constitute a young team and having fun is certainly important for all of us. As our team has to put in twenty-four hours of work many a time, we ensure that we enjoy our work.

- ❑ *The push-for-profit world of cutthroat competition in business provides little or no scope for sensitivity in business and corporate heads. Are women managers an exception?*

  Male or female, most successful businesspersons are wholly passionate about their business as their sensitivities are linked to business. Until very recently in our country, you were frowned upon if seen as a person interested in making profits. Why should monetary growth be a taboo? If our country is to grow and develop, we need to generate a larger volume of wealth.

As Priya continues to grow her business of operating and managing a large chain of luxury boutique hotels, upholding global standards in quality and service, she aims at differentiation with a host of new projects she will be initiating in the upcoming future. "We are also working towards strengthening the bonds of intimacy we share with our customers," she informs. She is currently charting avenues to explore newer and increasingly interesting styles and design models.

The Lengthy Trail

A nation of thriving business communities, India can engender high levels of entrepreneurship. "The younger (25-44) age bracket makes up the majority of the tourist populations," Priya reports. "But we still have a long way to go before we can equate ourselves with the likes of China, Hong Kong, Thailand, Dubai and the Maldives."

In the last decade, international arrivals in India recorded a whopping 3 million in 2000 – a far cry from the figure of 15,000, which our growth records contained in 1950. (Source: India Tourist Statistics.) She is however contrite as she says, "India's share in world tourism has remained virtually stagnant at 0.38% for a greater part of the last decade."

Try quizzing her on the intricacies of the tourism and hospitality sector in India and you'll see that she has not only a vast cornucopia of information, but the shrewd expertise to offer her suggestions to Indian policy-makers too.

> "Asia is fast emerging as a chosen destination among globetrotters. India is a late starter in tourism. Overseas players view India as an emerging market in Asia. She has always been a strong contender with the USA, UK, Sri Lanka, France, Germany, Canada, Japan, Australia and Singapore as her biggest market sources. Attractive tourist spots in Rajasthan and Agra (from the North), Goa (from the West) and Kerala (from the Southern region) have lured a large array of overseas travellers from the foregoing countries."

> *"As a leisure destination, India offers a unique bounty of nature. Right from climbing and rafting to bird watching to basking lazily in the sun, one can do so much here! The variety that lies at the disposal of foreign tourists in India complements the rich heritage sights in our country."*

"The high luxury taxes in India nevertheless pose a major deterrent to inbound tourism. The approved state and central luxury taxes for rooms and F&B outlets should range between 10 and 12 per cent. Above and beyond, there exists a hidden dimension of Indian tourism that holds little place in the policy planning of most industry players, marking the rise of domestic tourism. Over a span of the last 10-12 years, the industry has witnessed an increase of over 100 million travellers. More than 176 million visitors travel within the borders of India. The growth we have seen is perhaps a by-product of economic development. People are beginning to use their disposable incomes more often. While a considerable portion of these earnings is used for religious purposes, another huge chunk is being put to use when people set out on sightseeing sprees. With the rise in earnings, people are looking for better and more expensive methods of travel and accommodation."

A la Carte

Goa is one of Priya's cosiest retreats when she takes off on a holiday. She enjoys discovering and re-discovering the mysteries of Morocco and has a liking for cuisine, meditation and reading. She dishes out scrumptious varieties of savouries from the kitchen. "I don't know what I can cook best though," she admits, laughing. "I can probably make a delicious sandwich."

She loves listening to different forms of music too. "I can't sing well, though," she confesses ruefully. "I did take lessons in classical music when I was small. But I realized that I was not gifted with a voice for singing."

An apposite mix of fun and solemnity, laughter and tears, light and shadow. That is Priya for you. Deciding whether it is the façade of Priya Paul's large group of hotels that towers over her personality or her personality that towers over them is a tall order. What is indeed clear is that Priya Paul is a woman who seeks to enjoy what she does. It is this approach of hers that propelled her to establish practices to repaint the ethos of Indian hotels and made her a rising star. In the times to come, she is determined to write a new history in the Indian hotel industry.

Rajshree Pathy
Chairman, Rajshree Sugars and Chemicals Limited

10.
The Candy-maker

Her candy glows bright and pink. The lustre of the pink is of the same kind as the vitality with which one should sprint forward in business, constantly exploring larger frontiers. The sweet harmony of its taste and colour synchronizes with the amiability and diplomacy via which one should lead an industry and a sugar factory at that.

Rajshree Pathy (Chairperson of Rajshree Sugars and Chemicals Limited – RSCL) has given the sugar industry a newfound stature with her amiability, diplomacy and vitality. RSCL recorded a net profit of Rs.7.83 crore on a net sale of Rs.117.52 crore during 2001-02. "We aim to be an aggressive leader in the FMCG space," she told *Hindu Business Line* in a confident tone, soon after RSCL introduced the Demerara sugar into the broad national market with its venture into the area of pure, organic branded sugar. Suffice it to say, Rajshree is a woman who can lead, command and deliver the goods.

The Opportunists

A fourth-generation entrepreneur, Rajshree Pathy was born into the Kamma Naidu community, which migrated from Andhra Pradesh and settled in Coimbatore, raising a breed of prosperous cotton textile pioneers and philanthropists in the 1930s and 40s. The Kamma Naidus contributed to the development of the city of Coimbatore by building charitable hospitals and schools for scheduled castes and orphans.

Business came very naturally to Rajshree. She grew up in a legendary family, which gained its status as a clan of industrialists in 1911 when grandfathe PSG Ganga Naidu set up a ginning factory. Rajshree's father, the late G Varadaraj, was renowned for his dedication to social causes. Under his stewardship, the PSG Educational Institutions, an autonomous university grew to include a private medical college and a hospital. G. Varadaraj servec the Rajya Sabha for a full term. Rajshree loved meeting many groups o people who visited her home as guests and was motivated to achieve somethin of consequence when she grew up.

Since she got along well with people who belonged to the older age category her father encouraged her to participate in discussions with his friends anc acquaintances, many an evening. "A lot of interesting people – politicians business personalities and foreign diplomats – frequented our house," Rajshre recalls.

Young at heart, Rajshree's parents always brimmed with fresh vigour, whic they passed on to their daughters. Rajshree and her sister were given all th freedom and choice to do what they wanted in life. "My sister Jaishree and were never gender-differentiated," Rajshree says. "And we didn't know hov serious the issue was until we faced the real world as full-fledged adults."

Rajshree was a tremendously curious child. She enthusiastically participate in many extra-curricular activities so much so that her interest in any tas could be aroused very easily. She learned tennis, took formal training in classical Carnatic music and Bharat Natyam and played the piano. Holidays meant Goan beaches, churches, temples, food, fun and exciting car journeys to different parts of the country.

She had never known boredom and loneliness in her life. "Life with all its challenges has been a big roller-coaster ride for me," she reveals, adding, "I have been blessed with great mentors in my life. But a few especially need to be mentioned." She is grateful to author Paolo Coelho, whom she met several years ago during one of her extensive travels. A good friend of hers, he reinforced in her a belief in Karmic relationships. "He taught me to pursue life with passion," she recounts.

Swami Dayananda Saraswati, who was a part of her life since she was 18, taught her the philosophies of Vedanta and narrated verses from the Gita. "He never let me quit when I wanted to," she tells us solemnly. "His wisdom was incomparable. He guided me through the most difficult situations."

She also drew a lot of inspiration from Tarun Das, Chief Mentor, Confederation of Indian Industries (CII), who raised her confidence and self-esteem. This saw her unfurl from a small, shy town girl into an emerging business leader.

"My parents lavished unconditional love on me and set standards of ethics and honesty by their own examples," she acknowledges. The benchmark they set serves as her guiding principle in life. "Many people in my organization have stood by me through the highs and the lows, giving me the strength to continue the journey effectively," she adds.

Rajshree was married before she turned 18. Shortly after her graduation, she delved into the intricacies of cotton sampling and cotton spinning at the South India Textile Research Association in Coimbatore. Being the first-born, she found it logical to walk the trodden path of the family lineage and hop into the family textile business. She equipped herself with a degree in commerce and began assisting her father with sister Jaishree.

Unconventional in his ideas as he was, her father was always one to believe that a woman had to effectively play the role of a wife and mother before setting out on new ventures or managing an enterprise. In this aspect, his traditionalism did not provide him much leeway in encouraging his daughters to involve themselves hands-on in the family business. Little did he know that Rajshree was strongly self-motivated to prove that a daughter could equal a son in all respects.

Constructing an Empire

When opportunity struck, the fiery young girl seized it. She was barely 24 and in the family way, when she began managing the textile mills as soon as her father moved to Delhi as a Member of Parliament in the Rajya Sabha. It was not long before she built a new textile mill, managing the old one independently.

Recognizing her father's contribution to developmental activities, the State Government granted him permission to build a sugar factory in 1989. The factory was established in Andipatti (a most backward area in the southern region of Tamil Nadu) with an objective to generate agro-economic prosperity in the area and around.

In the meanwhile, Rajshree was pregnant with her second baby. Yet, she gamely accepted this new challenge. Not one to get to discouraged, she soon began giving shape to her empire. On the business front, she floated a public limited company, declared herself the Project Manager and toured around the country to interview consultants and engineers, with her two-year-old second-born in tow. She interacted with multiple contractors and watched foundations and cables being laid as she cradled her baby in the crook of her arm. She soon began canvassing for sugarcane in the villages – politician style – clad in a sari and driving through the mud roads in a jeep, holding village meetings.

Since she was busy building the business and mothering two small children, she could not find time to attend a regular college to acquire a formal education in business. When there was a lull in the growth phase of the business, she enrolled at Harvard University in 1994 to pursue a three-year-programme in Executive Education.

The Roller Coaster

Rajshree's father expired at the age of 52 while leading a business delegation to Europe. She felt as though the world around her had suddenly fallen apart. Following his tragic demise, she gathered the courage to face the responsibilities that had abruptly been thrust upon her, growing up overnight to fill in the position as Chairman of the group.

There were many sniggers when she sat on her father's chair. Her family and colleagues were quite unsure of her business skills and feared that she would tarnish the family's reputation, losing all the credibility that had been established so painstakingly over the course of several years. The more she heard negative remarks, the more she told herself she would succeed. And succeed she did. Since Rajshree took over the company, the annual turnover has grown nearly a record seven times – from Rs.60 crore in 1990 to over Rs.400 crore in 2003.

Seeking yet another challenge, Rajshree decided to build a sugar factory in Vietnam. She spent three years in obtaining permissions and identifying a potential area for growth and expansion. She respects the Vietnamese for their diligence and gender equality in society.

"There was no gender differentiation on any count," Rajshree informs. The women put in the same number of man-hours as the men and received wages on the basis of their equity of labour – a phenomenon fairly uncommon in India.

Alas, the project was unfortunately shelved when the financial institutions opted out on account of the huge south-east Asian recession in the late 1990s. The lessons learned were, however, invaluable, she says.

> *"There are moments of triumph and turmoil in one's personal and professional life. One should accept them as mere reminders of the lessons learnt and grow wiser."*

Rewarding Sensations

The volatility of monsoon plays a great role in defining the profits of the agro-based sugar business. Even today, the sugar business is a sort of 'regulated' industry in the country. "The sugar industry involves a lot of politics," Rajshree states as a matter of fact. The sugar sector works on alarmingly low margins. Undaunted by limitations from within and without, Rajshree nevertheless absorbs every facet of the industry. Her greatest challenge lies in fulfilling the goals that she has set for herself.

Her most fulfilling experience was personally seeing what had been a barren land with marginal farmers working tirelessly on it 13 years ago, transform into a luxuriant belt of sugarcane fields with a large number of prosperous owners who supplied cane to the factory. Rajshree introduced scientific methods of cultivation and freed a debt-ridden community by advancing loans and supplying them credit.

Her efforts augured well, when a farmer once wept with joy and told her that she had made him a "crorepati". "Redeeming a social predicament provides you immense satisfaction," she states. "Personal satisfaction arises when you see smiles on the faces of people whose lives you have impacted."

The Rendezvous

As the sugar expert takes us on a sojourn through the intriguing world of the sugar industry and its politics, she highlights the technicalities of the sugar industry and offers innovative suggestions for the growth and development of sugar mills in India. *Excerpts from an exclusive interview...*

- *Sugarcane production in Maharashtra has been braving a declining trend. What impact do you feel it would cast on the ambit of sugar mills in India – especially in the event that other lucrative crops have begun to serve as substitutes for sugar cane? What policy changes would you propose to counter this situation?*

  It is not a switch to other lucrative crops that is responsible for this decline, but rather, inadequate rainfall. Sugarcane continues to be the most lucrative crop vis-à-vis the inputs required. A switch to other crops is not only a question of price, but also one of geography, especially since terrain, climatic patterns, cropping cycles, pests, disease and potential yields exert higher pressure. The cultural orientation of the local farming community plays a significant role in the choice of crops too. And Maharashtra has always been a traditional sugarcane belt, accounting for over 30% of the country's sugarcane production. Policy change may support the industry. But the aspiration to grow sugarcane as a remunerative crop is a separate aspect.

- *How can we strengthen the basis of the public distribution system in India? Do you think it is essential to impose price controls on the purchase of sugar through the PDS?*

  The public distribution system was introduced in India to ensure the availability of essential commodities at fair prices to economically backward segments of the community. However, excessive dependence on the PDS has led to a drain on the exchequer due to the abuse of what could otherwise have been a perfect delivery mechanism.

  A larger effort to advance the cause of sustainable agriculture should be the cornerstone in our march towards the goal of national food security.

A commodity should remain in the list of essential items only as long as the country takes to build up its production base. Thereafter, market forces should be the key-driver. When the sugar industry is ironically the only sector that supports one of the Government's subsidy bills, the Government itself noisily trumpets the need to withdraw all subsidies. Shockingly, individual buyers are reported to consume only 30% of the sugar produced in the country. Soft-drinks manufacturers, ice cream producers and other industrial users sop up the remainder.

Given this scenario, the need to control sugar prices in the open market is no longer relevant today. The existing system of pricing and control is outmoded and needs to be rationalized. The control of the prices of sugar through the PDS is only indicative of attempts to keep in place a subsidy the Government wishes to maintain for political expediency. If the industry is to generate higher profits and pay higher prices to farmers, deregulation is the need of the hour.

> *"The vast vote bank and an eye on the elections have led many a state to hastily undo the hard victories gained in the battle to control fiscal deficits in the face of adverse criticism. Fiscal prudence and political reality are not converse; rather they complement each other."*

- *Does the cooperative sector continue to play a critical role in expanding the total output of sugar?*

  The very nature of the cooperative sector imposes limitations on its ability to synchronize with the changing business environment. I see a strong future in the expansion of conglomerates, which would make their mark by way of capacities, economies of scale and value addition through various areas of by-product diversification like power generation, ethanol, fertilizers and agri-biotechnology.

- *The Government intends to lay more emphasis on generating sizeable export surplus and ensuring adequate supplies for domestic consumption as well. How can we strike a judicious balance here?*

  Well, that is more in the hands of the rain gods than in the hands of mere mortals. (*Laughs*) With the projected growth patterns in the domestic consumption levels of sugar, the country would have to increase its sugarcane acreage by 10% every year. Considering the vagaries of the monsoons and their adverse effects on agricultural production, this is a rather tall order. An effective scheme to process imported raw sugar continuously would offset the effects of decline in sugar production. When the country wields a domestic surplus, raw sugar (processed into white sugar) could be re-exported as a regular operation. And a percentage of the volume of sugar could be retained in the domestic market during years of shortfall. If India were a constant player in the international market, price volatility would diminish, widening the base of profitability for sugar players.

- *Do you feel the Indian sugar sector is globally competitive? How can the free-market sales of cane and decontrol policies increase the level of competitiveness among the sugar mills in India?*

  Releasing the sugar industry from the shackles of price and release controls is not a panacea for the ills of the industry. In the absence of statutory controls, the industry may as well come up with a self-regulatory mechanism of its own. However, the regulation would be dynamic to the business and market environment and devoid of the stifling bureaucracy of the Government and the vicissitudes of politics. The market would be the driver of growth for the industry and expand capacities more efficiently, facilitating an optimum utilization of resources. Were it not for the imposition of price controls on cane and sugar, the Indian sugar industry would be the most efficient converter of sugarcane into sugar.

- *Has India tided over the barrage of high international prices successfully?*

  Many a time, the sugar traded in the international market is subsidized indirectly by artificially held high domestic prices in the countries of origin and protectionist policies like exorbitant import tariffs. The recent ruling of the WTO that the subsidies on sugar in the European Union are illegal is a victory for large sugar producers in the Cairns group, which has lobbied long and hard for the removal of unfair trade practices of the Union, as they depress international sugar prices. Given the level-playing field that the Indian sugar industry is, it does not need any overt support to compete in the international market.

Everyday is a Milestone Crossed

Bottom-line, shareholder value and corporate governance are the current buzzwords that dominate corporate performance, today. Rajshree religiously respects and practices these concepts. Rajshree Sugars prides itself on their excellent labour relations. The company has maintained a healthy win-win situation for both the management and the unions. For Rajshree, running an industry is all about building trust and integrity. "Trying to outsmart someone is an indication of short-sightedness," she believes. "As long as you display a sense of fairness in the way you treat people, success is a sure-fire phenomenon."

Once these values have been tried and tested over time, people begin to trust the management. Being a woman CEO, gender issues within the organization have not been major issues. In a lighter vein, she quips that her male colleagues have often complained that they are the ones who are being discriminated in the company! Rajshree hopes to grow larger in her core business (sugar and allied products).

> *"India lives not in the plush, air-conditioned rooms of the cities, but in villages. It is necessary to integrate the two to achieve a healthy symbiosis."*

The World Economic Forum, Davos (Switzerland), conferred the *Global Leaders of Tomorrow* recognition on Rajshree in 1996, at a time when few Indians were members of the forum. "It was truly an honour," Rajshree states. "It gave me the opportunity to meet intellectuals, business magnates and political leaders, who were drawn from a select and discerning group of one hundred young people, chosen the world over."

Elected as the President of the Indian Sugar Mills Association (ISMA) for the year 2004-2005, she is the first woman to head the previously powerful and male-dominated Sugar Association.

> *"I am honoured to note that my peers and colleagues have so graciously accepted me. Not that I require any endorsements or approvals, but it is an indication that society has opened up to women, accepting them as equals in conventional male-dominated businesses."*

An active member of the CII National Committee of Women Empowerment, Rajshree firmly believes that women would avail of greater employment opportunities in the era of globalisation, especially in light of the rapid growth of the service sector.

She has given several enlightening talks, emphasizing the importance of literacy for women for the overall growth and development of the nation. Furthermore, she has introduced various initiatives to empower women by eliminating gender inequalities, recognizing the achievements of meritorious young women and encouraging them to occupy higher positions in the business and corporate sectors. "Women should grab the opportunity and be more competitive," she opines.

Breaking Barriers

Women are beginning to make a mark in a wide range of service sectors which are mushrooming today. Rajshree draws our attention to the glass ceiling that continues to persist even today and their success in shattering it and swelling the ranks of the tertiary industry.

> "Although growth in export manufacturing may create a surge of initial, low-paying jobs for women with the globalisation of business, it is subsequently the growth in the services sector that often creates the greatest long-term benefits for women in the workplace. Women draw more benefits from jobs in the realms of banking and financial services, tourism, recreation and commercial services. In addition, they are perceived to put their special skills to use in certain nurturing service sectors, like healthcare and education. The marketplace offers increasing opportunities for women to work in traditional sectors too. Increased trade and investments breed an environment more conducive to a vital, growing economy by enlarging the scope for employment. In particular, the growth of industries that produce exports for external markets prides on a proven record of job creation. When jobs are available aplenty, they are less likely to be taken up entirely by men.
>
> "Barriers to advancement of women continue to remain although globalisation has spawned many more work opportunities. The larger numbers of managerial posts, which globalisation has churned out in top-notch companies, does not necessarily imply that women would be advanced automatically to executive-level positions. Women, who have managed to secure high-level managerial positions in large

organizations, are often restricted to the ambit of human resources, administration or other areas, which are less central or strategic to the organization. They do not have much room to move laterally into strategic areas like product development or finance or hike upwards through central pathways to key executive positions in the pyramidal structure, which is characteristic of big companies. I refer to these barriers as glass walls. However, these barriers are fast being broken – and perhaps at a much quicker rate in India than in the West."

"The Government and corporate entities have begun to address various concerns of women empowerment at all levels. Comprehensive surveys are being conducted through industry bodies to discern the patterns of gender recruitment in different types of sectors. Moreover, anti-sexual harassment policies have been formulated to tackle the issue of sexual harassment at work. These policies will be applicable to all companies. Furthermore, companies should be encouraged to set up high-quality crèches in their premises. Mothers find it more convenient to leave their children in the crèches so that they may work undisturbed. A lot could be done to identify other small and medium-scale organizations on the issue of women empowerment. Currently, various schemes are being compiled to encourage young women entrepreneurs under the Directorate of Employment."

A Natural Leader

Women, who are innately good at multi-tasking and compassionate in nature, do have the potential to emerge as natural leaders, Rajshree believes. Indian women in particular are blessed with supportive home infrastructures, which grant them the freedom to work. "Sometimes women do not opt for a career in business for two main reasons. To begin with, they lack the personal motivation to do so. Secondly, their families do not encourage them in their endeavours. They should understand that running a business requires a certain dedication of mental, emotional and physical stamina," Rajshree avers. "Neither the balance sheet nor the shareholders are sympathetic to one's gender. Business is a level-playing field and performance is the key word."

As Rajshree's male colleagues watched her grow over the years, their respect for her led her to take on numerous prestigious positions in the industry. She is not a woman who looks for sympathy or patronizing attitudes. You can find her constantly encouraging women to stand up for their convictions and put their heart and soul into what they believe their path in life should be.

Living by Convictions

Rajshree strives to give her son and daughter ample freedom, education and exposure to expand their ability to take decisions independently and choose their career paths. "Rajshree Sugars is a public limited company managed very professionally. I expect my children to prove themselves if they want a place in the company," she states matter-of-factly. Of course, she leaves the decision of working elsewhere up to them too. Always one to believe in the freedom of the individual, Rajshree Pathy lives her life with certain convictions that she has set for herself. And she respects her children for theirs.

Rajshree has a rare multilingual talent, which has her think and voice her views in English, read and write French and converse in Telugu and Tamil at home. Constantly in pursuit of contemporary art, she enjoys designing and reading books on art and culture. A voracious reader of non-fiction biographies and philosophy, she especially likes Paolo Coelho's *The Alchemist* and Richard Branson's *Losing my Virginity.*

She has been a PADL-certified scuba diver for the last twenty years. Photography, travelling, swimming and catching up with friends are her fun-time pursuits too. Mick Jagger, the Doors and Annie Lennox are her favourite singers while the movies of Fellini, Quinton Tarantino, Polanski and Pedro Almadovar appeal to her the most.

"Sir Richard Attenborough's *Gandhi* is a must-see movie, especially for the younger generation, for whom he has become a lost memory," she declares. White cotton clothes, a tall glass of fresh coconut water from her garden, a few laps in a swimming pool and a dash of "Vetiver" by Guerlain are her recipes for a perfect summer. Give her a holiday and you'll find her in Tuscany and the Chianti Vineyards.

The profundity of her principles contrasts strikingly with her young, peppy persona as she quotes her favourite lines on what freedom means to her, stressing that they sum up her philosophy in life:

> "Physical, emotional and financial freedom mean the world to me… they give me the power to live by my convictions, be fearless in my vision, cross set boundaries, shout from the rooftops for the causes I support, be a voice for the women who are afraid to speak, dance to gay abandon with people I love, travel to the extremities of the Earth with my children, cry without being weak, and most importantly give without asking… Freedom is living without living a lie…"

Ranjana Kumar
Chairman, National Bank for Agriculture & Rural Development

11.
Twists and Turns

The hare and the tortoise decide to participate in a race. "I can beat you hollow," the hare boasts to the tortoise. During the course of the race, the slow tortoise patiently moves forward inch by painful inch while the overconfident hare enjoys a long, restful nap, certain that the tortoise would still hobble along while he zoomed across the 'finish' line once he recharged himself with the refreshing nap. The tortoise beats the hare hollow. Applying the same principle to the corporate world, companies should never be complacent and rest upon their laurels. The story will continue but she had successfully applied her innovative story to the corporate life with a splendid success...

Here goes the story. The hare slumps his shoulders in defeat and walks away. The hare challenges the tortoise for yet another race. With the same pace and commitment, he beats the tortoise hollow this time. It goes without saying that companies too, should adopt a policy of being fast and reliable in keeping with today's fast-paced, dog-eat-dog corporate era.

Now, the tortoise challenges the hare to race him again. This time, the tortoise chooses a different route. In his greed to teach the tortoise a lesson for routing him in the first race, the hare hastily accepts the offer. Alas, the hare discovers a lake on his way, which he cannot cross. The tortoise swims across comfortably and reaches the shores on the other end. Likewise, companies should think twice before moving to territories that lie outside domains where they cannot use their core competence. Obviously, the hare learns a lesson.

Now, the hare and the tortoise have had enough. They believe that they can cover the distances together if they run side-by-side, each helping the other to achieve his goal. If competitors would join hands together to leverage their strengths, they would achieve stupendous results, contributing to the growth and development of the industry and the country's economy.

The narrator of the story is ***Ranjana Kumar*** (Chairman, National Bank for Agriculture & Rural Development – NABARD). A role model for nationalized bankers, she is the first-ever lady to head a nationalized bank as well as an apex agriculture refinance institution in India.

The Anti-Magnetic Radium Dial

A proud grandmother of two, Ranjana had a happy and eventful childhood. As her father worked in the Air Force, her family travelled extensively during her early years. Ranjana studied in different schools in Mumbai, Kolkata, Kanpur and Coimbatore, often finding herself 'the newcomer at school'. As a student, she was every teacher's dream. She aspired to become a doctor. Her disappointment knew no bounds when she did not obtain a seat in a Government medical college. But perhaps the banking sector gained what the medical field lost. She completed her graduation at Women's College, Hyderabad. Conscientious as always, she had a strong foothold on the fundamental principles she had learnt. For her final BA examination, she revised and re-revised the entire portion of her syllabus fourteen times, ate only *chapattis* and didn't watch a single movie.

Ranjana completed courses in Sangeet Bhushan (in music) and Virashad (in Hindi), briefly learning Bharat Natyam and Kathak too. She was an excellent orator, who represented her institution in several intercollegiate elocution and debate competitions. She enrolled in Osmania University to pursue a post-graduate course in Public Administration. At a time when job offers to women were rare, the Bank of India presented her a tempting proposal. Keen to make a career for herself at the age of twenty, Ranjana quit her Masters programme and joined the bank as a probationary officer in February 1966 while other girls her age lived fun-filled campus lives and revelled in shopping sprees.

Soon after Ranjana married, her grandmother worried that she was off to work all the time. "Don't forget to look presentable when your husband returns home from work," she would chide her granddaughter playfully. Acting diligently upon this golden rule, Ranjana would fly to the washroom as soon as she got back home from work, freshen up and hastily change into a new dress, regardless of how difficult the day had been.

She was once dismayed to find that she had a voluminous pile of work on her desk at the office and would not be able to complete it on time to return home and await her husband's return. Seeing no other alternative at the moment, she frantically phoned her husband at his office and asked him to come home late, as she wanted to return home before him and get 'ready' for him. Amused though he was, he agreed to return late. When he did, Ranjana explained to him in sheepish giggles what her grandmother had told her and why she was doing what she was doing!

Thanks to the effectiveness with which Ranjana juggles numerous personal, corporate and social roles, she is known to function like an anti-magnetic radium dial. "Women play many roles in our society. A clear understanding of the demands of these roles coupled with a well-balanced approach in life can go a long way in enabling a woman to do justice to her balancing act," she asserts. And that is precisely what she has done. Many a time, she too was tempted to throw her hands up and yell, "That's it – I can do no more." Pushing back the urge, she only chose to strengthen her resolve further. "Life requires a lot of adjustments," she observes in retrospect.

Ranjana wields a judicious blend of qualities she has acquired from both her parents. Her mother started a school and ran it for thirty years. "She was extremely hard-working," Ranjana mentions. "It was from her that I learnt not to crib for small failures in life." Her father held strong spiritual values. Ranjana imbibed from him the philosophies of responsibility and integrity. She has two brothers too; she never faced any discrimination vis-à-vis them. Her family was highly liberal in thinking and broad in vision.

Today, Ranjana's assertiveness in approach and aggressiveness in business combine well with the love and compassion we typically view as archetypes of femininity.

A Moment of Reckoning

Every woman passes through a phase during the course of which she contemplates whether to continue working or not, when posted to a different city or country. On joining the Bank of India, Ranjana Kumar worked in different states and capacities, heading various branches and offices. She steadily ascended the corporate ladder before she was positioned as the Vice President and Chief Executive of the US operations. She faced the first challenge when she received her first transfer. "As you escalate the corporate ladder, you cannot avoid transfers," she states sensibly. In the early 1980s, it wasn't common for a woman to receive a job transfer, leave her home, family and children and settle down in new, unfamiliar terrain. Moreover, living in a joint family made the decision more complex. Unafraid of these social constraints, Ranjana chose the tougher route.

Her stint abroad presented her with a dual challenge, as she not only represented the bank but a foreign country too. Under the tight scrutiny of the Federal Reserve, she managed to obtain a strong rating from the agencies for the first ever time in the history of the Bank of India in its twenty years in the USA. Shortly after she returned to India, she was made the Executive Director and soon assumed charge as the Chairman and Managing Director of Canara Bank. As a person equipped with immense expertise in the core modules of international banking, she was entrusted with the charge of heading Indo-Hong Kong International Finance Limited, a wholly-owned subsidiary of Canara Bank Limited.

The Swift Turnaround

"It is a punishment posting." That was the opinion of many, when Ranjana took on the mantle as the Chairman and Managing Director of the Indian Bank in 2000. "How can we just write off the bank?" Ranjana argued. "The bank is 95 years old and its fundamentals are strong." She played a pivotal role in managing one of the most challenging turnarounds in performance in the annals of banking in India. While many others declined, Ranjana capitalized on the solid foundation the bank had, and boldly took up the challenge of transforming a crisis-ridden public sector bank into a profitable enterprise.

During 1995-96, the unprecedented losses the bank had incurred amounted to Rs.1336 crore. Moreover, there was a negative capital adequacy of nearly 13%. Ranjana tactfully brought down the gross NPA from 43% in March 1998 to 15% in 2001-02 and pulled off additional recap assistance to the tune of Rs.1700 crore, turning the bank around gradually. Unsurprisingly, the *Economist*, UK labelled her 'India's Turnaround Queen'.

Boosting the sagging morale of employees was one of Ranjana's chief concerns. The bank authorities delegated powers to the branch managers to enable quick decision-making. Ranjana Kumar personally visited each of the branches and explained to the staff her formulae for the turnaround of the bank. The core strategy consisted of getting to know the customer, assessing the return on the assets, analysing the spreads and carrying an in-depth study of the volume of total income and expenditure.

Ranjana brought her excellent people-management skills to the fore, when she transformed the bank into a three-tier organization. Her masterstroke was the introduction of the Voluntary Retirement Scheme, which gave a golden handshake to 3300 employees. More than 120 officers had received training in the realm of credit recovery and many young recruits were hired to project a new image of the bank. As a constituent of cost reduction measures, more than 100 loss-making units were merged together.

> *"Corporate governance is very important for any and every organization. If we speak out what we think, we would have no need to worry about recalling and remembering data, figures and events for the simple reason that we would be reporting facts. Communication is an indispensable criterion. Every organization has its weak links. We must share our beliefs with the people down the line and tell them why they must work harder and even sacrifice their personal interests sometimes. Telling them that a persistent approach would benefit the organization at large will re-infuse in them their loyalty to the company too. But goading our employees to work hard and opening their eyes to certain implications if they don't perform will not suffice either. Organizational problems can be easily evaded if channels of communication are open and effective."*

The Indian Bank also established a plethora of rehabilitation units. Restructured in three years, the bank achieved a remarkable recovery, posting a net profit of Rs.33.22 crore. The bank returned to black within a timeframe of six years – one year ahead of schedule – re-enforcing the confidence of customers and the morale of the staff, alike.

The bank advocated the policy of direct marketing. The company's staff travelled far and wide to aggressively market various products and schemes the bank announced. So committed were they to their tasks and beliefs that they worked tirelessly even beyond the regular office hours and on holidays. The bank plunged into full-fledged action by linking many more ATMs to widen the range of connectivity. It also planned to open evening counters in select locations for the benefit of customers. Under the influence of Ranjana, the bank consistently made efforts to expand the business. Ranjana initiated talks with major public sector banks to share good loan accounts, moving on to build a portfolio of approximately Rs.50 crore.

She also established a friendly tie-up with HDFC Standard Life to venture into the area of distributing insurance policies. Besides fine people skills, it was transparency in the workplace that helped the bank reinvent itself, so much so that it even began a credit-restructuring department. The foreign branches in Singapore and Sri Lanka were quickly restored to the pink of health. The story of the turnaround grew so popular that Ranjana was invited to Sri Lanka to address bankers on issues revolving around restructuring. The University of Washington, Seattle invited her to address Senior International Bankers at the Pacific River Bankers Association Training Programme.

Paving the Way

After Ranjana's stints with commercial banks, NABARD was the most unglamorous posting she received. But she was determined to perform her best. She was a visionary in the spheres of pricing and post-harvest management, both of which were integral constituents of rural credit management. Keeping in view local necessities, rural infrastructure creation is her prime area of focus today.

Re-examining the provisions of regulated market acts, Ranjana understood the need for suitable amendments to extend free marketing facilities to farmers and to enhance the business climates. In this connection, she established a series of farmers' clubs to offer a forum for exchange of information, knowledge and technology and linked farmers' consortiums and self-help groups to business houses and industrial enterprises, expanding the gamut of marketing services, which every farmer could avail of. "The farmers' club forums are also functional in checking the quality of seeds and manure," Ranjana informs.

> *"While existing infrastructures like cold storages and godowns are not being utilized on one hand, farmers from other areas have an incessant demand for them. We need to take initiatives to link the forces of supply and demand to optimise the demand for these infrastructures."*

Under Ranjana's charge, the thrust on agricultural lending instilled in every soul a positive mindset, resulting in higher prospects of growth. The main roles of the bank lay in promoting agricultural development in rural areas by refinancing commercial, cooperative and regional rural banks. Instrumental in funding rural infrastructures by initiating road development programmes, building rural bridges and introducing irrigation and flood control measures, NABARD has offices in each state, with responsibility vested at the district levels.

An investor of rural entrepreneurship, NABARD forms self-help groups to supply opportunities for rural women to equip themselves through training and entrepreneurship development programmes, enabling them to acquire loans and start businesses of their own. The bank established an NGO to conduct numerous agricultural and rural development ventures in this regard. Ranjana is making arrangements for the final-year students of the National Institute of Fashion Technology (NIFT) to impart designing skills to women in select rural areas during the course of their three-month break.

In her latest assignment, Ranjana has pioneered an extensive series of projects and evolved fresh rural banking concepts, hitherto virtually non-existent. An awareness creation among farmers about various insurance schemes and the development of special schemes for marginal farmers were Ranjana's brainchild. She forged the model of Think Global, Plan National and Act Local to mitigate the hardships of farmers.

Banks could grant financial and non-financial incentives to borrowers who had good repayment periods. Now, Ranjana didn't believe in treating the farmers as intended beneficiaries or borrowers; she believed in viewing them as clients. "They should be provided a realistic scale of finance," she says vehemently. She worked to provide banking services at the farmers' doorsteps and has toured several villages to enhance the welfare of the farming community. A comprehensive risk mitigation plan is currently being envisaged under her leadership to ward off uncertainties faced by farmers.

Input-management issues such as those that covered quality, availability and cost were dealt with a firm hand. Many extension services like technology transfers and coordination efforts were heightened to an optimum. Ranjana strengthened the *Krishi Vigyan Kendras* (KVK) programmes with a view to rendering better technology transfer services. Stressing the pressing need for government agencies to play a more proactive role in the training of farmers and the supply of agricultural inputs, she undertook efforts to expand the network of agri-clinics and agribusiness centres, countrywide.

Hope Unbounded

A large chunk of cooperative banks faced a tragic state of affairs in the face of erosion of their capital. Raising cheap funds to refinance both cooperative and commercial banks is NABARD's main focus. "If commercial banks begin to monitor farm loans closely, in spite of the resultantly low volumes and high transaction costs, we would have the muscle to raise the rate of provision of loans to the agricultural sector by 30%," Ranjana declares optimistically. "Regional Rural Banks should indulge in lending activities instead of parking their funds in Government securities."

Alas, one-third of the entire population of Indian farmers is known to approach moneylenders to meet their financial requirements. Indeed, Ranjana has a tough job at hand. However, she remains unperturbed. Instead, she is optimistic about freeing the farmers from the unrelenting trap of moneylenders by providing them greater access to personal loans and mobility to shop for the best loans, increasing the level of flexibility in the loan terms and bringing down the insurance cover simultaneously. If she could achieve these tasks, it would be no less than a revolution, for we know that the small and marginal farmer is not a wilful defaulter!

A Long Repertoire

Ranjana is a woman who is popularly known for discharging a vast list of responsibilities. Besides serving as the director of a host of companies like the National Commodity and Derivatives Exchange Limited (NCDEX), Deposit Insurance and Credit Guarantee Corporation Limited and Agriculture Finance Corporation Limited, she is the Chairman of the governing council of the Bankers' Institute of Rural Development (BIRD) and an active member of the governing body of the Entrepreneurship Development Institute of India, which her keen interest in entrepreneurial activities urged her to join. Previously the Director of Discount and Finance House of India Limited, she was also a permanent invitee in the Advisory Committee on the Flow of Credit to Agriculture and Related Activities from the bank system of the RBI.

The KG Foundation chose Ranjana as the recipient of the *Personality of the Decade Award* for her contribution to the revival of the sick Indian Bank. The Institute of Directors, New Delhi, conferred the distinguished *Golden Peacock Women Business Leadership Award* in 2001. She also bagged the *Best Professional Manager Award* in 2003 and a series of *Best Banker* awards instituted by different bodies. In 2004, she was facilitated with the Sadguru Gnanananda Fifth National Award in recognition of her excellence in social services.

She is however as unassuming as she is conscientious and anxiously tells us: "Every time one receives an award, one feels the need to shoulder a greater sense of responsibility and live up to much higher expectations. Recipients of numerous awards and titles should accept their accolades with a sense of humility, keep a sound head on their shoulders and plant their feet firmly on the ground." A tinge of gratefulness is evident in her tone as she mentions that the honours and awards were the sweet fruits of the labour, consistency and team spirit of her colleagues.

Interface

Ranjana elaborates on the status of Indian agriculturists and the functions NABARD has undertaken to promote their welfare. We take a curious peek into her knowledge, expertise and profound philosophies in life, as she pronounces her thoughts with untold precision. *Excerpts from an exclusive interview...*

- ❑ *What would you suggest to ensure farmers get reasonable prices for their products?*

  Sufficient and scientific methods of storage are essential to enable farmers to keep their produce and sell them when prices are high in the market. They should be able to transport their produce to the marketplace without compromising on the quality. Middlemen should be routed out first; they take away a major chunk of the poor farmers' produce.

- ❑ *What measures can we adopt to promote sustainable development among the farmers and maximize their benefits?*

  We should encourage farmers' associations to set up grain and seed banks at the Gram Panchayat levels. Villages serve as the base units for assessing crop damage. Moreover, crop diversification, which is based on competitive advantage and organic farming practices, would further the cause of sustainable development. Apart from devising constructive crisis resolution mechanisms to handle natural calamities, we should initiate afforestation and watershed management programmes and consolidate land holdings through appropriate legislations to frame a model village development plan. This is what NABARD is aiming at.

- ❑ *What role has NABARD played in introducing initiatives that promise a great potential to marginal farmers?*

  With the involvement of NGOs, banks and industries, many initiatives are intended to expand watershed development, horticulture practices and the growth of medicinal plants to improve the plights of marginal farmers. NABARD has to be very aggressive. The bank has a vast reservoir of latent talent and special knowledge in the spheres of organic farming, animal husbandry and horticulture. Harnessing this energy lies solely in our will and power. Even if the schemes we formulate are first-rate, the delivery of credit continues to pose a problem. Expediting work at the grassroots level can rectify this problem.

> *"With nearly six lakh villages across the country, there is an increasing need for advocacy. In my opinion, benefits should percolate to every pocket of the country. The State Government undertakes responsibility to support its cause. To this end, I am meeting several chief ministers for discussions."*

- *What is your mantra for handling dicey gender issues at the workplace?*

(*Laughs*) Well, I've had no problems on that score! I have been very comfortable working with male colleagues. A sense of responsibility and an in-depth knowledge of what you are doing are necessary to be able to work alongside them. When I interact with people, I do not do so on the basis of their gender. Also, I don't just hear people. I listen to them. Listening requires effort and an act of intellect while hearing is merely a physical act.

> *"Bringing domestic problems to the workplace is not very professional. To stay focused, it is important to concentrate on your job once you are in the office."*

- *What have you gained and lost in the game of life?*

I gained the love and respect of people around me, all through my career. But I missed out on the tender moments of seeing my children grow up. I was with my children as they blossomed into ambitious teenagers. Nevertheless, I feel that I could have spent more quality time with them. I spent whatever time I had with them; the time I had at my disposal was very limited though. I used to bring piles of paperwork home with me. My granddaughter tells me that grannies don't work but stay home and make delicious cookies for their grandkids instead. She is in the USA with her parents now and I miss her fervently.

Life Makes You Strong

Right from an early age, Ranjana has invariably been hard on herself. Relegating personal comforts to the margins of her priority list, she has always executed every task she undertook with utmost commitment, sincerity and promise. Her powerful voice tapers to a sad whisper as she informs that she was unable to spend enough time with her daughter before her daughter's marriage because of a pressing engagement at work. "It is something I regret in life," she discloses. Indeed, a mother desires to share the happier moments with her daughter before the latter takes her flight from home permanently. That Ranjana met her daughter many more times after her marriage is an entirely different matter, altogether. "A woman's pre-marriage days are those that her mother would cherish with her daughter and hold closest to her bosom," she reckons.

Ranjana's hectic work schedules gave her no time for a sunny social life. The different and varied places that she had travelled to with her family as a child, when her father received postings in different cities, developed in her the ability to be flexible and to adapt and adjust. During the course of her career, she was posted in the USA, Mumbai, Chennai, Bangalore and Madhya Pradesh. While she garnered rich personal and professional experiences from her varied and wide-ranging stints, she compromised on a happy, intimate life with her husband and children, living away from them for years on end.

On select weekends and holidays, she would eagerly take off for Hyderabad to be with her husband. On travelling from Bangalore to Hyderabad to meet her husband one day, she met with an unfortunate accident that sent her to the ICU for one week. She was listed in critical condition. Nevertheless, she returned to work soon after she was discharged. "The displacement factor cast a major effect on me," she reflects. With the progress of each stage of life, Ranjana has only become tougher and stronger. Her unflagging perseverance speaks volumes for her ability to withstand and absorb.

An Earful of Wisdom

A strong supporter of women empowerment, there is a lot that Ranjana has to offer to the next-generation women. She candidly expresses her views on the status of women, today:

> "Every woman must strive for financial independence. However, it should not lead to arrogance or the belief that she will not devote enough time to manage her home. She should take care not to assume senior positions at the cost of her personal life. She can simultaneously

continue to keep herself engaged in viable sources of business. This is especially necessary as women begin to experience a lot of problems and uncertainties when they touch their forties, especially since their husbands take on senior positions, which may compel them to embark on many business tours. The demands of their husbands' careers are much higher at that juncture. Their children are independent and busy with new friendships and career pursuits and the women find a void.

> *"One must understand that men and women are two different entities altogether. Women are mentally much stronger than men. Men cannot handle their homes and careers with the same level of adeptness and efficiency of women. Young women of the modern era must take careful note of the fact that we do what we do to seek and find happiness. To a large extent, the strength of a family rests on the shoulders of a woman. While society does overlook a few idiosyncrasies of menfolk, a woman cannot afford to slip at any point in time."*

"When the joint family system was widely prevalent in earlier days, members shared their thoughts with women in the family. On account of the changing culture today, many men and women are passing through a phase of purposelessness in life. With effort, women are, however, emerging successful today. Like men, they too must be told that they can perform. Their efforts call for motivation, good guidance and appreciation."

Close Connections

Children of working women are known to mature faster, express greater understanding and be more independent. Moreover, they acquire a newfound confidence in their ability to take decisions effectively and analyse their intrinsic strengths and weaknesses in the face of demanding circumstances. Both of Ranjana's children grew accustomed to her unpredictable travel regimes; they have been tremendously accommodating and supportive of her beliefs and endeavours.

"My son got married recently," she informs. When Ranjana's children were earlier away and unsettled, she passionately wrote to them everyday. Both her children are independent and well placed today.

Ranjana discharged her family responsibilities with careful and meticulous planning. Her husband came from a joint family. Even as the chairman of a bank, Ranjana hasn't shied away from the role of a classic Indian *bahu* in a traditional joint family. Time and again, her husband encourages her to dress with the times. But Ranjana had long since given up her fervent attempts to impress her husband with her charming looks – much to her grandmother's chagrin. "Now, I tell him it is too late to change my style," she laughs. She has worn the same hairstyle – a simple bun at the nape of her neck – for several years. "My husband firmly believes in and supports my dreams and visions," she adds fondly.

In the realm of classical literature, the name 'Ranjana' means 'being happy'. "Happiness at home is extremely essential for mental and physical well-being," she declares. Ranjana finds happiness in revelling in the small pleasures of life. She has acquired a passion for Vedanta philosophies and can devour any book on it. She is also fond of reading anecdotes, Thirukural and books authored by Deepak Chopra. While the idiot box at home is tuned on to the National Geography channel many a time, she loves watching films starring Sanjeev Kumar or Madhuri Dixit.

Ranjana has always been a hardcore workaholic. For her, putting her feet up and relaxing doesn't mean lazing around. So engrossed in her work was she that she hasn't had a single holiday in years. It was in 1979 when she took off on her last vacation!

A quiet, lush garden amidst the hills and dales would be her ideal retreat. "Now, I am thinking of holidaying with my granddaughter in the USA," she tells us eagerly. Indeed, there is no ideal way of leading a happy life.

> *"Have a good head on your shoulders and you will see sure-fire success."*

Ravina Raj Kohli
Media Personality & Former President, STAR News

12.

Maiden of the Media

"You only get a short time
To grab a little glory
I want to have a good life
Not a sad story
To stay within the boundaries
Seems so formal,
If that's what life is
I don't want to be normal."

–Randy Crawford

Our news media's darling ***Ravina Raj Kohli*** is a personification of these lines of Randy Crawford's, which incidentally belongs to one of her most favourite songs too. Ravina Raj Kohli was appointed President of the STAR News channel, after it broke its alliance with ND-TV. Formerly in charge of spearheading the Nine Gold operations in DD Metro, she wasted no time in STAR News. She recognized the importance of regional languages in improving the reach among the masses and introduced Hindi news in STAR for the first time. As soon as she took the reins, the first week's ratings shot up skyward.

Under her headship, STAR changed its positioning and revamped the content of STAR News, shifting gears from English news (produced out-of-house) to 24x7 Hindi news, making it an in-house production.

Promising Media Aspirant

Born in Kolkata, Ravina spent the first five years of her life in Kolkata and Mumbai before moving on to Bangalore, where she schooled in Sophia High School and pursued her college education at Carmel College. She joined HTA in 1986 and Lintas in 1988. Aspiring to gain international experience, she moved to Singapore to join Grey in 1990.

Ravina jobbed in South-east Asia for six years before flying to New York in 1996, where she enrolled in the New York University to study Feature Films and Broadcast News. A year later, she moved to Mumbai and joined Sony Entertainment Television (SET), where she secured the post of Senior Vice President, Programming and Marketing division. Ravina had not lived in Mumbai earlier. Yet, she merged with her surroundings and circumstances with the absolute ease and adaptability of a chameleon, given her natural tendency to make herself at home anywhere.

Unafraid of change, this raring-to-go lady can always be seen gearing herself up to take on tougher challenges. "If someone extends an offer to back you in a high-risk event, plunge into it and make the most of it," she counsels.

Although she took up undergraduate courses in Psychology and Economics, she is known to have forayed into journalism right from college. Equipping herself with a degree from the London School of Journalism thereafter, she trained to write for the media. The rare mix of opportunity and spunk reveals itself as Ravina avers, "One need not pursue a particular line of education to become good in any field."

The Women in Her Life

"I have never made any decision because of a man," Ravina declares proudly. "It has always been a woman who has influenced the decisions that I have taken in my life." Right from her grandmother to her mother's friends and her own, the women whom she had encountered played their part in moulding the personality that she is today.

As a little girl, she found an intriguing conversation with a woman at a party immensely encouraging. And the interesting legends and stories her grandmother would narrate to her in bed heightened her fascination for mythology and stimulated the desire for achievement and recognition. "Both my grandmothers were very independent," she avows.

> *"More often than not, a woman is influenced by the older women in her immediate environs. Success is indeed very subjective. Nevertheless, every ambitious woman who has consistently succeeded and set her country's annals ablaze with her remarkable intellect and knowledge has, for the most part, drawn a large chunk of her inspiration from another woman."*

One of Ravina's foremost inspirers and the greatest driving force behind every endeavour of hers was her mother. Ravina's mother was a sterling example of an older woman in the family who did not allow herself to succumb to societal pressures. Instead, she gave her daughter wings to realize her dreams.

Undaunted by the compulsion to adhere to the rules of the traditional game by marrying, procreating and settling down, Ravina was a non-conformist. She believed in doing what she felt was right. Egging her on to do just that, her mother said she would take all the flak from society. She is known to have constantly told her daughter, "As far as I am concerned, you shall stand on your own feet. Marriage is not a necessity. It is an option. You will be 'settled' when you are financially independent."

Ravina calls herself an 'international child of India'. She does not believe in planning every phase of her life. She is not the kind of woman who would work in an organization for thirty years and approach them for pension after retirement. "Had you studied me several years before, you would have probably uttered a silent scream: 'This woman is a lunatic!'" Ravina jokes.

Dressed often in blacks and whites, she is a total mixture of opposites. Right from writing plays and musicals to learning how to be a travel agent, she has dipped into many exciting activities, garnering a wide repertoire of experiences from her versatile endeavours. She has indulged in several different activities during the course of her lifetime and just prefers it that way. The varied sensations she has lived through with every activity of hers provided her a strong foundation for anything that she aspired to do.

Life is an Open Book

At the threshold of her career, an excited Ravina waltzed in for an interview with HTA. She was posed the question, 'Why would you want to join HTA?' Pat came the ridiculously honest reply: "Well, your building is just across my house!" Bowled over by her outspokenness, the interviewer granted her the job. No sooner did she begin her stint as a copywriter in HTA, she moved quickly upwards in her career graph. Her activities soon gained momentum.

Likewise, she met the board of directors at Singapore, before she chose to join Sony. The board was in a lousy mood. The ratings were slipping. Numerous disasters they had invariably rubbed shoulders with in the past made them sceptical of Ravina too. They felt the need to introduce a national flavour in the form of Hindi programming.

"What would work in Hindi entertainment?" they queried solemnly.

"I have no idea!" Ravina piped up cheerily. And she just didn't! They took her in without batting an eyelid.

"I admire those people who have taken great risk by roping me in. I daresay I have been really lucky," Ravina says gratefully. Ravina has always been renowned for her candid expressions and ingenuous replies. Ironically, her implicit frankness in speech and action has turned out to be her most arresting asset.

Broadening Channels

In more ways than one, Ravina's career has taken a swift turn away from the path a run-of-the-mill career would have taken her through. Walking down the lanes of the entertainment industry in Bombay seven years ago, unknown, and perhaps even undesired, continues to be the greatest challenge that looks Ravina point-blank in the face to date. In her opinion, she didn't have her bearings right either. To add fuel to the fire, she had no knowledge of satellite television, broadcasting, TV personalities and silver screen stars when she joined Sony.

What's more, she candidly told one of her colleagues, Kunal (who was not even the Chief Executive Officer at that point in time) that she was entering the field as a non-entity. Making him promise not to spread word around that she was here, she requested him to give her six months to prove her mettle, failing which she would leave as quietly as she came.

Beneath that façade of insecurity and hesitation lay a stern resolve to work industriously and show the world what she was made of. She promptly got down to the brass tacks. For three years, she watched TV, read scripts, pored over pilot episodes and scrutinized completed serials detail by minute detail from 9.00 a.m. to midnight hour without a single break, nearly everyday. She had no social or personal life. Work was her passion, her lifeblood. Over time, she began dealing with actors and other entertainment celebrities. The cumulative expertise and knowledge she had gathered from her earlier connections with theatre helped her groom them well and recreate contemporary personas. The bond she shared with them was akin to the bond brothers and sisters would share with one another. The ideas she reaped from her interactions with different people inspired her to churn out bigger and better creations.

When Australian media tycoon Kerry Packer desired to promote Channel Nine in India, Ravina was the obvious choice. In India, Doordarshan was the only channel that had introduced the concept of terrestrial broadcasting in the electronic media. Ravina had to struggle to obtain licences to run her terrestrial networks. The switch from an urban satellite channel to a medium that created opinion and influence turned out to be a smart one.

A big group of nearly fifty, Ravina and her team-mates came on board to the very launch.

"My Channel Nine colleagues were warm-hearted and genuine people," she remembers. "However, they were taken in by the tall claims and promises Government officials made."

When the Channel Nine team decided to present terrestrial contemporary entertainment, Ravina enjoyed every minute of the show. Fuelled by the hope that she and her team would receive a longer licence, she directed all her energies to motivate them in the face of uncertainties. "Make sure the programmes are on air and pay all your producers. Keep up your end of the bargain with advertisers and see that you are not a defaulter," Ravina is known to have counselled her team, time and again. Their uncertainties vanished when their ingenious ideas and neat performances began to make a vast difference to viewers. "We would have achieved greater results if the licences had come through, though," Ravina mentions categorically. Never one to sit back and let failures overcome her, she continues in a tone that spells not a trace of disappointment: "It was the toughest yet most fulfilling management experience of my life."

And she learnt well from it.

A Free Feather

Ravina is a tough, iron-willed lady who says "No!" to nothing and concocts a wonderful creation from zilch. She has always been happy in places that have granted her complete authority and independence. "I am not a corporate politician," she asserts. "I can't play that game."

Her soiree with STAR News was no different. In 2002, not a brick, nail or person existed. Every asset of STAR News belonged to ND-TV. Ravina's hard-hitting approach took rein as she painstakingly created the channel, put her successor in place and let the channel move smoothly and effortlessly.

> *"The ratings of a channel are a function of two variables: The first is the distribution factor, which principally centres on how many people receive your channel and the level of its acceptability among the watchers. Secondly, the reach of a channel occupies a position of prime importance. The channel's market share can be calculated by multiplying the 'reach' by the amount of time spent on the channel, and dividing the resultant figure by the number of people who tune into your channel and stay tuned for at least a minute a week."*

Running one channel wasn't a challenge for her. What did pose a challenge to her was the question that came up in connection with whether she would be able to float an entire international news network in eleven months. And the question that followed was how she would set it up in Mumbai (a place where Hindi-speaking journalists were few in number) within a short span of time. Unperturbed by these constraints, Ravina hollered an enthusiastic "Yes!" to the project and accomplished her task before the midnight of 31 March 2002! Ravina's unflagging enthusiasm shielded her from a lot of stress that would have been natural in any endeavour of so great a magnitude. And in spite of the tension that gripped the workplace, the corridor would always ring out with laughter. Ravina's approach is simple: "If you can't laugh together, you can't work together."

The purpose with which Ravina enabled herself and her team to grow has been her biggest payback. She created bonds and lasting friendships while many of her counterparts sought commercial benefits.

At the Coffeehouse

Ravina gaily chatters with us over a mug of steaming coffee, expressing her ideas and philosophies, besides bringing to light her views on contemporary media issues. *Excerpts from an exclusive interview...*

- ❑ *What factors does the selection of your news broadcasts depend on?*

  As we have to take a quick decision on our course of action, we break our resources into stories we chase as well as stories that chase us! Deciding what is nationally, economically, politically and socially relevant is particularly important. You invest a larger volume of your resources in what you feel can develop into a bigger story. The budget or the elections are examples of such events. But we do not ignore a small human-interest story that could have a far-reaching impact.

- ❑ *We recall that you once said "The look of the channel is as important as the content; we will be subjecting our viewers to grave injustice if we appear shabby and frumpy, while reading the news"* (Asian Age, *June 15, 2003*). *How will such an approach pitch in to enhance the channel's TRP ratings?*

  In the discipline of television, one has no business to look unkempt. In any news forum on TV, national or international, being well groomed is vastly important. Moreover, this approach has redefined the concept of how one should present oneself. (*Laughs*) At a recent tour in London, I observed that all the television news presenters had painted and glossed their lips, glittered their eyelids and worn plunging necklines. This doesn't make them unintelligent or non-credible. It is what the person says which casts a lasting impression on viewers' minds.

- ❑ *What measures would you recommend to introduce more professionalism in media circles in India? What yardsticks should we locate to this end?*

  The degree of professionalism certainly yoyos in India and other countries too. Professionalism arises when companies cultivate people and allow them to grow and blossom, enabling them to establish security in their jobs. Non-professionalism creeps in when companies breed non-professional principles and qualities within their premises. Training people is an ongoing process. People have to be groomed well and this task can be accomplished to fruition only over a span of years. So, here is my advice to new professionals. 'Stick to your company and firmly abide by your principles. And give back to the company that you work for'.

- *How far will the Indian media have to go to be on par with international standards? What efforts has STAR News initiated to approach global heights?*

  We certainly need to go a long way. With the sophisticated technologies, which we have incorporated in our systems and the hosts of international experts we have introduced, we match international news networks both in technical acumen and intellect.

> *"Constitutionally speaking, we enjoy the right to information and the highest degree of freedom of speech. Paradoxically, we are also a most ill-informed lot. We don't have access to substantial information. But we have adequate leeway to choose our own channel/newspaper and process any information that we want. Viewers always make judicious choices. They also reject something you think is great. The power ultimately lies in the hands of viewers."*

- *How do news channels mould the choice of the public?*

  The role of the news media is to inform. The news channels should present stories just as they are giving the public both sides of the coin. They should not create a bias. Unless news editors cover their chosen events in as unbiased a manner as possible, their channels' credibility will take a nosedive. The media has entered the cosy snugness of millions of living rooms and bedrooms. In India one doesn't watch TV in isolation. One watches TV with a large circle of family and friends. This creates opinion. So, newspersons cannot afford to frame their own agenda.

- *Unfortunately, most events are being sensationalized to promote sales. What can we do to reduce the degree of commercialism in journalism?*

  Well, you can't control every journalist. In my line of business, people constantly plan stories about one another. I have been misquoted often too. Journalists are prone to brainwash. As a programmer, it is important for one to protect one's credibility. Trust is critical to our business. Once you lose people's trust, you're dead-meat. You wouldn't want to violate it in a hurry. Also, you can't allow others to buy you. I am very conscious of that when we frame our editorial policies and guidelines.

A New Face

Creating a clear identity for a brand is an integral component of any brand-building exercise. STAR News was always thought of as a full-fledged English channel. Hindi-speaking people weren't comfortable tuning in to STAR News although a few shows were telecast in Hindi. Under Ravina's presidency, STAR News was re-launched as an entirely new product, which whittled a niche for itself in a competitive market. When STAR News reinvented itself, it shot to the coveted Number 2 title. Ravina continued to create new teams and new technologies, holding up the channel's position.

> *"When I created* Poll Khol *with Shekhar Suman during the elections, the ratings skyrocketed. This programme became the top news show, countrywide. Our anchors received tremendous adulation. After the elections, the ratings slipped. Also, week-to-week fluctuations are inevitable."*

Ravina has introduced the principles of impact and immediate and fair coverage in STAR News. With her extensive exposé of the Mumbai blasts, STAR News' ratings and channel share picked up remarkably. "Merely breaking the news is not sufficient," she reiterates. "It is all about impact." She methodically categorizes the news media into bulletins (which are anchored live) and coverage of live news.

> *"Breaking news live definitely attracts a lot more attention if it is relevant to the viewers. A politician taking out a* rath yatra *is not a piece of news that would excite people. What they want is 'something relevant to me' – be it a natural disaster, a big election, which would cast a direct bearing on several lives or a news story, which brings to light humanitarian concerns."*

When STAR covered the horrendous Mumbai bomb blasts, it refrained from telecasting images of charred bodies, torn limbs and sickening rubble. Ravina was the heart behind it. Even during her spell at Sony, she insisted that she would not programme any image of violence of men against women and children and the abuse of drugs, alcohol and tobacco. She didn't propagate such characters on TV as they were meant to serve as role models to the public. Moreover, she believed that the foregoing problems were entirely private concerns.

> *"Violence is a fact of life. Violence and horror are glaring examples of entertainment in books, videogames and on television – they can be found everywhere. Glamorising events of carnage and violence and encouraging children to emulate unethical values is wrong. When we present our news, we consciously do not show disturbing images. If we do show gory scenes, we apprise our viewers of it well in advance. Before the programme goes on air, we might forewarn them, 'We will be coming up with images that are not suitable for all. Please switch off your television if you are not comfortable watching them.'"*

Journalist by Instinct

In many a case, people who haven't been trained professionally, have been known to become some of the finest journalists by pure instinct. Ravina belongs to that league. "A basic education will definitely come in handy when you handle a vast and diverse range of topics as a journalist or a media personality," she asserts. "You must be educated enough to do what you want to do. You don't have to master the subject though. You turn into a master when you work." This is an especially valuable piece of advice from the fiery media baroness, given the fact that it was exactly what she did.

Quality education has always held a place of utmost importance for Ravina Raj Kohli. She is glad to note that a much greater volume of effort is being initiated to introduce highly experienced faculties in colleges, universities and media institutes across the country, especially in the face of an increased demand for fresh faces in the media. Since time immemorial, hordes of foreign universities have been prize catches for media and journalism aspirants. "While a course in media studies or mass communication does provide an insight into the fundamental principles of various aspects of the media, one gathers the most valuable experience only by learning on-the-job," she opines.

With the explosion of the media métier, there has been a need for many more professionals in the fields of news and television. Ravina foresees a bright future for training institutes and schools to fine-tune the communication skills of writers, journalists, photojournalists and media aspirants, equipping them to face the industry with the expertise of corporate executives.

> *"The media grants ample scope to enable you to take the path of excellence in your career. You get greater recognition when you are on air. Off air too, expertise is largely in demand. Job prospects are particularly upbeat for programmers from varied spheres of IT, broadcasting or editing. Broadcast journalism is a new and young field, which holds great promise too. It does not have any experts yet."*

"We need to capitalize on our talents," Ravina informs. "What the Indian television industry is seriously lacking in is good scriptwriting. Isn't it surprising that we cannot produce a hundred talented writers in a country with a population of over one billion? What's more, the few who are truly talented remain unrecognised. That is the saddest phenomenon."

Ravina has constantly striven to encourage newer streams of people through the adventurous yet bumpy path of the media. Enthusiastically nurturing fresh sources of talent, Ravina keeps her mind and doors open for all.

Wedded to Office

Entertainment icons and television personalities are known to lead hectic, imbalanced lives. And Ravina's work schedule is as volatile, if not more. She has no time to call her own. Many a time, she has lived in the office more than she has at home. "However, I am slowly trying to spend more time on my personal life," she states. "Achieving balance is essential after a certain stage."

Her achievements have only humbled her further. The excited expression on her face transforms to one of modesty as she acknowledges that she is indeed grateful to have been able to realize the opportunity of being skewed to her work.

> *"Success is feeling good about yourself when you get out of bed in the morning. What others think about you doesn't matter. It is what you think about yourself that does. Look in the mirror and ask yourself, 'Do I like me? Am I happy with me?' If your answer is a big 'Yes,' that is success."*

She doesn't regret not having chosen a companion for herself and raised a family earlier. "The unpredictability of my job would not have permitted me to give them my full attention," she states practically. Making wise choices is a primary determinant of one's happiness. And Ravina has struck perfect harmony with the choice that she has made in her life.

Finding a Story Within a Story

For Ravina's tall, proud stature, lithe hourglass figure and childlike beauty, she may have as well been on camera, igniting worldwide sparks with her radiance. "My job doesn't call for being on-screen," she staunchly declares. "My job is to create stars, people, programmes and television." Beneath the hard-nosed veneer lies a softness that borders on the more sentimental aspects of life. She still mourns the loss of the signet ring her father gifted her before he died.

Ravina enjoys the dialects of various languages and can pick up new lingoes and styles with the ease of an eel. She watches movies most often during her leisure time. When she is free enough to relax, she loves horse-riding, water-skiing and holidaying in London and Goa. Architectural styles of different patterns have always enraptured Ravina to the core. "The best story is depicted through art," she muses. "On a recent culture trip to Spain, I spent a lot of time in the museum, sighting the beautiful chapels and fabulous masterpieces of art. Most of the sculptures I saw had been created because a large segment of the population could neither read nor write."

"For me, an ideal writer is one who can hold me with his style and peace-loving characters" she reveals, mentioning that *The Fountainhead* is one of her most favourite books and one she has read and re-read, time and again.

Ravina left STAR to explore larger frontiers. She might have stayed back had STAR continued as a 100% company. "My initial phase in STAR was my most rewarding time," she enthuses. You need to be more than a journalist to run a media company. And the media giant hopes to start her own powerhouse one day. She has the option of starting a magazine and a music company. That isn't all. Also on the anvil is a humorously anecdotal non-fiction book on being a working woman in India. "The book is going to be great fun," Ravina exclaims, with the merriment of a child. And here, we will be sure to find a story within a story.

> "Plan for the long-term without expecting miracles to happen overnight. Dig your heels in and go for the long haul. All the stars you admire today have been at it for over two decades."

Renuka Ramnath
Chief Executive Officer, ICICI Ventures

13.
Uncharted Ventures

The eagle's eyes shrewdly comb the entire expanse of the Indian capital market. For many years, they have spotted, seized and conquered. They belong to a wilful risk-taker who continues to create the right investment opportunities and back the right people to make supernormal returns for the fund investors.

One of the very few women in the male dominated citadel of private equity investment, ***Renuka Ramnath*** started ICICI Eco-Net Limited to exploit new value-creating opportunities that arose out of the Internet revolution and later consolidated her investment structures into the legal entity that we all know as ICICI Venture today.

ICICI Venture was founded in 1988 as a joint venture with the Unit Trust of India. Buying out UTI's stake, the company became a subsidiary of the former ICICI Ltd, now known as ICICI Bank Ltd. Under Renuka's guidance, strong parentage and affiliates were transmuted into a broad spectrum of financial and analytical resources, enabling increased accessibility to people and a better understanding of the entrepreneurial ethos in the financial markets of India.

The Persistent Go-getter

Belonging to a traditional South Indian middle-class family, Renuka was always an avant-garde Mumbai girl at heart. She was raised in the suburbs of Mumbai along with her brother and sister. Affectionately considered a mischievous rebel even during her earlier years, "How not to follow rules happened to be the driving principle in my life," laughs Renuka. A brilliant performer in academics, her focus at all times lay on being the topper, as she constantly pushed herself to achieve more and set higher benchmarks for herself. "Even in the smallest of examinations, I could never accept not being at the top," she exclaims in recollection.

She was no less in extra-curricular activities. "Learning skill-based activities was very important for me," she states. She studied many an art. She stitched, painted, and cooked with passion. She even tailored frocks and skirts for herself, steadily providing her brother and sister new supplies of clothes only to leave them hankering for more! She also gained knowledge of the intricacies of classical music, which she had learned for a period of twenty years. "I wasn't a great sportsperson though," she confesses. She didn't play sports to win games; rather, she indulged in them to experience the joy of being with people.

Renuka Ramnath aspired to be the Managing Director of a company, even at a very young age. When she was fifteen, her aunt told her father that she was a special child who was going to make it big one day. And make it big, she has. "Today, my biggest thorn in the flesh is the fact that I am busy and bustling around for 48 hours a day," quips an excited Renuka.

Completing her education in Chembur she moved on to VJTI and graduated in textile engineering, becoming the fourth woman to do so from the college. "The programme wasn't very woman-friendly," she narrates. Numerous conversations she had had with the principal of VJTI, who attempted to dissuade her from signing up for so rigorous a course, are lucidly etched in her memory. The assertive facet of her personality rose to the surface as she intrepidly declared that she would take decisions only on the basis of her own convictions.

Despite her initial stubbornness to take up a course of her choice, she later discovered that her chosen subject had little to do with design. "The course dealt with textile machinery, where getting productivity out of men and machines was the main focus of dimension," Renuka tells us. Always one who adapted to change, the dynamic young lady absorbed every nuance of the course like an eager sponge.

After graduating, she had the option of either pursuing a fully aided PhD programme in Technology in the Texas Women's University or venturing into a more adventurous career in marketing and finance. She chose the latter. "Making a dent in a textile company seemed pretty much a far possibility given the limited industrial scope that lay at its disposal," Renuka recounts. She promptly enrolled at Mumbai University and obtained a degree in Management Studies.

She topped her batch and joined Crompton soon after. Meanwhile, ICICI was looking for a textile technologist; Renuka fit the bill to the hilt. However, when the company's representatives approached her, she wrote to them, thanking them for her summer internship. She boldly informed that she preferred to work in the industry before she considered joining a financial institution.

Post-summer, she began working in Crompton. Such was the degree of confidence she had in herself that she aspired to move mountains and herald major changes in her capacity as a management trainee. "I may have been naïve in thinking so," laughs Renuka.

> *"Cowardice surfaces from within oneself. Blaming society in this connection is futile. Society allows us to live the way we please. On the other hand, people who tend to modify themselves to adapt to expectations others have of them, only remain perpetually confused as they have no idea of* whom *they are trying to please. Many people live for others all the time. In doing so, they make themselves, as well as those whom they are trying to impress, perennially unhappy."*

Steady Moves

Eventually, Renuka Ramnath did join ICICI in 1986. Much against her desires, she was chosen to lead the Merchant Banking division of ICICI. However, she quickly discovered that her talent and aptitude lay in the realm of merchant banking. She was later shifted to ICICI Securities to head the Corporate Finance and Equities Businesses departments. Here, she set new benchmarks as always and optimised the revenue potential.

She returned to ICICI in 1997 to set up a Structured Finance business before moving on to supervise ICICI's e-commerce initiatives. Appointed as the Managing Director and CEO of ICICI Eco-net Limited in September 2000, she took over ICICI Venture as the Managing Director and CEO, subsequent to the merger of ICICI Eco-net with ICICI Venture.

In line with her strategy to support every business with strong fundamentals, Renuka set up a real estate fund, which aimed at offering flexible investment opportunities for retail and institutional investors in a wide range of high-return properties, without tying them to individual 'immobile' properties. The bar on FDI in the real estate sector shut out foreign funds. To all intents and purposes, she positioned the asset management fund well to counter the situation.

Renuka Ramnath was one of the pioneers in investing in attractive mid-cap companies. "Indian companies have worked diligently over the last five years. And this strategy is one that drew in large numbers of private equity investors," she says.

ICICI Venture roped in many more foreign investors and succeeded in expanding the corpus of its flagship *India Advantage Fund* from Rs.750 crore to a swelling figure of Rs.1200 crore.

> *"We all need to take decisive breaks to prevent the inevitability of monotony, which can creep in even in the most challenging and adventurous of careers. Stress management programmes are decisive breaks that take us away from work. Moreover, they supply you with opportunities for introspection. We throw annual in-site and off-site parties where everyone would enjoy cutting cakes on small occasions!"*

Renuka intends to apportion funds to a diverse scale of sectors, which range right from groundbreaking real estate to management buyouts. She recently set up a team for mezzanine funding, which entails presenting unique opportunities for companies that seek financial alternatives yielding no significant dilution for existing shareholders. Here, she artfully structured subordinate loans with the opportunity of participating in the upside of the company.

The Game Plan

Setting her sights on chalking out a different strategy, even in traditionally sought-after areas for private equity funds, the company plans to set up a venture capital fund to provide backing to start-ups. To this end, Renuka has a different plan of action in mind. This strategy is well on its route to being acknowledged as a different and most innovative measure.

ICICI Venture has invested in and engineered exits from more than 130 transactions, with an average return of 38% since 1988. In 2002-03, the company raised the largest Indian private equity fund, enhancing the value of its existing portfolios.

On a macrocosmic note, Renuka hopes to invest in companies that require additional funds to restructure their systems and reposition themselves globally. "Seed funding can avail of the best opportunities in the biotechnology industry, which suffers from a dearth of adequate venture capital funds," she views clearly.

She has tied up with funding agencies to establish a consortium that would pitch in to put financial resources together. Inclusive of leverage, the sizes of the current deal vary between 15 and 30 million dollars, opening up a plethora of investment opportunities across sectors. Co-investing with international funds is her next strategy.

I 'Dare'

Renuka has always been an enigma to the world. She has skilfully structured several breakthrough deals through sheer brilliance, intuition and conviction. With her clever strategies and mysterious temper, she never fails to hold us in suspense and keep us guessing her next move. She unfolds the mystery behind her unparalleled successes. *Excerpts from an exclusive interview…*

- *What is your mantra for effective equity investments?*

  Developing excellent teams and establishing a firm focus receive primary consideration. We abide by a combination of detailed analysis and an intuitive approach to manage our stakeholders' expectations and the opportunity cost of money, during the process of decision-making. The overriding factor continues to be our belief in the promoters of the management team in terms of vision, the execution capability, and their willingness to adhere to Corporate Governance.

- *What kind of equity investments are you effective in taking charge of?*

  ICICI Venture is a well-diversified Private Equity player that participates in a host of investment opportunities, which include providing growth capital, buy-outs, restructuring, mezzanine funding, etc. In terms of sectors, we follow a broad-based approach; we are actively exploring the pharmaceutical, manufacturing, IT/ITeS, textiles, media and retail sectors.

- *What was the rationale behind the merger of ICICI Eco-Net Limited and ICICI Venture?*

  ICICI Eco-net and ICICI Venture carried similar objectives of funding entrepreneurs to create opportunities. Therefore, ICICI Bank decided to merge the two entities.

- *Can you describe a unique feature of your vision statement?*

  We wrote our statement nearly three years ago. To date, we have been checking its relevance, once in three months. The best part of our statement is that it carries in it the certitude that each and every employee in the organization has the power and desire to make life happen and our hardwearing belief in creating world-class companies. We wish to be pioneers and shape the landscape for investing a multitude of opportunities in new and emerging industries. We intend to invest in different sectors across a wide geography in the country.

- *With the dawn of liberalization, how crucial a role should Indian businesswomen play in shooting up the economy?*

  It is important to have a global mindset. Building locally competitive companies will not bring you fruition. When I use the term 'global', I don't mean 'foreign'. Some of the best global practices have been established the Indian way. Moreover, setting sustainable benchmarks can make Indian women stand apart from the crowd.

Affection Vs Ruthlessness

Businesspersons and women in particular, have always maintained their composure in the face of the most catastrophic events. Moreover, they are largely known to remain unruffled in the face of heartrendingly touching instances. Do their dispassionate temperaments extend to their personal and social lives too? Renuka contends that the probability of such an occurrence is highly unlikely. Business crusades do not by any measure dilute the humaneness, sensitivity and compassion of truly exemplary business leaders, she believes. One can be ruthless about business decisions and still be a most loving person.

"If you don't take appropriate decisions in a business environment, you are performing a disservice to everyone, including yourself," Renuka concurs. "If I think a person is destroying value for my shareholders or displaying a high degree of inefficiency in his tasks, I don't hesitate to fire him. Of course, I would still find a job for him elsewhere." The no-nonsense financier doesn't see the slightest confusion between helping people and saying "No" to a proposal, which might momentarily make the entrepreneur unhappy. "If I complied with his request even if I were not entirely convinced by his proposal, I would be setting up my company for sure-fire failure," she states candidly. "Declining upfront when I do not approve of an idea or proposal is a far superior existence to saying 'Yes' to it and eventually causing unhappiness to him and myself too."

> *"Being firm in business and resolute in your decisions doesn't have anything to do with what you feel about the person in question, at a personal level. You are not attacking him personally. I would be very happy to counsel persons who approach me for guidance and would gladly put them on to other experienced people, even if I may have turned down their proposals. So, the two are not mutually exclusive."*

The Quick Learner

"I got a useful insight into various aspects of business and finance from my well wishers, particularly Shikha Sharma, Lalita Gupte and Kalpana Morparia," Renuka enthuses.

Her husband was deeply affectionate, caring and proud of her talents and achievements. He gave his all to encourage his wife and fine-tune her intuitiveness and decision-making skills. Her love and admiration for him are evident in that pair of piercing, crystal-clear eyes. She lost him nearly ten years ago. She didn't let the tragedy throttle her. She aggressively pursued her career ambitions, casting indelible imprints in the corporate world. "Had I sacrificed my career after my husband's death, I would have been a complete wreck," she informs, sombrely.

She handled her children impeccably well. She cleverly integrated life at home and life at work. This 'integration' approach involved bringing her son and daughter to her office during weekends, explaining gently to them that she had five more children, whom she had to take care of in the office.

Today, her little children are focused, goal-driven teenagers who possess equal knowledge of equity investments and their mother's clients (if not more!). Ask them what a 'debt to equity' ratio is and they'll provide you the answer in a jiffy! "My children are my greatest sources of ideas," Renuka smiles. "I pose challenging problems to them and obtain most interesting answers and suggestions in return."

She continues, "Lack of application of mind is irksome; nothing is more peeving than seeing that my people have all the right analyses and wonderfully arrive at an incorrect conclusion!"

A Trace of Simplicity

Beneath that well made up countenance, chic designer sari and sleek jewellery lies a very simple person. At home, you'll see her cooking bland food (she is not too fond of oily food) and fluttering around in an old faded maxi. "Old clothes are what I'm most comfortable in!" Renuka exclaims. She confesses that she had always aspired to embark on a full-scale PhD programme. The demands of her job and her hectic lifestyle haven't provided her much time to follow her passion. So engrossed is she in business that the prospect of enrolling for a PhD in the near future is minimal.

In spite of her business pressures, the child in her is very much alive as she tells us, "I am far from punctual. In fact, I feel embarrassed when I do make it on time somewhere!" Kamal Hasan and Waheeda Rehman are her favourite stars and Mohammad Rafi is her favourite singer. We also asked her to recommend a book everyone should read. She promptly said, "Stephen Covey's *Seven Habits of Highly Effective People*."

With her sharp business acumen, Renuka Ramnath holds many of her senior colleagues – males and females alike – spellbound. Aside from numerous mentions in the media, she was presented with the *IMM Best Women Entrepreneur Award* in 2002. Her single-mindedness shall continue to see the eagle soaring to newfound heights in the imminent future.

> "Always try the best and incorporate the concept of global competitiveness in every venture you undertake. Behave and act in exactly the same manner in which you wish to act at the point of time you wish to act."

Ritu Kumar
Fashion Designer

14.

Refashioning Indian Glamour

She has made many a woman's life with her infusion of an authentic character, which is both indigenous in innovation and international in look. A catalyst in placing India on the world's fashion map through the revival of traditional Indian attire, she shaped the identities of a battalion of global beauty icons like Aishwarya Rai, Sushmita Sen, Jemima Khan, Princess Diana, Manpreet Brar, Rani Jairaj and Sandhya Chib.

Ritu Kumar (Fashion Designer) requires as brief an introduction as Giorgio Armani. She is not only the creator of the first chain of exclusive boutique stores in India but also a pioneer who culled the bewitching wealth of Indian heritage and integrated tradition with modernity, weaving a unique, exquisite blend of her own.

The desire to own a Ritu Kumar original has been every Indian bride's dream. The design diva was rated the best fashion designer in India for designing the fortune of aesthetics in the country.

The Knowledge Seeker

Ritu's parents were originally from Mint Kumni (currently in Pakistan). Born into a forward-thinking upper-middle class family in 1944 in Amritsar, the city of the Golden temple, Ritu was only three when India gained independence. Ritu schooled in Amritsar. She spent her primary years of schooling in Sacred Heart Convent and completed her intermediate education in science from Government College. She later graduated in Home Economics from Lady Irwin College, New Delhi and obtained a B.Ed degree from the same institution before travelling to Briarcliff College, Westchester Country on a well-earned scholarship to study the History of Western Art.

"During my college days, I was passionately nationalistic," she remembers. "I later realized that my strong feelings for India stemmed from a certain insecurity that the affluence of the Western world generated." A most well-read and highly qualified woman of her times, she held her education in high regard. And why not? Her future inspirations were tempered by education. Destiny however wrote marriage in her fate. She joined her garment exporter husband in wedlock and returned to Kolkata, thereafter.

The Fateful Question

The city a designer lives in is usually believed to inspire him/her enormously. Ritu Kumar was no exception. She instantly fell in love with the quaint charms of Kolkata. She was, however, besieged by the pain of knowing little about the intricacies of Indian culture and heritage. Following her urge to delve into the mysteries of the History of Indian Art and its aesthetical foundations (a subject rarely taught in the country during that time), she signed up for a course in Museology at the Ashutosh Museum, a musty, dilapidated old building on College Street.

During the course of her study, she received considerable exposure to classical arts and gleaned widespread knowledge of the craftsmen who worked in various media of folk art in West Bengal.

As Ritu plunged deeper into the intricacies of the subject, she could always be found to ask herself the question: "What can we do to improve the status of arts and crafts in India?" She silently mulled over the question for many days. "If no action is being taken to improve the situation, why don't *you* take the responsibility of doing so?" Kamala Devi Chattopadhya shot back to Ritu, when the latter revealed her thoughts to her one day. Her mentor's words were to change her life.

Fuelled by concern for the artisans and craftsmen, Ritu took the first step with the small boutique store that she opened at Wellesley Street in Kolkata as part of a grocery shop with a rent of Rs.150, little knowing then that this single step would magnify into a massive revolution.

Fever of Fashion

Ritu's tale began with hand-block printers and two tables in a small village near Kolkata in 1968. "I would attend college every morning and stroll down the lanes of Kolkata in the afternoons, experiencing the true flavour of India," she recounts.

Very soon, she built a stock of textiles. At this juncture, she had no clue of how she would market the designs. "Compared to the current trends, people were not acquainted with the culture of purchasing readymade garments from shops," Ritu explains. When the tailor was especially available round the corner, she found it particularly difficult to convince people to buy from shops too.

When one of Ritu's aunts opened a flower-shop a few days later, Ritu tied up with her to set the ball rolling. Kolkata, a swinging, cosmopolitan city at the time, reacted to this phenomenon with spunk and courage. "There were fun folks in town," Ritu laughs. "The dress codes varied widely." Fashion shows were conducted with great fanfare at Trincas in the famous Park Street. The Bengali gentlemen oscillated from the true essence of Brit elegance to the semi-babu panache from semi-Brit to Bhadrolok dressing.

Junie Bose looked like an elegant painting with the ethnic handloom saris she draped around herself; Amitabh Bachchan grew immensely popular for the boyish poses he struck with his bell-bottoms; Deepa Mehta could be seen prancing around in pretty ruffled blouses; and the regular jeans-clad Victor Banerjee looked funky, as always. And ladies resembled exotic orchids as they brandished their pearls and floral chiffons. In other words, Kolkata was swathed in every form of fashion imaginable and Ritu adeptly drew down on the city's enthusiasm to sell her designs.

"I too contributed to the sartorial confusion that existed," she confesses with a giggle. She mounted a futuristic exhibition that displayed macho-styled kurta-pyjama sets. Keen to experiment with new concepts, large swarms of customers thronged the venue and took their pick from the exhaustive variety.

The following day, Ritu received an exciting review from *The Statesman.* The glowing report was particularly surprising for Ritu as the new collections were labelled 'The Zing of Leather'.

The Threshold to Fame

The crafts and fabrics of India had always fascinated Ritu and she soon began experimenting with them. "The colonialism that prevailed then wiped out the craftsmanship in India," Ritu reports. On the brighter side, the ambience provided a rich reservoir for the development of various handmade products.

In 1970, Ritu held a fashion show that portrayed forty varieties of inexpensive yet inimitably styled outfits, which encompassed catchy labels that read 'A Woman needs four pockets; maybe more!' and 'Lungi-Loungee-Loiter.' "We did the show with a tea-break as we couldn't acquire a sufficient number of models for our clothes," Ritu reveals with a lopsided grin. The show received numerous accolades from the press.

In the 1970s, Ritu expanded her frontiers to western India and opened two other boutiques in Mumbai. Her boutiques stocked saris and continued to sell ready-to-wear collections aimed at the young Indian urbanite. Her collections held a strong element of indigenous design. The redefined prints and patterns began characterizing the collection, which was soon to become Ritu's distinctive signature statement.

During the course of her long career, Ritu Kumar's accomplishments lay in her revival of traditional Indian crafts like Zardosi, vegetable printing, painting, tie-and-die, Kashida and Kantha works and other forms of delicate embroidery. She ignited innovations in the use of printing techniques in Tanjore and researched diligently on the minutiae of traditional design motifs. She transferred their conventional applications to leather and textiles. She also developed a specialized printing unit at Balabhgarh, employing modern techniques of screen-printing. When the extensive research she conducted on designer clothes received a warm welcome from the Indian market, Ritu became the media's favourite topic of conversation.

Following the success of her boutique ventures in Delhi and Kolkata, Ritu Kumar wove a collection of western garments in the mid-seventies and carried them to Europe to explore the level of interest European countries had in the textiles and workmanship of India. In those times, the export trade for garments was in its very nascent stage. Ritu's attempts to capture the European market did not achieve much fruition, perhaps in light of the fact that European outfits were far too structured.

Meanwhile, signals flashed in India, indicating a major revolution in the fashion industry.

Ritu's dear friend, Kamala Devi Chattopadhya and pioneers like Pupul Jayakar raised the issue of the survival of crafts of the country in the national forum. In an era where saris worn by society women were mostly made of French fabrics, Ritu came out with yet another exhibition of hand-printed saris. Her collection soon became popular and played a remarkable role in reintroducing Indian aesthetics to the country.

Ritu was undeterred by the high-cost variety of her designs. She was certain that customers willing to pay a premium for quality aesthetics did exist. Relying solely on internal funds, she thought wisely and grew slowly.

> *"There are two most engaging dissimilarities between the clothing of Indian women and those of Western women. The first line of distinction rests on the form of attire. Across many a nation, European and Western fashions have created an international semblance. We see few Kimonos and sarongs, with the exclusion of festival seasons. In India though, the sari is still trendy. The second difference lies in the colour factor. While international styles present a few select colours, one can find an exhaustive variety of colours in India. Notwithstanding the changing patterns, India grasped the crux of her forte and captured a large world market share."*

Soft Talk

Embellished in multi-hued chiffons and silks, Ritu graced the 2004 winter collection show in Chennai. We caught her in the fray of activity and fired a volley of questions. *Excerpts from the exclusive interview...*

- ❑ *What degree of competition does the garment sector face today as against other industries? What advantages can one glean from a career in fashion?*

  The industry teems with a lot of small players. A definite knowledge of the ins and outs of the industry is essential. Those who do not possess sufficient knowledge tend to remain small-time designers/operators. If you are not confident about the people and functions you deal with, a career in any other discipline would be a much better option. We must take the bull by the horns!

- *Who manages your backstage activities?*

  What I'm sure of is the fact that I do not rely on men to do my jobs. (*Laughs*) I have women executing all our backstage tasks – they spend several sleepless nights to make a show happen.

- *What are the credentials that one requires to make a dent in the fashion industry?*

  A fashion designer learns a lot, even while he works with the crafts. A strong, full-fledged education helps you appreciate art and design. An in-depth knowledge and appreciation of art would generate fresh ideas, which you can implement. In the realm of fashion, few areas remain unexplored. One is therefore required to be highly innovative and distinctive in his approach.

- *In a career-conscious era, where personal grooming has become mandatory for all, right from contenders in the job market to corporate executives, does 'fashion' continue to be perceived as a sphere which confines itself solely to the rich urban elite in India?*

  Fashion isn't entirely affordable to the common man in India. Increased affordability will emerge only with growing economic maturity. India is genuinely in want of retail infrastructure. Nevertheless, huge malls, shopping complexes and super stores are springing up across the country. They bear testimony to the fact that fashion holds a very bright future in India.

- *Have gender issues affected your career?*

  Hardly. During the earlier stage of my career, I worked extensively with men who belonged to rural areas. They were extremely caring and supportive of me.

Spirit of Vitality

The exclusiveness of Ritu's creativity and originality as well as her yearning to reinvent herself and experiment with wide ranges of colours and concepts make her an undisputed leader in the fashion segment.

Ritu Kumar has secured numerous lifetime achievement awards from various forums like NIFT and *Kingfisher Fashion Fantasia.* In 1998, Ritu's *Tree of Life* Show (which has now grown to be a classic in the Indian design industry) drew delirious reviews from Hong Kong and Davos earlier in the year and was later chosen to represent India at the World Fashion Forum by NIFT. The PHD Chamber of Commerce conferred the *Outstanding Women Entrepreneur Award* on Ritu.

The Miss Universe and Miss World organizations selected her to bedeck twenty-three international beauties, of which five Indian beauties – Aishwarya Rai, Lara Dutta, Sushmita Sen, Priyanka Chopra and Diya Mirza – succeeded in bagging the coveted title.

Ritu Kumar won't hear of adding an upper limit to her endeavours. Belonging to the Board of Governors, NIFT, she is also a proactive member of innumerable executive bodies like the *All India Handloom Board at the Ministry of Textiles, Delhi Crafts Council, Delhi Chapter* and *Divyachhaya 'Save a Child' Trust* in Kolkata and Delhi. Ritu was incidentally credited with the launch of her book *Costumes and Textiles of Royal India*, published by Christie's in London.

Ritu ingeniously trained her husband and children to adapt themselves to the fact that they would not receive much attention from her. She placed her children in boarding schools to train them to be independent and self-adjusting. "My family stands resolutely by my convictions," Ritu acknowledges. "My husband and children have extended immeasurable support to every idea and suggestion of mine."

Not the slightest fear or hesitation in Ritu's mind has ever held her back from her goal. With the burgeoning market in India, she directs her focus on honing India's fashion potential aside from conducting five shows a year in Europe. India has over 60 million art workers. Ritu feels that efforts should be coordinated to elicit talent from skilled Indian artisans to increase their level of employability and bring them to limelight. Her contribution to the evolution of fashion remains unchallenged as many new pearls emerge from the oysters of the world.

> "Women today are more advanced than they were ten years ago. Over a span of the next ten years, I foresee an explosion of women in all sectors. Men-folk should brace themselves for a real tough fight from their female colleagues."

Ritu Nanda
Chief Executive Officer, Escolife

15.

Larger than Life

She rose like a phoenix from the virtual ashes of a not-so-lucky venture and recreated the magic of life. Hailing from a prestigious background, this ladybird decided to sing her own song. Her charms made the world listen to her song of life, which she diligently shaped into the classic high-technology platform of Escolife to provide services to the insurance sector, nationwide.

Ritu Nanda (CEO, Escolife) sold a record number of insurance policies and brought poise to the role of an insurance agent. "*Escolife* is my way of sharing with my agent colleagues the solutions to the difficulties that insurance agents typically encounter," she states unequivocally. She enhanced the productivity of her colleagues and agents through various productivity enhancement tools and facilities, which she single-handedly created at *Escolife.* Today, over 55,000 clients are on her roster of which about 8000 belong to the lower economic strata of the country. With *The Brand Ambassador* and *The Best Insurance Advisor of the Decade* awards, which the Life Insurance Corporation of India conferred on her, Ritu Nanda gained widespread recognition from the single largest nationalized insurance corporation in the world. What's more, she sashayed into the *Guinness Book of World Records* for selling a whopping number of 17,000 pension policies in a single day!

She now takes charge of *Raksha,* a third-party administrator, which runs a host of medical administrative services in the healthcare sector. Needless to say, she is a woman who has achieved her targets.

The Early Wedding

Ritu was born on 30 October 1948 in the family of Raj Kapoor, the legendary filmmaker. She went to Walsingham House School in Mumbai. She was not groomed to be the business professional that she is today. "Education wasn't given much importance in my family in the earlier days," she recalls.

Eight months before she completed her graduation from St. Xavier's College, Mumbai, she found herself engaged to industrialist Rajan Nanda. Since she was to be married in a few months, her parents withdrew her from college six months before she graduated and deemed it better that she join The Institute of Catering Technology and Applied Nutrition to recapitulate the fundamental principles of housekeeping.

The Insurance Regulatory Development Authority (IRDA) demands a certain level of educational qualification in the insurance sector, which she did not possess. Even though the RNIS College of Insurance and Management (which she ran herself) offered a masters' programme in Insurance business, she was not eligible to enrol, as she was not a graduate.

Although she achieved a distinction before completing her course in catering, she regrets not having obtained a graduate degree back then. But one can easily observe the satisfaction in her eyes as she says, "I am studying again today. I rise at five a.m. and give myself two hours to study for the Certified

Financial Planner every morning." The Certified Financial Planner is none other than the internationally recognized programme initiated by RNIS and certified by IRDA.

Down Memory Lane

Ritu's heart brims with fond memories of her father, Raj Kapoor, who was one of the greatest showmen of his times in the Indian film industry. "I could never spend enough time with him at home as he was constantly steeped in work," she says. "For him, work was worship and his priorities in life were directed towards his career, which really took all his time." Her father would be absorbed in work while Ritu and her brothers Randhir and Rishi were away at school. He would return home late at night when the entire house was deep in slumber. It was always her mother Krishna Kapoor who bridged the gap between father and daughter.

"On 26 January 1950 all the lights shone down on the city of Bombay to celebrate the newly acquired Republic Day," Ritu remembers her father narrating to her. Open-air trucks dotted the grounds. Baby Ritu wove her way through the heavy traffic jams to see the Victoria Terminus and other historic buildings, which were illuminated with the radiance of sovereignty. "It was like a carousal with papa," she declares. The child in Ritu surfaces as she continues: "I also remember driving down to Juhu Beach for fun-filled picnics with Papa." Ritu was the apple of her father's eye. The frequent trips she took to the Vihar Lake and Aarey Milk Colony with father Raj Kapoor are indelible in her memory.

As a child, she also wrote tiny notes and messages to communicate with her father. One night, she placed a note under his pillow, requesting him to buy a piano for her birthday.

And hey presto, no sooner did she rise the following morning than she found a glossy new piano by her bedside! It was the same piano which Raj Kapoor used while filming the song *Dost Dost Na Raha* in his film *Sangam.*

Raj Kapoor had his own reasons to believe that it was apt for men to make a foray into the film industry while women should find suitable grooms and mould themselves into what their husbands wanted them to be. Only once in one of his films, *Shree 420*, were Ritu and her brothers invited on the sets of R K Studios when the song 'Pyaar Hua Ikraar Hua' was being filmed. In one particular shot, the trio could be seen crossing the street under a rain-swept sky. "It was an unforgettable experience," Ritu laughs. "We thought we were big stars. We got a day off from school and a raincoat we could keep for ourselves!"

The Mentor

Work was always very creative, Raj Kapoor believed. "He taught me that learning was observing, as also grooming, training and education," Ritu expresses. Indeed, earning a degree is not as crucial as applying what one learns in life.

Raj Kapoor held that awareness was very important in life. The deeper one involved oneself in any subject, the wider it opened up, he was known to say often. He did not complete his matriculation. Aspiring to join the naval corps, he appeared for the exams. It was only after he failed that he made an entry into Indian cinema.

Had he passed with flying colours, Raj Kapoor would have in all likelihood established a career at the top rungs of the Navy and would not have mounted the proud stallion as the great showman that we all remember him as. "Everyone is endowed with a certain skill, a certain aptitude, a certain quality that opens up in some form or the other at every stage of life," Ritu conveys.

Raj Kapoor always taught his children to preserve the grace of Indian heritage and perform good deeds. Ritu Nanda imbibed her father's philosophies, acquiring from her parents the beliefs that were associated with certain value systems and commitments. Many a time, Raj Kapoor could be found telling his daughter that children were akin to advertisements for their parents.

When Ritu got married, Raj Kapoor composed a special song for her. "He said 'Always stay in the heart of your husband. Your sincerity to him is your jewel'," Ritu discloses in happy recollection. His words remain ingrained in her subconscious.

> *"Sometimes, the little self in you feels small or humiliated because you are always shining in another person's glory. However, it also gives you an incentive and motivates you to do something more in your life so as to create your own identity. But getting recognition can become a tall order when you are compared with someone who is so big."*

The difference between Ritu's showbiz family and the family of industrialists she married into was tremendous. "My husband Rajan (Chairman, *Escorts Limited*) is a total workaholic," she muses. "Had I not started working, our marriage would definitely have ended up in divorce," she adds jokingly. "A woman enters a man's heart through his stomach, they say. But she can stay there only through his brains."

The Sleeping Giant Rises

In the early 1980s, Ritu Nanda invested Rs.5000 in a home appliance firm Niky Tasha, which she set up in her kitchen at home, naming her company after her children Nikhila and Natasha. During the initial phase of her work life, her parents phoned her time and again and solemnly queried, "Do you have a problem at home? Do you have financial difficulties?" It was a time when working women were yet to be perceived as financially and emotionally capable individuals.

"Innovations emerge from needs," Ritu explains wisely, before moving on to cite a personal experience of hers: Soon after marriage, Ritu would cook for the entire household. One day, there was a gas strike and she ran out of gas. An idea sprung up in her mind when husband Rajan suggested that women should have stoves that worked on both gas and electricity. When there was no gas, they could switch to electricity without batting an eyelid and the show would go on. That was when she launched her first product Electro Gas. This saw the beginning of an occupation an industrialist helped initiate for his bored wife, who was eager to prove her credentials to the world.

However, there was a huge demand for gas stoves, which sold in thousands in striking contrast to Electro Gas, which sold in hundreds.

Niky Tasha soon became Niky Tasha Private Limited. The plant was located in Haryana. For reasons unknown, the consortium of five banks that had granted loans to the company could not accept Ritu Nanda as a professional. She was perceived as the wife of a very successful businessman who was the Managing Director of a massive blue-chip company. As Niky Tasha grew to be a household brand name, Ritu Nanda came face-to-face with innumerable instances of rivals and imitators who sought to compete with her products on a massive scale. In spite of these instances, the company expanded meteorically.

The Vacuum

Unfortunately, mismanagement spun disaster along the way. Products were over-marketed. Moreover, the regressive tax regime of Haryana bred a non-conducive environment, which compelled her to bring production to a halt. Alas, the company folded up prematurely. The crisis placed Ritu in an awkward situation, where she was confronted with financial stringencies. While she wallowed in the midst of her harrowing experience, her husband stepped in to help her restructure the company. At this juncture, she withdrew from a full-time job and gave her husband complete authority to run Niky Tasha. When the systems were revamped, the show ultimately became a hit. But Ritu never forgot what she learnt from her oversights.

> *"A good qualification carries immense value and provides instant confidence, credibility and recognition. It is very important for a woman to qualify herself if she is to be a highflying professional."*

The Brave Jump

One morning, a female friend of hers suggested that she could become an agent of Life Insurance Corporation of India. Stepping into a new line of business, Ritu began selling insurance policies to the cutthroat corporate world. Her idea of selling insurance was met with a lot of initial scepticism. Moreover, she was an untrained agent. Undeterred from her mission, she set forth to dispel the myth that losers became insurance agents. In a short span of time, she went ahead to become the country's path-breaking LIC agent.

Figuring in the list of the top 1000 insurance professionals in the world, she made it to the LIC Chairman's Club-A list of best-performing agents for an astounding eight years in a row. She was a member of 'Top of the Table' and 'The Million Dollar Round Table' associations for seven and fourteen years respectively. Ritu also endorsed the Life Insurance Corporation of India in an advertising campaign on TV as part of its image-building exercise, which was intended to glamorise the profession of an insurance agent.

Yearning to give back to the profession from which she had obtained so much, she aimed at developing skilful insurance professionals who, she believed, possessed the drive to make a mark and leave traces of their footprints in the competitive world. With this philosophy in mind, she established the RNIS

College of Insurance and Management, setting up many branches across India. Over 75,000 insurance agents and brokers have been trained, so far. Ritu created an online insurance portal www.escolife.com. The portal serves as a neutral platform to provide various services to the insurance sector. The Asia Insurance Review rated this portal among the top four best insurance sites in the world, through a competition whose winners were judged by a distinguished panel of professionals and regulators from the insurance industry.

A Holistic Agenda

Ritu's father was a man of the masses. He identified himself with them and was always beholden to them for his fame and popularity. The Kapoor family, long involved in many non-profit charitable organizations, formed a trust, Raj Kapoor Jana Kalyan Sanstha (RKJKS) on 14 December 2001 (Raj Kapoor's birth anniversary) to keep his spirit alive by continuing his mission in their own humble way. The trust aimed at uplifting the conditions of the economically weaker sections of society. In concert with her brothers, Ritu contributed substantially to it. Under her guidance, the trust offered Life Insurance and educational scholarships to the underprivileged in India.

In 1990, the former Soviet Union honoured famous film personalities worldwide to commemorate one hundred years of global cinema. Her father Raj Kapoor was one of them. The others were Ingrid Berman, Jean Gabin, Charlie Chaplin and Marilyn Monroe. To mark the occasion, Ritu Nanda wrote her first book *Raj Kapoor*, which was a pictorial tribute to Raj Kapoor and the hoydens of Indian cinema. The 'Issukutskovo' publishing house in Russia published a Russian translation of the first edition of the book, which boasted 10,000 copies. The book was also translated into Chinese, Hindi and English. Penguin published her second edition titled *Raj Kapoor Speaks.*

The stylish, state-of-the-art office at Okhla Industrial Estate in New Delhi, where you can see Ritu Nanda seated today, is a proud workmanship of art and corporate ethos – a product of the blood and sweat she put in to build it painstakingly. The walls of her office are adorned with artworks from her other business enterprise 'Rimari Corporate Art Service' – a niche business, which was created exclusively to provide services to architects, interior designers, hotels and corporate offices.

Rimari has been functioning for fifteen years now. As the daughter of an artiste, Ritu is well aware of the complexities creative persons face when they choose to market their own products. "Rimari is a window for unknown talent," she informs. Rimari represents over 200 artistes gifted with different skills nationwide, stocks over 18,000 artworks and prices art pieces at wholesale corporate rates and supplies them in varied sizes, colours, mediums and frames chosen by customers themselves.

Soul's Core

In a heartrending soiree, Ritu narrates the experiences and teachings that shaped her personality, reflecting on the principles she learned from each of them and diligently applied to every aspect of her life, thereafter. *Excerpts from an exclusive interview...*

- *What insights did you receive from your first venture with Niky Tasha?*

  It was tough to gain acceptance from professionals. Every year the company doubled its turnover. So quick was its growth that it was mismanaged. I realized that I was perched at the top only when I fell down. It took thirteen years for me to restructure the heavy loans the company had incurred. I learned that the largest problems arose from the consequences of misuse and abuse, besides inefficient delegation of authority. Moreover, the regulation of state policies can seriously hurt the potential of a business enterprise. I openly saw the power of bureaucrats and the magnitude of trouble unplanned growth could lead to. Eventually, I would say that every incident that life has to offer carries a certain meaning. No experience is wasted. We must apply the lessons we learn from our previous experiences to perform better in the future. The application is however different in each situation.

- *How did you apply this learning to your new career in insurance and initiate the turnaround?*

  Soon, I realized the insurance profession was one that was not respected. Insurance advisors were embarrassed to accept the fact that they were actually agents. I have never forgotten or forgiven those who laughed at me, when I became one. This provocation and contempt motivated me to work hard and make an effort to bring respect, recognition and credibility to the wonderful domain of insurance. I applied my 'Niky Tasha experience' to market life insurance schemes. I had a different vision in mind. Exposure to company law made me replace mandatory, statutory accident coverage to the blue-collar working class with a plan from the LIC of India. The company benefited as it gave additional insurance coverage to employees. Under my scheme, the company obtained the money (which it had paid as premium income after a stipulated period of time) in the form of tax-free income instead of losing the premium. And the rest was history.

- *Did you believe in the school of thought which contended that women make better managers?*

  Female genes are much stronger than those of males. The nerve connectors in women exceed those of men by 40%. Women possess the versatility and capacity to handle so much more than men. They are also better at lateral thinking and have greater perceptiveness, intuitiveness and expertise in prioritising their activities and managing their time. It is this quality that enables them to play the different roles of daughters, sisters, wives, mothers and professionals. (*Laughs*) This is not my statement. Science has proved it.

- *What inspired you to write the book? Was it a planned exercise?*

  The idea for the book was born shortly after Papa's death on 2 June 1988. Suman Seghal, a business colleague of mine, told me that the peoples of Russia required a book on Raj Kapoor. I asked him to contact Bunny Rueben, who besides being a dear friend and a colleague of my father's, was also the author of a biography titled, *Raj Kapoor: The Fabulous Showman*, which was completed during Papa's lifetime and published shortly after his death. Sadly, this proposal was not commercially viable for Bunny Rueben. Suman Seghal consulted me for further advice.

  I then guided him to approach Simi Garewal. She too was a star colleague and a very dear friend of Papa's. She had made a documentary on Papa for BBC. Ironically, when her documentary (titled *Raj Kapoor, the Living Legend*) was telecast for the first time on Indian television, Papa was battling for his life at the All India Institute of Medical Sciences, oscillating between what sciences could offer and what destiny had designed for him. There was a lot that even I, Raj Kapoor's daughter, had discovered about the legend, through this wonderful documentary and I was certain that Simi would do a great book. Unfortunately, the publisher in Moscow was unable to meet the terms and Suman was back to me again.

  There was another book on Raj Kapoor called *Raj Kapoor's Films: Harmony of Discourses*, which had been authored by Malti Sahai and Vimal Dissananyake. It was a research at the East West Centre in Hawaii, USA. Papa's work was used to illustrate how a true showman knows the pulse of the nation, also bringing to light how he used the powerful medium of celluloid to communicate with the masses. The book was a great tribute to Raj Kapoor. But it was not a reflection of the person that he was. I did not feel that this was the kind of book the Soviet publisher wanted.

It was at this stage that I thought of a photographic book on Papa. I made a dummy of the concept and sent it to the publishing house in Moscow. The project was accepted and I received a telegram stating the date on which the delegation from Moscow would arrive on to commence work on the book. I panicked and went to a publisher-friend of mine, Aroon Purie, for guidance. To my astonishment, he said, 'Why don't you do it?' Till then it had not even occurred to me to attempt such a project! I thought it was a crazy suggestion and went on with my usual preoccupations, hoping to find a suitable person to author a record of Papa's life for posterity.

The delegates arrived in Delhi. I left with them for Mumbai. At this time, my brothers were busy completing my father's unfinished film *Henna.* My older brother had an assistant director, Khalid, who was also a writer. I requested him to advise me on the storyline I could frame. Khalid promised to come and help me. He did not keep his appointment. It seemed like a hopeless situation. I remember going to my father's room and breaking down. I wept. Here was this great honour the Soviet Union was planning for my father and I had kept the idea alive, but now I did not know what to do next. I was convinced I couldn't write the book myself: I might be the daughter of Raj Kapoor, but I did not know the great showman in the perspective required to produce an enduring record of his contribution to cinema.

I prayed to my Guru Shri Sai Baba to help me. In the holy book, the author Sai Satcharitra addresses God in the very first chapter: 'How can I write a book on You, Almighty? I am a mere human being.' God appears to him and says, 'You write and I will write through you.' I implored Sai Baba to help me likewise; I would in return offer the first copy in his name at his shrine in Shirdi, Maharastra.

I believed that God was communicating with me. As Papa's video with his interview was on, an idea flashed in my mind: Why couldn't Raj Kapoor write his own book? And then I became completely focused on how I wanted to create this book. I locked myself up in my room with the project for four months, researching vastly and weaving a narrative with Papa's own words. Four months later, the book was printed in Moscow.

Reality in Death

Ritu is not a non-life agent. All the same, many companies have approached her to become one, stating that every life insurance agent was free to do so. "I am not an agent of any non-life company because I don't feel for it," she announces. Indeed, the chemistry of her personality is such that she sees what she calls the 'reality in death'. "I am not confident I can handle a fire or accident insurance," Ritu confesses.

Not surprisingly, several splendid offers were extended to her. She politely declined them all. "I would deem my mission successful if an insurance agent came up to me and told me that I had done something which helped him/her do more," says Ritu.

"Usually, you don't find agents talking about themselves," Ritu declares fiercely. "They like to hide and be quiet. Well, *I* am very proud." And the larger-than-life Ritu is indeed true to her word. A burnished plaque that bears her name and designation 'Ritu Nanda – Insurance Advisor' is the first sight that would catch your eye if you strode into her office.

Right from *Niky Tasha* to *Escolife*, she has come a long way in opening the public eye to the striking combination of gentleness, shrewdness and expertise that defines Ritu Nanda, the insurance agent. She has many more interesting projects under her belt. A lot of unfinished dreams await her. She holds us in intrigue with the gravity of her curiosity-arousing statement: "And wait with bated breath – this is only just the tip of the iceberg!" For the glamorous grandmother of two, 'life has just begun'. Yes, we agree that life is indeed insured.

> "Faith believes in something you cannot see, and the result of faith is seeing that which you believe in."

Shahnaz Hussain
Chief Executive Officer, Shahnaz Herbals

16.
The Herbal Crusader

She conquers the spiritual boundary with the words, "Let not my life be a series of days and nights, of hopes and sighs; so that when I die, I will close my eyes and say that it was all worthwhile." This isn't a saint we are talking about.

A winner of numerous national and international awards, she is both the pioneer and the undisputed queen of herbal care. She is one of the top twenty billionaires in the country and India's answer to Anita Rodericks. An advocate of natural splendour, she built a global kingdom of Ayurvedic formulations and naturopathic beauty products, challenging the ethics of the synthetics cosmetics companies. Her products have graced the faces of the most beautiful and eminent personalities in the world. Right from the late Indian Prime Minister Indira Gandhi and Princess Diana to writer Barbara Cartland, she has served them all.

This herbal queen was offered the role of a Mughal queen in a multi-million dollar Hollywood blockbuster titled 'Taj Mahal – Lover's Story', which was to relive the grandeur of the Mughal era and immortalize the legend of Mumtaz Mahal. Estimated to cost over $100 million, the film was to be produced by First Light Entertainment Limited. With her arresting patrician features, exotic kohl-lined eyes, commanding screen presence and powerful Indian ethnicity, she was tailor-made for the role of Noor Jahan. She turned down the offer. In a persistent attempt to accommodate her rigorous working schedule, the Hollywood epic makers promised to build the sets for her in Delhi and offered her a whopping sum of $10 million. The stubborn queen refused to shift her stance.

It is the same stubborn streak that has made ***Shahnaz Hussain*** (CEO, Shahnaz Herbals) a legend in her lifetime. A first-generation woman entrepreneur in her family, she traded 5000 years of Indian civilization in meticulously bottled jars and refurbished the international beauty market, materializing as a superstar across the globe.

We walk into the priceless treasure trove of beauty and several years of memories and associations, which is her home. "Well, home is where my heart is," the princess greets us, as she emerges from her cubicle, her long, luxuriantly hennaed hair entwined in slender golden threads. Her famous nose-stud catches the light of the Delhi sunshine and winks at us with a gleam in its core as she radiates her most disarming smile. "I am an avid collector," she admits. "I constantly pick up masks and curios during my extensive travels. I especially have a fetish for birds, fish, flowers and potpourri too."

Gifted

Originally from Samarkhand, Princess Shahnaz's family rose from a royal lineage, which encompassed eminent legal luminaries. During the pre-independence era in India, her family members held prominent positions in the royal governments of Bhopal and Hyderabad.

While Shahnaz's paternal grandfather Mir Yar Jung was the Chief Justice of the Hyderabad court, her maternal grandfather Osman Uddaula and his father Sir Afsar Ul Mulk served as the commanders-in-chief of the Nizam of Hyderabad. Educated at Oxford, Shahnaz's father N U Beg was the Chief Justice of the Hyderabad High Court and his brother H U Beg was the Chief Justice of India.

Born into an orthodox family in Hyderabad in 1944, Shahnaz was compelled to conform to the existing customs and traditions her family imposed on her. Her father's secular outlook and broadminded horizons urged him to send his daughters to *Queen Mary's*, an Irish convent in Allahabad. He instilled in Shahnaz a penchant for poetry and English literature. "My father was always my pillar of strength," she avows. "He encouraged me to have faith in my own abilities. Abandoning the differences that existed between religions, he highlighted their similarities and taught me that every religion upheld love, peace, fraternity and charity."

As a child, Shahnaz never was a beauty buff. Over the years, she acquired a fascination for herbal products from her grandfather, who exerted a tremendous influence on her. She was brilliant in her vocabulary, a zealous debater and an active contender of numerous poetry and essay-writing competitions at school. Many a time, she would even find herself presenting plays and dramas along with other dramatics enthusiasts. Shahnaz's competence in reciting verse after verse of poetry stemmed from her lyrical temper and razor-sharp memory.

When she was ten years old, she and her parents went to Pandit Nehru's residence. Eager to unravel the girl's talents, Nehru asked her to dance and recite poetry. Uninhibited by the fact that she had had no formal training in dance, the curly-haired doll swirled around to music in gay abandon in her mother's bright red sari, clutching a long-stemmed flower in her hand. An eloquent recitation of 52 verses from the *Life and Death of Abraham Lincoln* ensued.

Nehru sank into a pensive mood after that. A luminous bulb flashed in his inward eye as he looked up suddenly, smiled at Shahnaz's father and exclaimed in pristine wonder, "You have a genius in the family. Please educate and enlighten her; don't make haste in getting her married."

A Child's Child

Shahnaz and her sister rode to school in a curtained car everyday as a mark of the purdah system, which her family believed in. One morning, a handsome young man fleetingly saw her part the floral curtains of her car curiously (as she did all the time) on her way to school to sneak a peek at the world that lay beyond its confines. She instantly became the woman of his dreams. On returning home, the gentleman requested his family to send Shahnaz's parents a marriage proposal. Now, while Shahnaz's mother insisted on handing her daughter in marriage to a prospective groom, her father was much keener on empowering her intellectually. Giving in to his wife's wishes nonetheless, he agreed to the young man's marriage proposal. She was engaged at the age of fourteen and married at fifteen.

Nelofar Currimbhoy was born just before she turned sweet sixteen. Early motherhood proved to be advantageous to Shahnaz in more ways than one. "We felt like school girls," she admits. "There is nothing more beautiful than growing up with your own child. And Nelofar and I grew up together – just like two sisters." When Shahnaz later began attending International Beauty Congresses in Paris, New York and London, Nelofar flew with her in her personal capacity as a beauty therapist.

The Gateway

After Nelofar was born, Shahnaz's husband received a posting abroad and the family travelled westward. "I decided to delve into the intricacies of beauty during my sojourn in Iran," Shahnaz reminisces. She seized the opportunity and schooled in some of the world's most reputed beauty houses like Helena Rubinstein, Christine Valmay, Lancome and Lean of Copenhagen to study cosmetology and cosmetic chemistry.

> *"I also refused to offer certain treatments and salon services people asked for. For instance, I didn't allow bleaching of the skin or facial steaming. I educated my clients about the dangers of bleaching and the damage it could cause to the natural beauty of the skin. At this time, the market didn't offer products that catered to individual needs. Moreover, such concepts were unheard of."*

While she was training, she observed with horror the gruesome ill effects of synthetic products and the irreversibly devastating impact they cast on numerous hapless casualties. Gory instances of burnt scalps and impaired vision urged her to abandon chemical concoctions in a trice and seek solace from exotic herbs. A certain discontent gnawed at her. She resolved to discover a solution to revolutionize the concept of cosmetic care and reform the dismal scenario. In 1971, she borrowed a capital of Rs.35,000 from her father and set up a modest yet exclusive herbal clinic in the verandah of her home in Delhi. Rejecting the existing salon treatments, she adopted the principle of 'natural care and cure', introducing 'protective, preventive and corrective care' beauty treatments in her nature care salon.

The Big Break

Ever since liberalization, striking competition has been a challenge Indian businesses have had to contend with. Despite the economic slowdown that followed, there were enterprises that not only held their own, but grew steadily too. The Shahnaz Hussain Group belonged to that consummate league.

Shahnaz waded through torrential economic difficulties. Unlike other existing companies, she didn't have adequate financial stock to invest large sums of capital in the business. During her time, India had no representative to take her to the global dais in the arena of beauty. Shahnaz took the lead and filled up that void. Many a time, she financed her trips abroad to attend International Beauty Congresses and fight for the recognition of Indian herbal beauty care in far-reaching international platforms.

Sashaying into the international market with Indian Ayurvedic formulations and procedures was no piece of cake. Shahnaz explored the caverns of the international market for the first time in 1980, when she chose to remain solo and stand behind counters at the Festivals of India in London, Paris and New York.

A satisfied client is the best form of advertisement. Shahnaz kept this policy well in mind when she rubbed shoulders with the biggest international brand names in a market, where millions of dollars were pumped into packaging and advertising. She never advertised; she let her products speak for themselves. "The 'word of mouth' is more powerful than we usually think it is," Shahnaz points out.

When Shahnaz was granted a counter in the perfumery section in Selfridges (London), she sold the entire chunk of her consignment in three days, breaking the store's cosmetics sales record. The following morning, the headlines of the *Daily* screeched: 'Herbal Hell Breaks Loose in Selfridges'. Impressed beyond measure with the sound business insight with which she had accomplished so extraordinary a feat, Selfridges offered Shahnaz a permanent counter.

The Shahnaz Protocol

Every so often, a pioneer is confronted with the hurdle of making people accept new ideas. Shahnaz developed her own products for the treatment services that she rendered and initiated a tremendous volume of effort to create an awareness of the importance of a glowing complexion and healthy hair and convince the sceptical masses that her beauty products worked well.

She never allowed a ripe business opportunity to slip through her fingers ever. She calls to mind the occurrence of a particularly stupefying incident during her spell at Galeries Lafayette, where she had to quote the minimum sales target for the store to provide her a month-long display. Totalling her resources, she discovered that sales fell short of her target figure by a few hundred francs. Only one more night was left.

Shahnaz sat and thought hard, ruminating over the options and the possible outcomes of her decision. All of a sudden, a brilliant flashbulb exploded in her mind. She sent her staff members back to the hotel room to fetch some of the Persian carpets, which she had incidentally brought. She swiftly made a gift pack and announced in the store's microphone that each person who bought a hamper would be gifted with a free Persian carpet. The long, jack-in-the-box queue that followed persuaded Galeries Lafayette to put her face on their show window for a month.

Shahnaz always places human values before anything else. "I believe in interacting with each client as an individual and establishing a distinctively special rapport with her," she informs. Those who have a higher level of affordability consider her treatments expensive. For those who can't afford them, the services are free. *Pay if you can, pray if you can't* – that is her slogan. Shahnaz reaped rich spiritual dividends from this policy of hers. Over the years, she fostered strong spiritual liaisons with customers and their untold goodwill and blessings reflected in her outstanding achievements.

Shahnaz engineered an integrated business that consisted of a chain of clinics and product ranges, each supporting the other. She established her brand with long years of commitment. While many more players exist in the market, the Shahnaz Hussain brand name remains secure against the swirling winds of change. And behind this magnificent enterprise stands a stoic Shahnaz, the brand ambassador of her products and ventures. Within Indian frontiers, Shahnaz now has 460 outlets and a well-established distribution network of beauty clinics, which extend to smaller towns in India too. The impeccable brand equity that she revels in today has classified her products as those that belong to a special guild.

> *"I firmly believe that every woman can be beautiful; and this is the idea that I have tried to convey. I have been told that my methods defy every code in the books. All the same, they have proven to be successful."*

As a leader in product innovation, the Shahnaz Hussain group has developed more than 80 formulations for skin, hair and body care and 300 Ayurvedic formulations for the treatment of skin and scalp disorders. "Ayurveda can help to make India a major tourist destination with mass concentration on fitness, rejuvenation and stress reduction as well as the universally acclaimed 'back to nature' trend," she affirms briskly. Tested under actual user-conditions, Shahnaz's peerless product ranges evolved from the model of clinical usage. This matchless collection encompasses unusual lines of therapeutic products, which rope in specialized cleansers, masks and moisturizers for the treatment of specific problems like acne and pigmentation. The immaculate clinical measures the company offers include the famous Vegetable Peel and the Thermo Herb. There are no equivalents for such products in the market.

The Shahnaz Hussain group provides a massive feedback programme. With the personalized techniques the company has integrated en suite into its approach, Shahnaz's clients have easily established a personal rapport with her herbal chain. In an attempt to encourage holistic lifestyle patterns, the group supplies health tonics and provides advice on diet and lifestyle to eager clients.

Extending over 138 countries, the Shahnaz Hussain Group has 400 franchise clinics that span the globe today. The Shahnaz Hussain label dominates the most exclusive chain stores and retail outlets across the world, including Blooming Dales in New York, Galeries Lafayette in Paris, Seibu in Japan, Harrods and Selfridges in London and La Rinaeccente in Milan.

A Mark of Distinction

Shahnaz's achievements are not confined to those of a cosmetic era alone. She has attended many press conferences, promotional fairs and Festivals of India worldwide. She visited China as part of the CII delegation, when the former Prime Minister was away on his official visit. Besides being a skin-care specialist, Shahnaz's untold dedication to research and practice in yoga won her unprecedented universal acclaim and innumerable awards, like the *World's Greatest Woman Entrepreneur Award*, which she received from *Success* magazine, USA.

The *Flying Falcon Award* from Dr Taylor, Chairman of ITEC, U K in 1982, for the promotion of Indian herbal cosmetics abroad, the *Udyog Jyoti Award* in 1992 for her individual contribution to economic development, the *Rajiv Gandhi Award* in 1995, the *Lata Mangeshkar Award* in Mumbai (2000), the *Golden Peacock Businesswoman Leadership Award* (which she received for outstanding achievements, worldwide acclaim, high commitment to excellence and total dedication to her career) from L K Advani, the *Priyadarshini Award for Women Entrepreneur of the Millennium* (which she received from Sheila Dixit, Chief Minister of Delhi) in 2000 and the *Outstanding International Personality Award* are just some amongst the many.

In 2002, Shahnaz Hussain received the *Global Quality Management Award* for quality excellence and the *Outstanding Woman Entrepreneur* in London. In September 2003, she was selected for the prestigious Global Indian *Woman of the Millennium Award*, presented by the Global Indian Congress, based in California, USA. With several awards the group secured from the Government of India for Export Excellence, exports have played a central role in the activities of the group too.

Shahnaz always believed that India had a great deal to offer the world. "This belief has been my guiding force," she reveals. She has never failed to keep up the pulse of her enterprise with new products, innovations and applications. Her efforts were geared towards transporting the Indian herbal heritage to all corners of the globe with a level-headed crusader's zeal.

> *"India can be a major destination for spas as most spa treatments originated from here."*

Besides a captivating line of healthcare products like Ayurveda tonics and medicines, health drinks, herbal teas and immunity enhancers, the company introduced the Astro-Gem Therapy Range and Spa Collection.

Upfront

We launch into an in-depth question-and-answer session, where Shahnaz unravels her unique business plan and her suggestions for furthering the cause of the beauty business. *Excerpts from the exclusive interview...*

- ❑ *Are animal-free cosmetics a myth or reality? How has the Shahnaz Hussain Group championed its cause?*

  Animal-free cosmetics *can* be a reality. During the initial phase of my career, I ensured that we did not practise any form of animal testing in our R&D laboratories. Using ingredients derived from animals has always been an absolute no-no for us.

- ❑ *You have made a foray into men's cosmetics as well. What inferences have you drawn from the market response in this regard?*

  Beauty isn't only a woman's prerogative. Looking presentable is crucial to win your employers over, particularly in the hospitality and tourism industries, front-office jobs and full-time careers in television, modelling and marketing. Men are beginning to realize the importance of personal grooming in today's competitive, corporate era. Broadly speaking, that is the market response. We received a large bulk of mail from many men who sought remedies for skin and hair problems. Although our clinic was exclusively tailored to meet the needs of women customers, men would often drop in to purchase our products. These factors prompted me to formulate an entire product range solely for men too. I called it *Man Power.* (*Laughs*)

- ❑ *How do you propose to counter the challenge of foreign nationals?*

  With the ample scope the beauty business provides in India, there is ample room for many players. Today, my contesters meet me on my home ground. With months of backbreaking study of Ayurvedic beauty-care, 34 years of experience and my wide network of clinics and distributors, I feel that we have got a good headstart.

This unbeatable begum never sits back on her laurels and preens at the world. Sleepless, ambitious and raring to go at fifty-seven, she plans to trail new blazes in hitherto undiscovered domains, identifying potential avenues to capture newer markets and expand her global ventures to larger prefectures.

Shahnaz Hussain medi-spa clinics are springing up in Toronto, Athens, Brunei and south-east Asia; Shahnaz plans to spread her roots further. Exciting new ventures are in the offing in the USA, south-east Asia and the former Yugoslav countries.

> ***Propagators of the Feel-Good Factor***
> *"I believe that a woman has an added advantage in the field of beauty, especially in an enterprise like mine, which encompasses a huge chain of clinics where women constitute our main clientele. With the wonderful people skills that women possess, they are more efficient in handling clients. Furthermore, they can understand one's desire to look and feel beautiful, within and without of oneself."*

In-built Mechanism

Do Indian women have everything it takes to be successful entrepreneurs? "They do," Shahnaz insists. "As a woman efficiently juggles her roles as wife, mother, homemaker and career woman, she acquires the values of patience, time-management and budget handling. She is no less than a man in spheres of intelligence, talent and creativity. Creativity generates a wide gamut of innovative ideas. Business involves translating these intriguing ideas into practical terms. The strengths of Indian women entrepreneurs lie in their dedication and single-mindedness as well as their ability to work hard and survive rough patches. They can rectify weaknesses by strengthening their mechanisms to cope effectively with their home and work lives. Most importantly, it is imperative for a woman to realize and acknowledge her own potential as an equal member of society."

The determination to succeed, the drive to excel and courage are the core recipes for sure-fire success. One should not only be innovative and enterprising, but also endeavour to adapt to changing trends and demands of markets. Shahnaz keeps trying tenaciously and never gives up until she gets what she wants.

> *"A vast segment of well-qualified women do not join the ranks of entrepreneurs. Lack of time, confidence and adequate capital and an unbridled fear of risk-taking could be constraints. The Government does provide incentives and opportunities to encourage women entrepreneurs, especially those who seek to explore the realms of kitchen or cottage industries. Further, the Government and other agencies need to identify other areas where women can be successful entrepreneurs and discover their markets. Certain states have adopted such regimes to promote the trade of handicrafts."*

The Gain-Loss Equilibrium

Achievers have sacrificed the small pleasures of life and compromised on their personal needs and desires, many a time. To gain in one area, they've had to lose in another. The world knows Shahnaz gained. But what did she lose? "Well, I have no regrets," Shahnaz declares. She pauses emphatically, runs a bejewelled hand through her tresses and continues, "I once wrote, 'There is a price tag to everything in life. There is a mind-boggling price one has to pay for success. When you skim through the waves of success, you can miss the finer values of life'. Perhaps, I would have spent more time with my children were it not for my career commitments." It is pretty lonely to be at the top too. However, the lady has made it mandatory on her part to take family vacations and/or spend long, lazy weekends with her family at her herb and flower farm.

Shahnaz makes it a point to build relaxation into her daily lifestyle through a hard-core fitness regime, which includes aerobic exercises, deep breathing and yogic asanas. When she has some time at her disposal, she pampers her passion for painting and writing poems. She has recently channelled her creativity through her African Art collection, which consists of sculptures, paintings, miniatures, statues and accessories. She plans to make the collection available to people at showrooms in Santushti and Khan Market.

As Shahnaz had first opened her clinic at home, she didn't have to wrestle with obstacles in her personal life, unlike numerous other career women. She was always available for her children. Nevertheless, as her empire grew, she was compelled to find the middle ground on the home front.

Her family stood by her through thick and thin. Her second-born son Samir always exuded vitality, which gave her fresh joy and strength. Shahnaz recalls that she used to love riding with him on the motorbike he was given when he entered his teens. "It would just make me alive!" she whispers, her eyes shining. He is now twenty-eight and has carved a niche for himself in a high-profile career, which he enjoys to the core.

Ask Shahnaz about her post-retirement plans and she will laugh teasingly at you. Shahnaz continues to oversee her business. Plans to retire are light years away from the queen-bee's mind.

Full Circle

Shahnaz has groomed her children with painstaking care. "I taught them to value 'time' and live each day as if they were leading a complete life," Shahnaz informs.

"With each breath, I am coming closer to the grave," Shahnaz states philosophically. "This business is extremely important to me. It is my lifeblood." The land of beauty the herbal queen has built is now left for Nelofar to perpetuate. She is confident of Nelofar's ability and willingness to hold together with indomitable pride and courage the beautiful world that her mother has built, when the responsibility of taking the baton finally lands on her young shoulders.

The circle shall be complete; Shahnaz's halo shall be immortalized and her Mughal opulence shall live on through her children and their progeny for generations to come.

Sharan Apparao
Proprietor, Apparao Galleries

17.
Painting a New India

In the classical literature of Sanskrit, Shakti is defined as an inexhaustible form of energy, a blazing fire, which serves to replenish and resurrect itself, providing an impetus to the rise of a newer and stronger phoenix from its previous vestiges.

Sharan Apparao (the proprietor of Apparao Galleries) appears to symbolize this *shakti.* Combining her aptitude for colour with her aspiration to create a market for the unique ideas she developed, she launched herself into the art business in 1984, at the age of 21. Thus, the Apparao Galleries was born. With her new venture, she was instrumental in tapping unexplored markets and harnessing the latent interest in contemporary Indian art. Originally called 'The Gallery' Madras, Apparao Galleries has grown to be one of the most important and widely recognized art businesses in India today. Sharan is an established brand in the Indian art world.

"I gave my gallery the name 'Apparao Galleries' in 1997," the kohl-lined, kurta-clad lady informs with a smile.

A Woman of Purpose

Sharan Apparao hails from a family which enjoys a long-standing Zamindari stature. She grew up in a liberal environment, where she was granted full freedom to chase her dreams and do what she aspired to do.

A legendary figure in the field of tennis, her landowner father M V G Apparao devoted himself to the cause of tennis, initiating pioneering efforts to market and promote the sport in the 1960s and 70s. The conviction with which he invested in the Amritaj brothers helped to promote their names and cultivate a brand for them, placing them on the international map as the world's most famous Indian tennis stars.

As a much acclaimed sports journalist, he redefined the practice of sports writing in India and his reports from Wimbledon were looked forward to by ardent tennis fans every summer. Sharan lost her father when she was just sixteen. Sharan inherited her father's writing skills and integrity. She herself wrote extensively on art and travel for a plethora of newspapers and magazines.

Sharan graduated in Art History from Stella Maris College, Chennai. Even while at college, she was a repository of vibrant energy, which she longed to give expression to. She felt that the austere ambience of the college provided her little leeway to do so. On completing her graduation, she applied for a Masters course in the same college. Her application was rejected.

"The authorities probably found me too wild and rebellious," she says. Nevertheless, she has never had to regret that. Once she completed her graduation, she found that she could release her unspent energy by pursuing her passionate interests with greater freedom.

She worked as a summer intern at the Smithsonian Museum in Washington D C in 1985 and later at Christies' Contemporary Art in London in 1987. She met her future husband in London and joined him in wedlock in 1988. Unfortunately, the marriage did not work out well. Frequent travels and work pressures kept them apart and culminated in a divorce in 1991. Sharan didn't let the divorce shatter her.

Thereafter, she invested a lot of time in honing her communication skills with a course in art writing, which she enrolled in at the Harvard University. The programme moulded her appreciation of contemporary art, providing her gainful insight into the mass interest Indian art had garnered worldwide. With a firm resolve, she threw herself deeper into work, laying a solemn focus on expanding her business aggressively.

A meeting with D K Mukherjee, the Chief Joint Manager (CJM) of the erstwhile Grindlays Bank in 1986, dramatically changed the course of events. The bank had recently begun an art gallery, which it wanted Sharan to run.

Sharan was not enthusiastic about the proposal they put forward. She rather suggested that she could enter into collaboration with the bank to organize and promote art shows. The bank agreed and they got right down to it. The valuable experience she gathered from working with the bank gave her the confidence to open her own gallery.

Making an Alcove

Sharan's soft skills and organizational efficiency rose to prominence when she organized an exhibition of Chinese paintings in the Chola Sheraton Hotel in Chennai, fresh out of college. She had no knowledge of hosting an exhibition. "When I saw the basement where I was to conduct the exhibition, my eyes nearly popped out of my head with horror! It looked like a huge, cold grey dungeon," she recalls with a sheepish smile. "Sleep eluded me. All night, I tossed and turned in bed, wondering how I was going to pull through." Her never-say-die attitude saw her conjure up new themes and patterns to enliven the place. She finally decided to transform the basement into a Chinese garden with a large cornucopia of potted plants and flowers, which she bedecked the hall with. She was adventurous enough to even suspend the paintings in midair.

Numerous companies volunteered to sponsor the exhibition. At the end of the day, Sharan happily pocketed profits to the tune of Rs.6000 – a figure that comprised a volume of capital which she found sufficient to create her own business, a year later.

Sharan wanted to give her gallery the rustic look of a town. She moved into the first floor of her family house in Chennai. She met several builders and incurred a substantial expenditure to build additional space on the first floor. Located on a long narrow strip of the terrace, the gallery stands proud and large in Wallace Garden in the heart of Chennai today, with pictures of antiquated beauty along the poky stairway, traditional sculptures in front of the walls and a grotto of scented potted plants lining the railings and window wills.

Learning how to run the business, balance the books and prepare her financial statements posed the greatest challenge during Sharan's journey through the art business. A complete novice in finance and business, she consulted her family auditor, soon after she built her gallery. The auditor indiscreetly told her to return to him when she made some money. His words didn't discourage her.

Although Sharan had extensively studied and researched on various aspects of art history during her stints abroad, she desired to explore the realm of art marketing and fine-tune her business acumen. She signed up for short-term courses on finance and management, studied carefully and thoroughly and directed her energies on running her enterprise successfully.

Crossroads

Sharan had always wanted to take art to unconventional alternative avenues. Like many historical overtures, her untiring art crusade took shape when she learnt through several conversations she held with people that upcoming artists who were being encouraged in their endeavours were few in number.

It was a movement which was to showcase the Rembrandts, Picassos, Hussains and Ravi Vermas of tomorrow. Motivated to provide a platform for their talents, she decided to market artists who held promise. A veteran in planning and conceptualising, she has held numerous shows and exhibitions across the country, showcasing the works of young and gifted yet unrecognised artists.

Apparao Galleries has conducted multifarious art activities on different themes in Delhi, Mumbai, London, Singapore and New York and successfully catered to the aesthetic needs of the Indian Diaspora, opening windows to the emerging trends in India. "A vast segment of NRIs in these areas make up a considerable section of our audience," Sharan says. Over the two decades of its existence, the gallery has built an impressive portfolio of artists who have scaled international heights today. (Yusuf Arakkal, Anjolie Ela Menon, S H Raza and Shakti Burman, to mention just a few names.)

Apparao Galleries also functions as a consultant company with a view to authenticating and documenting every facet of contemporary art for a large gamut of private and corporate collectors. Apparao Galleries has been a major force to reckon with in promoting the globalisation of art. It has expanded its activities worldwide today. Besides locating exhibitions in different avenues and assisting in a wide variety of displays and presentations of contemporary art, Sharan Apparao has been coordinating overseas activities on an extensive scale with her export sister-concern *Art Route.*

Art Attack

Sharan has been more of an art professional than a patron. Over the years, she has become increasingly perceptive in judging the calibre of artists and helping them realize their true potential. The pictures and visitors around us fade imperceptibly into the background; only Sharan remains in the fore, looking younger and more determined than ever, as she gets ready to voice her views on the status of art in India. *Excerpts from an exclusive interview...*

❑ *How have religions influenced our Indian art forms?*

Art grew from religion. It is essentially a part of religious life in India. The wonderful intricacies of our art forms can be seen in various Tanjore paintings, illustrations and venerable icons. The aesthetics of art have shifted today. Contemporary art isn't about beauty, vivid art techniques or pretty images. Art involves engaging minds. It is how effectively you communicate your ideas and concepts, which determines the rate of success in the art business.

> *"The perception of art changed with the advent of the Second World War. Urban imagery has become very popular. Visual impact inhabits a place of prime importance too. Art changes with time in keeping with the latest trends and fashions. And that is what sustains it."*

❑ *Can you discern any difference between au currant artists and artists of yesteryears?*

Well, there is certainly a vast difference. In the earlier days, artists displayed a higher level of enthusiasm. They painted for the sake of painting and enjoying life. The art we see today is highly commercialised. Today, the art business is just like any other show business. Primary importance is attached to sourcing work, which in reality is a very tedious task. It is not a presentation of aesthetics as it earlier was. It is a product which commands a high market share and a good degree of market viability. Images are built, stories are told and the final products are packaged in cartons and sold to the public.

> *"Most often, art is being run by bureaucrats. We need to develop the concept of* art administration.*"*

- *How can the media pitch in to promote art?*

  Sadly, the South Indian media is more interested in movies and politics. Consequently, their coverage of visual art is dismally low. The media should increase their coverage and contribute substantially to the upgradation of various gifted artists who work in and around Chennai.

- *What forces are at play in driving the art market?*

  The market itself. The free market forces of demand and supply determine art prices. As the availability of a commodity increases, prices will reduce. Also, it isn't fashionable to paint like Rembrandt today. However, if a Rembrandt does come up, it will cost millions.

- *Evidently, not all of your buyers are art lovers. On what basis do they purchase your paintings, besides their love and passion for art?*

  Clients have different needs. They may purchase for investments, matching their curtains and sofa sets with their living room décor or even because the artist is seemingly well known. Customers who buy art to make investments seek an assurance that prices will eventually rise. Furthermore, the reliability of the gallery's valuation is another factor which affects the purchasing patterns of customers.

True Cultural Ambassador

"Larger numbers of women are venturing into business and taking higher and higher risks in doing so," Sharan avers. Sharan was never really a painter. Many years ago, she dabbled in painting, sculpting and pottery. Nevertheless, she gave them up. Sports have always captured her interest. Windsurfing, parasailing and white-water rafting appealed to her most during her younger days.

In the fullness of time, she aspires to coordinate a joint collaboration of artists and craftspeople for an up-and-coming designing project and to market Indian art globally. Sharan has a lot of space in her personal life, which she channels for the purpose of expanding her activities and operations. "My mother has been tremendously caring and supportive of my endeavours," she acknowledges. Her mother takes care of her company in Chennai while she is away on business tours. It is her spirit of adventure that has seen her through every success and travail.

Sharan has daringly navigated uncharted waters, vanquishing the sea demons that came along the way. She has redefined art, giving it a new form, a new meaning. Promoting new talent, she has placed herself in the league of cultural ambassadors who have contributed substantially to the fortification of India's composite culture and heritage. She shall continue to build visions and monuments with a much greater momentum than we would have ever imagined.

"Nurture a spirit of adventure and the world becomes your oyster."

Simone Tata
Chairman, Trent Limited

18.

The Cosmetic Czarina

Lofty, snow-clad mountains rose to the azure blue Switzerland skies. In the farthest corner of a frozen mountain in a village near Geneva, a schoolgirl crashed down through the ice, landing on her back with a resounding thud. Though momentarily flushed, she hoisted herself up with steely determination and strode home sans her socks and shoes, regardless of the amused stares of passers-by.

This incident took place more than six decades ago. That elfin girl soon flowered into an enterprising business baron, who took Indian consumers on a joyride to the fascinating land of cosmetics. Credited to be the first lady to commercialise the cosmetics business in India, ***Simone Tata*** (Chairman of Trent Limited) redefined the standards of the fashion and cosmetics sectors via the same determination with which she picked herself up during that mountain fall in Switzerland years ago.

She came to India in 1955 and joined the board of Lakme six years later. Also the first lady to establish beauty salons and later launch 100% private label stores in India, Simone Tata was appointed the Managing Director of Lakme in 1964.

Under her spell, Lakme became India's leading cosmetics enterprise and made a swift dent in several overseas markets. Simone took over as the company's chairman in 1982 before she was appointed a director of Tata Industries in 1989. "Interacting with experienced veterans in the board of Tata Industries is an enlightening experience," Simone admits. "I can hear out people who emerge from different streams of business and hold diverse views on a large range of topics." Indeed, the knowledge and wisdom that one acquires from such interactions outshine any level of expertise that could be achieved if one were fettered in one's own company.

In 1996, Simone sold the *Lakme* cosmetics business to *Hindustan Lever Limited (HLL)* for Rs.200 crores, gleaning profits to the tune of Rs.93 crores.

Simone claims she is a very private person. "In fact, press interviews with me aren't very common," she states earnestly. "I consent for purely professional reasons. Our family members cherish their private lives."

The Evolving Industry

French by birth, Simone spent most of her childhood and youth in Geneva. Private schools were few in number and everyone went to the common village school, back then. For all the unsullied innocence of the earlier days, Simone's childhood was blemished with effects of the Second World War, the tension and animosity of which even countries like Switzerland suffered from. As the rancour of the war spread its deadly tentacles worldwide, Simone's family grew accustomed to the unrelenting restrictions on food, clothing and petrol.

"In Switzerland, it was very difficult to commute and no one had cars. We rode on bicycles," Simone recollects. Nevertheless, the war helped her develop an early sense of responsibility. As the world painstakingly reassembled the shattered remnants of the post-war era, Simone began high school with other girls her age. She lived her high school life to the fullest and especially enjoyed cycling to school with her friends.

Most of the upscale fashion entrepreneurs, who have escalated to global heights today, are believed to have attended finishing schools to fine-tune their etiquettes as well as their social, professional and people skills. And Swiss finishing schools in particular have always been regarded as the ultimate pedestals of pride and charm. Simone didn't attend one. "Finishing schools did not exist in my time," she says. "Finishing schools constituted a part of the early twentieth-century concept. The few that evolved usually roped in foreign girls as students, whose parents had no patent picture of what they could do with their daughters after school. Personally speaking, I feel they have lost their utility and value."

Simone relocated to India after her marriage to Naval Tata. She however found it easy to drop by her hometown during business tours abroad. Aside from a bachelor's degree, she had no business qualifications whatsoever. "I regret it to this day," she admits ruefully. "I do envy girls who hold MBA degrees. That is something I never had. I learnt as I worked, made all kinds of mistakes one could possibly imagine and learned never to repeat them again." Simone learned on the job. She didn't choose her career, though. Neither did she have her eyes peeled for one.

While she holidayed in Delhi shortly after the birth of her son Noel, her smooth alabaster skin began peeling. Alas, she could find no cream or lotion to alleviate the effects of the chilly Delhi weather on her dry, sensitive skin. "When Tata has Lakme, why can't we manufacture creams and lotions?" she casually queried to the group of Tata associates whom she was chatting with, one wintry morning. The question she posed served as a dramatic turning point in her life. When Lakme instantly sought her for a job, she told herself, "Why not? Let us see what we can learn." When she boldly asked her requesters how much time it would take, she was told that two hours would suffice everyday, for one month. "I replied 'OK'," she laughs. "And that was how it started."

Simone's newfound career unravelled before her a broad scale of options and possibilities, which captured her inquisitiveness and yearning to explore, invent and re-explore. She extended her daily work-schedule from two hours to half a day.

At the time, Lakme produced two broad types of products – skincare products and aspiration products. Some products clicked, while others didn't. However, those that were closer to tradition sold well during their initial phases. Simone located the pulse of the Indian market and churned out her talcum powder to exploit the 'fairness fever syndrome', which then prevailed in India. Simone provided a varied range of colour choices to her customers as the market developed from its embryonic stage. As the market matured, her customers picked up a few select colour choices.

Severe criticisms were levelled against the Indian cosmetics industry as the packaging of products had taken a severe beating. But there were no volumes to match. Initially, a tax rate of 120% was imposed on feminine vanity. Simone protested vehemently. She sent representatives to reason the situation with the Government. Convinced by her logic, the Government reduced the level of taxation.

Over the years, social barriers that sprang up in connection with applying cosmetics diminished as more women began working and gained financial independence. Simone anticipated this from the very beginning. "Cosmetics are largely relevant to the Indian market if they fulfil the consumers' needs," she declares. Her company sent beauticians to different colleges and clubs to educate women on various aspects of grooming and looking presentable. It was her vision to develop the market aggressively.

The Road to Fulfilment

Simone neither considered herself a professional, nor did she take herself too seriously. Nonetheless, she turned in sterling performances. Her career further nourished the fascination that she had felt when she beheld the warmth and simplicity of Indian life and the charm of Indian culture and folklore, on coasting eastward to the country.

It wasn't long before Lakme persuaded her to take over as the Managing Director. Their sudden request surprised her. "I did it for a lark," she exclaims. "And I became an unpaid Managing Director! Just call it destiny."

Husband Naval was happy with her successes. Simone and Naval rarely discussed business at home. They always found animated debates and discussions of current affairs and rampant socio-political and economic issues across the globe interesting. Simone believed in drawing a fine line of distinction between her work life and home life. "Had we harped on the demands of our respective careers, we would have each been bored out of our skulls," she grins. Nonetheless, they always derived strength and inspiration from each other. Naval's death fifteen years ago only strengthened her resolve. The steady support she received from him shielded her from numerous obstacles, which she might have otherwise had to face on the home front. "Naval was a very hardworking person; he struggled valiantly and braved several impediments," she reveals.

The Rebirth

All global icons have fought against the tides of an obstinate challenge during the course of their professional lives. Just as they approach a dead-end, they go through the proverbial 'Aha experience' and strike on a solution out-of-the-blue. The international acclaim they win soon after they circumvent the challenge restrains them from ever looking back. For Simone, it was no different. She confronted her greatest challenge the day she sold Lakme, thirty years after she began her career. It was more than the company she sold. Investing her energies in sustaining her company and giving it a new direction, she patiently upheld her poise during the transition phase between the sale of Lakme and the rise of Trent.

Simone was one of the earlier starters of the retail business in India. The slight degree of competition that existed at the time, screened her new venture from untoward responses on the part of rival players in the industry, except perhaps, one or two retailers who were in the up-and-coming too. "No one questioned my objectives or discussed my intentions," she informs. Even so, the industry she branched into took many years to gain acceptance from shareholders. The new concept she introduced naturally faced initial scepticism.

Competition built up slowly. Before Trent came into vogue, Simone's team held numerous discussions with *HLL*. Simone saw representatives of large international cosmetics companies move towards her office from every corner of the world. Her social network expanded to massive proportions as foreign players vied with one another to set up a joint venture with *Lakme*.

Simone was confident that an alliance with a financially sound company would strengthen *Lakme*. She struck a joint venture with *HLL*, stretching it to a period of two years. When *HLL* offered to take over the entire company thereafter, she relied on her conviction that accepting its proposal, keeping in view her shareholders' interests, was the right thing to do.

When Simone sold the cosmetic business, she sold the *Lakme* brand too. Subsequently, she had to abandon the *Lakme* tag and find a new trade name for her garments. She chose *Trent*, which proudly stands for *Tata Retail Enterprise*.

Finding the *Westside* name was not an easy task. Before her team picked *Westside*, the management put their heads together and looked through hundreds of names. Simone wanted a distinctive name which would be simple to pronounce, easy to remember and adaptable to new products that could be introduced to extend the company's product lines in the future.

Many names she chose initially sagged; they had either been taken up before or were too difficult for people to remember. *Westside* was a neutral name and one that would instantly spring to one's mind. The *Westside* label bore no elitist ring to it. Neither did it give away any information on whether it described a popular family chain or an upmarket one. Furthermore, *Westside* epitomized a timeless international approach to retailing. Building the *Westside* brand was not an overnight assignment. Simone's company studied and researched, at

> *"During the preparatory stage and the phase of planning, we spelled out the three pillars of the company. The first was value for money, the second, style and the third, quality. I would say that each of the three is equally important. This strategy that we charted established a firm foundation for our company. It is one that we scrupulously adhere to even today."*

length. "We took a few months to decide how we were going to operate," she admits frankly. Selling brands wasn't her objective. She chose to sell her own *Westside* brands. This model not only opened up profitable avenues but was best adapted to India too.

The Industry Wizard

Simone won the *Special Award for Innovation*, presented by the Bombay Management Association in Mumbai in 2003 for mooting and implementing innovative ideas in retailing. At the Images Fashion Awards (IFA) function held in Mumbai in 2003, she was also conferred the *Visionary of the Year Award* for her outstanding performance in the business of retail fashion in India. Simone teems with dynamic ideas and strategies as she notes the dramatic growth of the apparel industry with the progress of each year. *Excerpts from an exclusive interview...*

- *How did you identify the Indian market for the retail business? What potential do you think it has?*

  Initially, the retail business in India was undeveloped. However, in light of the changing lifestyles of Indian consumers and greater exposure to the international media, it was to be a sunrise industry, eventually. When India did not eschew technological developments and western influences of fashions and lifestyles, why should she escape retailing? We did not escape television, DVDs and the likes; they all *came* to India. So, large-scale retailing had to come to India, one day. With this belief in mind, I initiated a foray into the sphere of retail trade. The retail segment in India carries vast potential. Changing customs and lifestyle patterns drives this potential. With enlarging numbers of working women and talented young professionals, the Indian scenario has transformed. Cushioned within every bosom is the aspiration to achieve and accomplish. '*Look smarter, feel younger*' is the catchphrase, today. Our desire to shop in a better environment and project a trendy and fashionable persona constitutes part of this change.

- *According to some quarters, the NCAER had identified the 15-35 age category as the biggest contributor to the growth of the fashion industry. What is your opinion?*

  Why isn't the 35-50 age group seen as a major contributor to growth too? (*Laughs*) Don't we see young mothers and the not-so-young mothers who are fashion-savvy and fashion-conscious? Just look at the number of mature women who enrol in gyms and aerobics classes. They are impelled to do so by their children or the media. Women between the ages of forty-five and fifty-five want their pairs of jeans too, the plump and the slender ones alike. On the other hand, the younger generation is goading the older generation to adopt modern ways of dressing. One generation is pushing the other. And one can see that the third generation is materializing now. And the Indian fashion industry has the potential to serve them all.

- *Do you feel that emphasis on consumerism can have an adverse impact on the Indian economy in the long run?*

  As far as an impact on the economy is concerned, I would say, 'Yes.' People would have a greater propensity to spend. On this score, the general level of consumption would increase. India was always known to be a great country of savers – especially in view of the fact that the country had one of the highest savings ratios, worldwide. Our inclination to save will not disappear as it has been ingrained in our system. But with the higher salaries of professional, managerial and the higher-income segments welling up from many streams and flowing into the pockets of the elite and well-heeled circles in the country, disposable incomes are going to shoot up.

- *What influence would an increase in the level of disposable incomes exert on the purchasing powers of the masses?*

  We have seen the outcome of liberalization. Many buy their own houses and cars today. The construction industry is performing well. When massive construction takes place in Mumbai, a whole new city surfaces from those foundations. The extensive demand for houses, flats and apartments is fuelled by higher rates of remuneration. And the reduction in the interest rates to a level almost on par with the international rate is the biggest cherry on the cake. The liberalization of the economy and the drop in interest rates have not only brought forth a revolution in the construction industry but also increased the magnitude of demand for consumer durables, mobile phones and electronic appliances. (*Laughs*) Families want new curtains to match the shades of their living rooms, homemakers explore various models to revamp their kitchens; collegians shop for trendy new outfits they can wear to discos. Moreover, huge shopping sprees await us in the face of a wedding or a big family event.

- *E-tailing trends are beginning to catch up now. How do you propose to counter fierce competition from this area?*

  Well, I don't believe in e-tailing. The e-tailing concept fits well in areas like books or music. If we take the garment/apparel industry and the ready-wear market into consideration, e-tailing would be beneficial to consumers only if the sizes of clothing were absolutely standard. In India, we have an exhaustive range of colours, varieties and sizes. Moreover, the size of the outfits one company produces differs considerably from those of another company's. Perhaps a man can purchase a shirt via e-tailing.

  But e-tailing will not hold a candle to direct sales. As the consumers finger the tresses and trimmings, their eyes delight in the sight of sleek, elegant pieces on those racks; they yearn to try them.

  Furthermore, we have a postal system that isn't very efficient. Potential clients are reluctant to give their credit card numbers. So, I don't see e-tailing sprouting as a constraint factor or a source of competition for us.

Crafting New Ventures

Simone's ingenious mind isn't content with spinning colourful fantasies and fulfilling the dreams of every modish youngster. She has used every iota of her spunk and vivacity to make a plunge into the business of food retailing too. She plans to shape her food retail stores into a complex chain of hypermarkets, which targets cost-conscious consumers, roping in fresh and non-fresh items like pulses, tomatoes and carrots. "Hypermarkets are variations of superstores," Simone explains. "They provide a more far-reaching range of products than any other superstore/supermarket." Just like other supermarkets, routinely purchased items like saucepans, plastic buckets, FMCG products, electronic appliances, household goods and garments are being sold at attractive prices and discounts. The mass-retailing foray has been established under a new name *Star India Bazaar.* The company plans to open two more hypermarkets in Mumbai and Bangalore, each spanning over 50,000 square feet by the middle of 2005.

Sound knowledge of SCM (Supply Chain Management) is of paramount importance in running a hypermarket. For all their humbleness, Simone and her team members brim over with adept knowledge of SCM precepts, which would better equip them to skilfully handle various facets of the supply chain. Redefining the food-retailing culture in terms of quality, prices and the availability of foodstuffs, Simone intends to extend it across other parts of the country.

Her son Noel has provided her full support and encouragement in these new ventures. He began his career with Tata International (the international trading arm of the Tatas). A man of explicitness in thoughts and ideas, this 46-year-old Managing Director of Trent Limited has his mother's astuteness flowing in his blood too. He proved that retailing was a heart-warming area for the Tatas. He turned a single-store Trent to an eleven-store business, garnering revenues of over Rs.105 crore in just under five years. Under his direction, Trent has crafted a success story of the Westside chain with almost 14 stores across leading metros. Noel believed that a diversification into the grocery business would be crucial to reach out to a greater section of the masses.

A Distinctive Effort

Gracious at heart, Simone has contributed her mite to enhancing the country's social and economic development with numerous orders she has placed from NGOs and the assistance she provided in facilitating the sale of their products. Simone fondly recalls the glorious occasions of Diwali and Christmas. Community tables would be set up and Trent would purchase exquisite Indian handicrafts and artefacts, only to sell them at cost price.

Trent has developed bonds with several children's associations. Simone's interest in children has hurled her into many children's activities and causes. The *diyas* (lamps) and stars that she sells enable the company to collect ample money, building dreams, forging careers and restoring faith in the hearts of many a physically challenged, underprivileged and/or orphaned child.

> *"Both men and women are widely known to fight for social causes. A man might more often engage in such activities for his organization. But the tendency for a woman to involve herself in social and humanitarian concerns at a more personal level is much greater than that of a man."*

For the most part, businesspersons are believed to be aggressive go-getters. Could compassion be seen as a weakness in business, especially among women? Simone's response is a vehement "No." She mentions that business interactions do involve a lot of situations where one has to deal with compassion. "Compassion is recognizing someone's problems and listening to them," she avers. "Men and women are equally helpful in nature. Perhaps, I would say that a woman is a better listener; she has greater patience to listen to stories."

> *"Women are adopting a critical role in the LPG (Liberalisation, Privatisation and Globalisation) era. Not as many women may hold fort at the topmost levels; nevertheless, the number of women who make a mark and play a dynamic role is phenomenal. I can cite an unusual example. A few years ago, I made a visit to Tata Tea in Munnar. On entering the premises, I found two young ladies who were managers of the tea estates. Now, a tea estate would easily lose its identity in the large expanse of the woods. And these were particularly ones that were located at an hour's distance from the next tea estate. The girls' presence overrode all other considerations."*

Trent Limited has three or four women store managers too. The activities their jobs entail are those that are customarily undertaken by men. The cascading effect takes form; it grows bigger and bigger, burgeoning to a large size and intensity. This trend has galvanized a great upward movement into managerial cadres. "It is not fair to address only those women who are chairmen and managing directors of big companies," Simone states heatedly. "We pay little attention to women who are placed in the second and third rungs of the corporate and industrial ladders. We need to ask these women what motivated them to chase their dreams, aspire and achieve."

Perking Up Over Tea

Unruffled by the pressures of her career, Simone finds time to enjoy hosts of other activities. Summer holidays usually entail flying to her hometown in Geneva and relaxing in her home with sisters, cousins and nephews. While Tuscany is the tourist spot of her dreams, Rajasthan's time-honoured mores, welcoming peoples and vivid culture mesmerize her. "I don't have much flair for languages though," she jokes, adding that she is unsatisfied with her ability to communicate in Hindi.

Simone is an ardent reader too. Never failing to keep abreast of current national and global developments even at a very tender age, she reads fiction and non-fiction extensively, even today. You will always find an interesting book by

Simone's bedside. As a child, her fascination for history and literature further moulded her passion for reading. The course on Aesthetics in Indian Art, which she has recently enrolled in, has further kindled her penchant for Indian culture, which involves a lot of reading. The mighty effort required to absorb and correlate the events and episodes in a book makes her a pretty slow reader.

> ***A typical day in the life of Simone***
> *"I read newspapers in the morning before dashing to the shower and rushing to the office. A pile of office work awaits me at my desk. I hardly ever lunch in the same place! I get back to work after lunch, return home in the evening, deal with all the household quandaries, have my dinner, watch a bit of news on TV and then curl up with a good book to recline for the day."*

Simone's passion for reading doesn't rein in her outdoorsy nature. The fact that her Swiss family of origin lived by the lakeside in Geneva shaped her zeal for sailing. The winters won her undivided attention when she dished out her skiing gear and embarked on many skiing expeditions. White is her favourite colour. She was most often seen in white dresses when she was young. "It is a remnant of my childhood," Simone discloses.

Simone's respect for her colleagues is what draws them to her. Says an employee of the company, "As a leader, she is not only knowledgeable about her domain of business but also open to all discussions. Furthermore, she goes out of her way to solve problems that her employees face."

Right through, she developed wonderful teams and granted team-mates the freedom to explore any area they believed held promise for the future. Not one to let triumph or turmoil engulf her, Simone has taken every success and failure in her stride. "Looking back, I should say it has been a pretty smooth sailing though," she remarks humbly.

With her vivid plans for the future, the incisive 72-year-old businesswoman is ever on the go, just as always. Under her baton, Trent has consolidated its position in the retailing business.

> "Planning efficiently, organizing oneself well and having patience can be the perfect recipe for a near-perfect balancing act."

Sulajja Firodia Motwani
Joint Managing Director, Kinetic Engineering

19.

Riding to the Summit

She pumped a triumphant fist in mid-air, her face a mask of newfound victory. "I got six signatures from Dad this term!" she exclaimed in delight. Her mother and sisters stood around her, overwhelmed with pride and joy. It was a cheerful Sunday morning. The warm Pune sunshine streamed merrily through the windows of the neat little villa.

The wavy-haired girl and her sisters regularly strived to obtain the largest number of signatures from their father, who gladly did so when his daughters either stood first or acquired a cent percent in Maths. And that particular term, she had outshone them.

With the 'steal the show' attitude she wields to the world and the contemporary woman of style in business that she is today, she has pioneered sweeping changes in the automobile industry today, transforming the Kinetic group into a composite two-wheeler manufacturer with the series of new models she has launched.

Sulajja Firodia Motwani (Joint Managing Director, Kinetic Engineering) was voted among the top 25 business leaders of the present century in a poll of industrialists conducted by *Fortune India* and described as the 'Face of the Millennium' by *India Today*.

Truly Indian

Sulajja inherited the engineering skills and technical expertise from her grandfather H K Firodia, who built Kinetic Engineering and father Arun Firodia, who founded the Kinetic Group. A family of hardcore academicians, the Firodias always stood at the forefront of education. The powerful role Sulajja's forbearers played in leading various movements to strengthen India's struggle for independence only fortified them further. Mahatma Gandhi and Jawaharlal Nehru were among the illustrious few whom the Firodias regularly entertained in their home.

A renowned women's activist and a speaker in several sabhas, Sulajja's grandmother led many women's rallies. While Arun Firodia acquired MBA and MS degrees from MIT Sloan in the USA, his wife graduated from Harvard Medical School and is currently a high-ranking doctor in her own right. Sulajja and her brother and sisters travelled abroad to pursue their higher education too. Sulajja's lineage has been unswervingly sound, not only because of the industry the Firodias built together but also due to their sturdy value system and the fragrance of nationalistic education, which hallows their conviction.

The Genesis

The Firodias transformed their image from that of a politically renowned family to a family of industrialists, with their first venture in the automobile business in the post-Independence era. A harbinger of the first generation of businessmen, H K Firodia was a firm believer in science. He held that India could be a strong nation with her scientific temper and innovative approach. The automobile industry was a perfect vehicle to promote self-reliance in India. Taking up the challenge with full gear, H K Firodia joined hands with Bajaj. While Bajaj was the financing partner, his company was the managing partner. He split up with Bajaj in the 1960s and took over Bajaj Tempo before the Kinetic group emerged.

"I have been interested in the rigorous challenges of a business career ever since I can recollect," Sulajja declares. "Grandpa was my biggest confidence-booster and largest source of motivation; he made me believe I had in me everything it took for one to make it big in the business world."

Sulajja's father, mother and grandfather regularly had discussions of important family affairs or business developments over dinner at home. Sulajja and her siblings could sit with them and listen to the proceedings of the meeting if they liked. "Of course, we didn't have much to say during these meetings," Sulajja laughs. "We would even pose silly questions." Nevertheless, Sulajja always looked forward to participating in the discussions.

"We have been immensely fortunate to go to good schools," Sulajja acknowledges. Aside from the consistent academic records the Firodia children set at school, they were self-motivated to educate themselves by all other means too.

"Dad was particular that we should keep abreast of current developments by reading newspapers, magazines and journals extensively," Sulajja reveals. "We didn't. Undaunted by our indifference, Dad came up with the idea of quizzing us every Sunday on major news items of the previous week. Whoever provided the correct information and scored the highest would be granted pocket money of Rs.100, which was quite a sum of money in those times!"

Sulajja featured in the merit list when she completed her tenth grade with high scores and a solid distinction. She topped the entire state of Maharashtra in the HSC examination. The head girl of her school and a school team captain many a time, she could always be found indulging in her passion for sports. Particularly fond of gymnastics, she fractured her hand twice while experimenting with new acrobatic positions!

Armed with a management degree from Carnegie Mellon University, Pittsburgh, Sulajja Firodia joined Barra International, an investment consultancy firm in California, as a sales professional. Strategy, business planning and marketing were subjects that captured her interest. Her four-year stint in Barra provided her an in-depth insight into the ins and outs of finance. She acquired invaluable expertise travelling four days a week, working for commissions and meeting her targets, which she found very intellectually stimulating. While product planning, sales and dealer motivation and network development are some of the more challenging domains she dabbled in, she has always enjoyed product launches to the core. Inherently a forward-looking person, advertising has also been a fun-terrain for her. It was at this time that she met and married Manish Motwani who worked with Sun Microsystems.

While India provided a sturdier platform for her to develop and evolve further, Sulajja performed remarkably well in the USA too. "Heading an organization would have however taken me a much longer time in the USA," she reasons.

On returning to India, she handled the Indian operations of the company she had worked for in the USA while Manish established his own computer monitor-manufacturing unit. With the functions she performed, she established her credentials as a full-fledged professional. Her roots on Indian soil kindled in her the passion to run her family empire. A year later, she took charge as the Joint Managing Director of Kinetic Engineering. Since then, she has wholeheartedly involved herself in Kinetic's operations, designing innovative strategies to market her bikes.

Sulajja has accustomed herself to a stress-ridden work style and office culture. She and her father and brother are hardcore workaholics, she admits. With almost all of her family members steeped in business, conversations at the dining table invariably veered around to work-related issues, after making small talk for five minutes. "My mother doesn't involve herself much in these discussions though," Sulajja reveals. "She is our balancing factor."

The Product Makes the Company

Born as a moped company, Kinetic has several firsts to its credit. While Lunas grew to be a generic name for mopeds before it was placed among the proud pioneers of gearless scooters and motorcycles, Kinetic Honda became a runaway success too.

"Besides my father who constituted a part of the Kinetic Honda management, the Japanese were the directors of the company too," Sulajja informs. Kinetic Honda was the company's biggest acquisition. With its sleek get-up and unique style, Kinetic Honda revolutionized the market standards with its emergence. Moreover, safer and simpler methodology made the Kinetic model a superior option.

Sulajja considered Kinetic as a smaller company with an entrepreneurial spirit. She believed in laying emphasis on a solid value system and thrived on the basic principles of creativity and innovation. This belief urged her to frame a model, where the work style was directed to suit a smaller, quicker and progressive company, as opposed to that of a larger company, which she believed was more likely to be bureaucratic.

Realizing the importance of growth through innovation, Kinetic began its life with stiff competition from other players in the industry, which she faced boldly and effectively.

> *"We don't lose ourselves in bureaucracy. One of the primary advantages of being a small group is a broader leeway that we have to interact on a much closer level with one another. Getting to know everyone better would certainly help us accomplish greater feats."*

Well aware of the full implication of the phrase 'Survival of the Fittest,' Sulajja has been widely resilient to all odds. To begin with, the company's premium scooter Marvel didn't hit the success button. Thereafter, she shifted strategies.

Her group branched out from mopeds to a new, eclectic range of scooters and motorcycles in the core sector. She had the Kinetic Group focus on four-stroke technologies for its bikes. The launch of the Challenger and the GF range of bikes followed her foray into the motorcycles segment. Over the last few years, the Kinetic Group has taken large strides to build a future for itself in the core business of two-wheelers and diversified into related areas like auto components and engineering businesses, which are high-growth areas for the future.

Sulajja has also plunged into the domain of tools engineering. Looking to build up her business further, Sulajja set up two other companies to manufacture auto-electrical components (CDIs and magnetos to mention only a few!). JayaHind Sciaky, another smaller company in the group, has been building up the business of welding machines. The Kinetic kingdom also has a unit that provides finance products for two-wheelers. To this end, the group struck a joint venture with Citibank.

"The trend is upbeat. Futuristic scooters are the ones that are expected to change the status of the two-wheeler industry within the next decade," Sulajja declares optimistically. Kinetic has recently bought manufacturing rights and the entire production line for a range of seven scooter models from Italy. The scooters are expected to create major excitement in the domestic scooter market and promise the company a great future in the area of exports. Large volumes of investments have been made in this regard.

Kinetic was the first Indian company to buy out a majority of foreign partners. As opposed to reverse engineering, Sulajja has resourcefully brought in new concepts of technology to spur the success of her acquisition models.

Kinetic is banking on its wide group-distribution network and a pristine knowledge of its dealers and customers' tastes and preferences to leverage her skills for the service sector. The group struck a joint venture with Taigene (a company in Taiwan) to make starter motors. Having established an exclusive alliance with Hyundai to import elevators from them, Kinetic is now installing elevators and escalators across various cities in the country. Sulajja is focusing on exploiting the group's engineering expertise to give a firm direction to her new business. With this endeavour, she also had to contend with various instances of rivalry and imitation. To begin with, an Ahmedabad-based company began making elevators and branded them Kinetic. Sulajja boldly filed a case against them.

The elevator business is mushrooming rapidly. The returns garnered from the elevator-business bear testimony to the company's strategic outlook for the elevator management business and the impeccable installation engineering services it renders.

Always attempting to reinvent herself, Sulajja has been entirely experimental in her approach. Five years ago, she started a direct sales company to see if she could successfully sell two-wheelers. And successfully she did. Choosing traders are her main segments, she capitalized on the existing latent demand for two-wheelers. Once the sales graph shot up, she and her team travelled to forty cities to increase the prevailing level of awareness among people.

Sulajja experienced a desire to set up a company entirely different from a manufacturing company and one that she could run independently. Thereafter, Kinetic Marketing Services Limited was born. This venture provided her an opportunity to build her basic business and closely scrutinize relative growth areas. Consisting of 600 recruits, the company is employee-owned and has its presence in one hundred locations. Kinetic Marketing Services Limited encompasses three divisions, which market two-wheelers, financial products and consumer durables.

Designing a Niche

Sulajja has made several daring ventures in a large gamut of businesses, which she perceives as potential areas of growth for the future. Four years ago, Manish Motwani began Kinetic Communications, a company that works with various automotive companies to provide design and CAD/CAM/CI services. The Kinetic Group's knowledge of the automobile business has obviously stood them in good stead.

Sulajja garnered a management team that is predominantly knowledgeable about the automobile business, as well as a huge mass of software engineers. She hopes to garner more revenues by providing design services through her components, software and other future industries.

Does her core competence lie in marketing or design? "Well, I think common knowledge is my strength," Sulajja conjectures. She has studied finance and marketing in detail. Nevertheless, design is her passion. Known to contribute heavily to design, she has also conceived of innovative product lines. The design centre at Kinetic Engineering has been running for twenty-five years now.

> *"At Kinetic, we earlier made our products and sold them. Now, we spend a large portion of our time in collecting feedback from our customers, tracking down their needs and then tailoring our products to suit their needs to perfection. To this end, we have directed focus in bringing the consumer's voice into our company."*

Sulajja invested heavily in adopting sophisticated R&D technologies in her company. Kinetic blazed a trail with the new Nova that she launched. The scooter won the best-designed automobile of the year in 2003. Sulajja has never once defaulted on supplying the most durable, best power, best fuel-economy bikes, which contain low-priced spare parts and provide a higher ground clearance.

Although perceived as a scooter company, the Kinetic folks have worked hard to bring in new motorcycling values for customers. Obviously, the lady isn't content with her achievements. She hopes to broaden her range of motorcycles through these initiatives.

Capturing Her Goal

Aside from continuing to further develop her new businesses, she has an impressive product portfolio up her sleeve. In endeavouring to evolve new facets of areas she has recently ventured into, she hopes to build her businesses in components and design to fruition. "Both are to contribute equally to our group in the coming years," she predicts with a confident toss of her hair. Further, she nurtures the dream of building an assorted array of scooters from the Italian range.

"We must now create a new range, a new face of Kinetic, which will take us forward to the next decade," she reveals, her voice ringing with conviction. And that's exactly what she's working on. The Italian range of scooters would go a long way to strengthen the Kinetic image for the future. She is simultaneously working on building her motorcycle business in a meticulously planned step-by-step fashion, fabricating niche products, which brandish high images in the market.

> *"Kinetic Honda boasted of a sleek, international design, which gave it a proud global touch. But there are instances of products that haven't been suitable for international markets although their original design may be international. That's because they were highly domesticated. But today, Indian automobile companies need to design models made for international markets. We have now taken a route where we have acquired products suitable for international markets as our main thrust for promoting them globally. We can enhance our technical acumen and further create products for the international markets by building an international range and exporting them, especially capturing the European and American markets."*

Beyond Corporate Confines

Sulajja hasn't publicised what she does for society. Nevertheless, her company has all along served as a silent catalyst in supporting the ranks of deprived, browbeaten souls. Sulajja regularly donates scooters to disabled soldiers. Apart from running a school in Ahmednagar, Kinetic has a tie-up with a leprosy centre, which besides generating employment opportunities to the leprosy-stricken takes charge of the entire ambit of the spare parts. Kinetic has also been instrumental in creating the concept of Swapna Bhoomi. Under this programme, Kinetic has succeeded in providing gainful employment facilities to the unemployed and impacting the lives of rural citizens across the country. Kinetic has always shared a close relationship with society. The sound principles the company follows are attributable to her religious social commitment.

Out on a Cruise

Organizing her thoughts articulately, she proceeds to analyse the automobile scenario in India and enumerate the status of Kinetic on the world map. *Excerpts from an exclusive interview…*

- *Could you describe the average product development life cycles at Kinetic? Are they on par with global standards?*

  We expect our newer industries to be substantially more profitable in the future. In light of the fact that two-wheelers are consumer products, our margins are shrinking severely and our product life cycles are pretty short although it is a high-profile business. It is our bread and butter too! (*Laughs*) Three years ago, people wrote off India. They believed the economy would remain static here. They declared that China was the way to go. They acknowledged the depth of India's knowledge in engineering and her solid business ethics only after they burnt their fingers in China. Today, Indian manufacturing is back with a big bang.

- *What sort of revenues do you intend to realize for your global operations? What targets have you fixed in this regard?*

  Of a turnover of about Rs.1000 crores, the turnover of our two-wheelers is Rs.700 crores. Predominantly domestic, only 10 per cent of two-wheelers are being exported. As I look ahead, I expect our components business to enlarge to a business of Rs.200 crores within the next two years and attain a much higher level of profitability, particularly since it is a higher-margin business than consumer marketing. Our tools-engineering business currently has a turnover of about Rs.12 crores. We reckon that our components and tools businesses would obtain about Rs.30-40 crores together. The two-wheeler industry will continue to grow further. The export of scooters should pick up, though. On paper, we export to nearly 50 countries. Turkey, Argentina, USA, Sri Lanka and Bangladesh are our key areas of business today. However with the launch of Italjet range where an Indian company would be launching a truly international range in the world markets for the first time, we expect the export market to expand, as we will be exporting our scooters, worldwide.

- *Where would you say India ranks in the area of designing components?*

  Indians have an analytical bent of mind and a knack for innovations, especially in the realm of special software design creations. You can see hordes of good engineers in our country. India is certainly a nation where the threads of design and development can grow stronger as we continue to move up the value chain!

- *What are your views on the reliability of data contained in automobile magazines? How much truth do we find in the information they provide?*

  Journalism involves a lot of subjectivity. For instance, how one feels about product 'A' versus product 'B' and vice versa is rather subjective.

Likewise, the degree of authenticity of information from such sources really varies from magazine to magazine. Perhaps, some magazines are more principled than others and evaluate the models more objectively. Nevertheless, they adhere to the same process of examining a company's vehicles before featuring them.

- *Does corporate governance contribute to the goodwill of a company?*

  Relative to the earlier times, corporate governance has risen to greater prominence today. It is not only essential to abide by the duties companies are to perform towards their shareholders, lenders and customer, but is also a key to be being a good social citizen. I believe in establishing governance practices which have a social angle to them. Goodwill is very important for a company. And we see to it that Kinetic is viewed as a good company. One shouldn't be a good person because he is god-fearing or afraid that the cops will catch him at gunpoint and toss him behind bars! He should be good because he wants to be good. That is a simple logic I follow to establish good corporate governance too.

- *Do you feel the Indian educational system prepares us for successful entrepreneurial careers?*

  As opposed to the holistic education patterns we observe in schools in the USA, the Indian system still focuses on rote learning. There is a sizeable gap between what students memorize from their books, how they apply those concepts and how they express their views and ideas articulately. Also, Indian schools do little to hone their students' social skills. Even those who display a lot of interest in participating in numerous extra-curricular activities and competitions should receive more encouragement.

  As I have received ample exposure to both systems, I can perceive the difference. Business schools in the USA place tremendous value on case studies, group studies, presentations and application of knowledge.

  At B-school in Carnegie Mellon, I recall that we had series after series of open book exams. (*Laughs*) My colleagues and I would lug all our class notes to the exam hall. But if you think this was easy for us because we stood a grand chance of scoring high grades by merely solving from the textbook, think again! Our notes only consisted of concepts that we learnt. How we applied them to solve various twist-and-turn problems was a puzzle that we had to sort out ourselves. It was stimulating, nevertheless.

Driving Her Point

Sulajja's unspeakable pride for India can perhaps be traced to the political stature of her ancestry. As she unveils her philosophies and highlights the increased acceptance of women entrepreneurs and business heads, a strong sense of patriotism is evident in her approach.

Women in Business: A Social Evolution

"A few generations ago, women fought for their basic right to vote. They went through the stage of being restricted to their homes. Those were the days when women's liberation was a myth, in spite of all that was being said about it. Then came the backlash. Sexual harassment grew rampant at the workplace. To begin with, women were not treated professionally; they weren't accepted as professional colleagues quite so easily. The issues we face currently are not those of gaining acceptance in the organization but those of how women corporate executives can discover a right balance between the responsibilities they shoulder at the workplace and the responsibilities that emerge with motherhood. Most women are known to drop out of their jobs when they become mothers. So, the issue that we face now is more social in structure.

"There has also been an attitudinal change in the mindsets of men who are fresh college graduates; they express a desire to marry financially, economically and emotionally independent women with broad horizons, sharp intellects and minds of their own. Men have begun to respect women whose interests lie in non-domestic activities as well. This sea change has introduced lifestyle modifications too. With the incessant increase in the propensity to consume and enjoy the finer pleasures of life, careers have perhaps begun to suit everyone's image. We can discern a great difference in the India that we live in as this change has percolated to cities, countrywide."

> *"Today, women have not only acquired the confidence that they can contribute significantly to societal growth but have also fine-tuned their professional skills and proved their mettle in corporate circles, which are beginning to provide several opportunities for women in the sectors of advertising, media, research, journalism, marketing, software, ITeS (IT-enabled services) and services."*

The Indian Woman: Changing Roles

"Indian women hold immeasurable potential as entrepreneurs. Opportunities, which didn't present themselves earlier, are slowly evolving now. One can make a career out of running a small software company. Retailing and distribution extend ample scope too. In particular, the garment retailing and ready-wear sectors are booming like never before. Tying up with a retailer for many international brands or establishing outlets for a telecom company would do wonders to expand the development of our nation. Many more credit facilities are available today. Loans are being provided at concessional rates of interest.

"As a country, India is known to be resistant to unstable and precarious conditions, whether social, economic or political. Indian women have a high degree of patience, staying power and accountability. They are sure to perform well at any task. They are committed to their education, families and work. They are truly a sincere lot.

> *"Gender has never been an issue for me, as much as it hasn't for other corporate heads who are holding similar posts. When I can't change my gender, why should I worry about it? If someone has a problem with it, it is his problem, really! Anyway, there are many more issues to worry about!"*

"Women, however, require a strong social support system. Understanding husbands and in-laws can go a long way in heralding a newer, fresher breed of young women entrepreneurs. Unfortunately, lack of social support urges a vast segment of women to give up too easily. Intrinsic motivation is a core ingredient of success in any field. They should be self-motivated and all geared up to accomplish the impossible."

In the Scrapbook

Before the fiery young woman dipped into the realm of motherhood, taking a breather from work meant gracing social occasions and visiting friends during weekends. "Work life was very easy back then," Sulajja reveals candidly "Outside of our work, we did enjoy ourselves. So, it was a different life altogether."

With a small child to tend to, Sulajja is more conscious about the need to strike the right balance today than she ever was before, especially during the course of the last three years. While pregnant, Sulajja worked arduously till the last day. Her last working day turned out to be a Friday, she recalls. Feeling unwell, she took leave the following day. She was hospitalised on Monday and discharged on Wednesday. Soon after, she divided her time between the baby and meetings. From the fifth day after her son was born, she began exercising her grey cells for about seven to eight hours a day, working almost full time! She set up a video conferencing room at home and held meetings between 8 a.m. and 10.30 a.m. in the mornings and sometimes even between 6 p.m. and 8 p.m. in the evenings. On days when she had two-three video conference meetings, she took breaks time and again to breast-feed her baby.

Sulajja has been known to be media-savvy, giving scores of interviews and addressing huge gatherings. She judged a Miss India contest too. "But believe me, I have minimized my social activities today," Sulajja laughs.

Sulajja finds alternative ways to de-stress herself from the demands of her hectic career and family commitments. She personally drives her self-designed motorbikes and competitors' too. On Sundays, you can find her whizzing by gaily down the streets of Pune. "I drive all but the Kinetic Aquila, which is pretty heavy for me!" she chuckles. An advocate of the adage, 'physical fitness leads to fiscal fitness', she continues to make a beeline to the gym nearly four times a week to keep her lithe figure intact. "It is important for me to be physically fit for mental well being too," she asserts. "A rigorous workout really helps me sail through." Her penchant for running, reading and skiing knows no bounds either.

"Broadening your perspectives is critical if you are to grow as a person," she avers. "You tend to stagnate if you are bound by the fetters of a smaller world." In retrospect, she is very happy with the choices she has made. The euphoric sense of financial independence and the feel-good factor take rein as she continues to contribute her inputs and share her intellectual growth and development with her family and society.

> "Go out there and do something exciting. The world is transforming. Why should you be left out? You needn't be a career person, if you wish not to. But do strive for self-development. It enhances your personal growth and provides you an exalted sense of contentment and satisfaction."

Tarjani Vakil
Former Chairman and Managing Director, EXIM Bank

20.
The Pacesetter

The petulant girl kicked up a fuss to go to school because she wanted to taste the freedom her brother seemed to enjoy during the course of his post-graduate degree in the liberal arts. The fidgety young child could not comprehend why her brother didn't attend classes regularly while she was compelled to attend school everyday! She yearned for liberation from the fetters of schooling!

Fate wove a fascinating design for ***Tarjani Vakil*** (former Chairman and Managing Director of EXIM Bank) who went on to establish an enviable status as the first Indian lady to head a bank and financial institution – a matter of unspeakable pride for Indian women. She began her career with the *Maharashtra State Finance Corporation* (MSFC) and pocketed her first monthly salary of Rs.75 in 1958. She journeyed through the rungs of hierarchy in the banking sector, successfully impacting every financial institution she joined. She later joined IDBI in 1965. Her ensuing voyage to the EXIM Bank won her the status of the highest-ranking woman official in Asia. Here, she hired new technologies, built new ethics and revamped the entire province of Indian banking with the strong systems and procedures she established during her tenure.

She was also declared *The Woman of the Year* in 1996. In 1997, *KPMG Worldwide Business* recognized her as one of the top 50 women to prove her valour in the world of business.

The Emerging Banker

Born and bred in Mumbai, Tarjani Vakil was the youngest child in the family. She had three brothers who were much older than her. Tarjani completed her early education at HPT Girl's School before moving on to Elphinstone College, Mumbai, where she completed her masters in History – a far cry from what she was to do in her life later on. Back then, it wasn't certain which field she would enter. What was indeed certain was the firm belief that she would be a far-reaching career woman one day, which her father fervidly believed. Obtaining the best grades at school and college only strengthened this belief. Her family was well read, liberal and unconditionally supportive of her in all endeavours. "It was my congenial family background that helped me flourish in the job environment," she reveals.

Tarjani was mid-way through her masters' degree when her brother prompted her to take up a job with the Maharashtra State Finance Corporation (MSFC). Glad to avail of an opportunity of working and studying together, she walked into the MSFC premises with her brother. MSFC was a fairly small organization with twenty people on its payrolls. Meanwhile, her classes at college were on at full swing. She recalls the tough times, which saw her shuttle between her college and her job, trying to meet the demands from both sides. The job kept her hands full so much so that she even skipped meals many a time. "My mother began to worry that I was losing weight," she throws a laugh. She took leave when exams loomed round the corner.

She went back to work only after her results were declared, although she did receive calls in the intervening period, requesting her to join the institution.

Tarjani was given the position of an assistant when she joined MSFC soon after completing her education. At MSFC, she specialized in term lending. She was especially attentive to small-scale enterprises and enabled them to promote the development and expansion of their industries across the entire region of Maharashtra. At the young age of 27, her commitment and integrity to her profession and earnest enthusiasm in helping people out, even beyond the call of duty, helped maintain an impeccable reputation for herself as the star of the small-scale industries in Maharashtra.

Most people whom she had interacted with were semi-skilled and illiterate farmers, who barely had adequate finances to make their ends meet. There was one particular farmer who came from a Kolhapur Jaggery Unit. He struggled to write an application form in English. It was Tarjani who went out of the way to help him perform the task. Touched by her gesture, he wrote a letter to her after returning to his village. The letter addressed her with utmost respect: "*Tarjani Vakil bah' na, sastang namaskar.*"

Tarjani worked in MSFC for seven years. One day, she chanced upon an advertisement in a newspaper. IDBI, which had been newly constituted, wanted to recruit fresh personnel. The bank preferred to hire candidates who had a qualification or work experience in the realm of industrial finance. In Tarjani's days, professional institutes like the IIMs hadn't made a foray in India. So, recruiting talent was indeed a Herculean task. On a friend's suggestion, she applied and was selected, shortly thereafter. The other IDBI contenders were chosen from various State Finance Corporations and commercial banks across India.

Tarjani was the only woman among thirty colleagues who joined IDBI in 1965 and fourteen others who manned the IDBI team in the officers' cadres. As a young woman, she had long, lustrous hair, which swirled a few inches above her ankles. With her glossy tresses spreading out like a fan behind her while she leaned back in her office chair and spilling across the floors when she sat, she made a rare picture in the offices. During the time she joined, however, women were slowly beginning to dispel their inhibitions and make a bold entry into the business sector, revolutionizing the economic scenario, countrywide.

Self-made Woman

IDBI was a whole new organization with an excellent work culture, which suited Tarjani's temperament to the hilt. She enthusiastically addressed numerous issues like underwriting and disinvesting in the stock market. Innovative experiments like cash flow analysis, shadow pricing and turning loans into equity were gaining ground just then.

"A large amount was traded in the stock market on behalf of the financial institutions. That was very interesting," Tarjani says. Brokers could be seen in the traditional attire of long coats and dhotis. However, by the time Tarjani had established herself firmly in the Indian capital market, professionalism became the buzzword in all the stock markets across the country and young brokers wore business suits – ample testimony to the professionalism that had surfaced.

Most managers including Tarjani gleaned an impressive knowledge of these procedures during the course of their work. She and her team-mates pursued ideas to extend industrial finance to large-scale core sector enterprises and implemented several new and radically unique strategies by just grasping the fundamental principles they read from books. Towards the end of her tenure with IDBI, she was transferred to the International Finance Wing.

During the growing phase of one's career, training is always believed to be imperative. Though Tarjani performed exceedingly well in her career, her gender stood in the way of the training that she needed. Quite protective of her, seniors didn't send her abroad for training programmes since they believed it was impossible for a woman to travel abroad all by herself and were worried about how she would manage were they to send her alone. She was told she was performing brilliantly even without adequate training. Over the entire span of her 17-year career, she was sent for training only for ten days. Her shrewd intellect, extensive reading and numerous interactions with people helped her learn the ropes quickly. For a brief spell, she underwent training at the ASCI (Administrative Staff College of India).

"Perhaps, their hesitation to send me away for training programmes was a reflection of their concern for me as there weren't many working women," she avers. "Gender equality still warrants that every woman should receive opportunities to upgrade her skills and develop her expertise."

She had to wrestle with the issue of factory visits too. "I was told that my visits to the factories wouldn't be useful for IDBI because I was a lady. My fury knew no bounds. '*What if I am a woman?* I queried. Pat came the reply: '*There would be workers in the factories.*' I firmly told them that I would do my job of inspecting the workers and reviewing their progress. Such was the atmosphere in the 1960s."

> *"Don't think of your gender when you go to work. Be a professional."*

Tarjani also has great faith in the abilities of the youth. "The young should never give up the pursuit of knowledge, wherever they are," she advises. "At an age when we are young and eager to learn, our educational qualifications play little or no role in enabling us to seek that knowledge."

The Executive at EXIM

Tarjani's migration to EXIM Bank as the General Manager was quite a natural transition from her stint as the Deputy General Manager of IDBI. R C Shah was the first chairman of EXIM Bank. When Tarjani joined EXIM in the top management cadre, the institution was in the process of evolution. Numerous economists, academicians, commercial bankers and former World Bank and IDBI employees joined EXIM. Tarjani not only contributed to the development of the Bank as an atypical export credit agency, offering finance, information and advisory services at all stages of the business cycle but also maintained the bank, which had been set up as a flat organization sans peons or clerks.

Creating a cohesive environment was Tarjani's most stimulating challenge. The new institution's mission, vision, logo and code were communicated effectively to her colleagues and employees. Moreover, they were to prepare notes themselves. Even the general manager and the chairman wrote their own letters and notes – something unheard of at the time. "Don't create a file and sit still in your office. Move with your files. Walk up to the next person and give them to him," Tarjani is known to have instructed her personnel, many a time.

EXIM got its first PC in 1982-83, when computers weren't very common. The PC was given to the person who came from World Bank, as he knew the ins and outs of operating a computer. As the company grew wider, everyone had a PC on his desk. While Tarjani was the Chairperson, there was no cabin; the office was open.

"We had a small pantry, where we stocked all our necessities and prepared a cup of tea ourselves," she explains. Each floor had a machine room, which consisted of a fax machine and each person had a telephone and a computer at his desk. The tables were placed in such a manner that no individual was disturbed at work, while there was enough room between the tables. If desired, people could even maintain eye contact while they talked to one another over the phone from their workstations. When people unconsciously raised their voices while placing long-distance calls, their colleagues signalled them to lower their decibel level. Everyone eventually learned to speak in a soft tone.

> *"In today's world, looking presentable is essential if one is to meet people from different corners of the world and talk to them. As Indians, we should learn to look more presentable. The EXIM Bank has many delegations pouring in, every year. If officers are not smart enough and up-to-date in etiquette and subject knowledge, they can't dream of carrying discussions with them or clinching deals. You learn and improve your conduct through vicarious experiences."*

Before long, EXIM grew to be an efficient organization with Tarjani at the helm of affairs. Tarjani reinforced the basic principles in every mind, the experienced and the raw, alike. Amalgamating different minds to develop a strong ethical base was the primary principle behind every activity at EXIM Bank.

Tarjani organized the distribution of work on functional lines. Each group leader took charge of the men, money, machines and materials. Tarjani also believed in increasing the number of direct communication channels. EXIM imbibed these practices in due course of time. The bank continues to follow them to date. Even after Tarjani retired in 1996, she left the trajectory of her phenomenal achievements in the banking premises of the country.

Banking on Her Resolve

Tarjani was appointed the chairman of EXIM Bank in 1993. Around this time, the Indian economy had begun to extend its arms to foreign markets, throwing open vast opportunities that benefit industries. The volume of exports expanded remarkably. Under her stewardship, the bank grew at a rate of 20%, giving a token contribution to the Government too. Tarjani crafted mechanisms to build a work environment conducive for good performance. Her managerial abilities were put to test when she tackled three generations in the same office.

As the Chairman, she regularly met all the group heads at 9.45 a.m. everyday to discuss the events of the previous day, review the progress of current projects and put forward new project proposals. Tarjani ensured that every meeting at EXIM took place through an appointment – yet another indication of her professionalism.

The morning meeting involved sharing informal interactions with friends and colleagues over a warm cup of tea. No notes were taken. Instead, the meetings and sessions served the purpose of apprising the management of the bank's activities and instilling in the senior officers, the need for a knowledge-sharing perspective. This system injected a lot of transparency into the entire set-up. Just stroll into EXIM Bank and you'll see transparent offices on every floor, save for two closeted rooms where discussions are known to unravel in the presence of the senior management. One can easily spot those who enter and leave these 'transparent rooms'.

Tarjani was driven by a need to invest in advanced and sophisticated technologies. She transformed EXIM into a billion-dollar bank with 150 people and eleven offices in India and five abroad. The representatives of EXIM were sufficiently skill-rich to integrate information from various sources and pass it on to their colleagues via email and telephone. Tarjani and her team worked round the clock. "I used to receive telephone calls at six in the morning, when Washington was awake," she smiles.

An operator in international markets, EXIM had offices in Washington, Africa, Singapore, Rome and Budapest. In particular, Rome and Budapest were enriching products of Tarjani's single-handed efforts. "Rome was my chosen place because I discovered that Indians found it comfortable to stay there; London was too busy," Tarjani laughs.

Impressed with her conviction that the East European markets had a vast potential to exploit, the World Bank financed the construction of the offices in Budapest and Rome. Tarjani is also credited with the creation of world-class learning facilities in Bangalore. Apart from the officers of the bank, exporters could avail of these facilities too. It was an excellent initiative that adopted first-rate educational technologies. Exporters, importers, businesspersons and industrialists from India were invited to attend seminars and listen to distinguished people who would address relevant issues of social, industrial or corporate concerns. And it was invariably during the course of these congregations that brilliant ideas emerged to develop a strong vision.

Another radically different initiative of Tarjani's involved conceiving a knowledge exchange forum among the export credit agencies of the Asia-Pacific region. "Although, we were their competitors, we managed to get them in the same forum," she reports. Some thought it was a political initiative. Nonetheless, the first two interactions in India proved them wrong. Subsequently, every country began to host these knowledge exchange forums turn by turn.

Undaunted by the competition, rampant at every level, Tarjani continued to surge forward with passionate conviction, winning her superiors and subordinates alike.

Question Bank

As we sail through a brisk wrap-up session with Tarjani, we acquire a glimpse into the vast treasure trove of knowledge and expertise, which she has proudly garnered during the course of her experiences. *Excerpts from an exclusive interview…*

- ❑ *What benchmarking practices did you adopt for selection of your personnel?*

  The IIMs served as the basic entry point. The bank required skill-rich people. As the Chairperson, I had to ensure that each individual was given a sufficiently challenging assignment. Else, they would grow restless. Moreover, each of our trainees/employees was to contribute directly to the success of the bank. Our personnel consist of chartered accountants and fresh IIM graduates between the ages of 25 and 28, the middle management level, which encompasses persons belonging to the 30-50 age category and then those who are aged 50 and above. Freshers who emerged from the IIMs graduated to the middle-level and eventually stood as the backbones of the institution. Over a period of the first 3–4 years, they acquainted themselves with the bare

> *"I believe in hiring new blood because the young are familiar with new areas and well acquainted with more contemporary techniques, systems and procedures in every field. This way, older and younger persons can contribute collectively to the growth of the institution on a different plane."*

technicalities of the job, grasped the fundamental objectives and gleaned expertise from the tasks they performed. It was always the top management that took the final decisions while recruiting fresh talent. It becomes much easier to fit employees into proper organizational goals if they are moulded right from their initial stage in the Bank.

- *How quality-oriented are Indian companies?*

  I am very keen on the movement for quality. I am on the board of one of the foundations that advocates the cause of quality improvement in the Indian industry. Success will elude us unless we position ourselves as the best players in terms of products and processes. The means to an end must be good. We should adopt the right systems and processes if we are to enhance the quality of our products and services and market them globally.

> *"We can see that Indian companies are at the top of the world, today. One of the first Indian multinationals to set trends, Asian Paints has spread its muscle across 24 countries. Several other companies like Ranbaxy pride themselves on their global aspirations too. However, the key to becoming a truly global enterprise lies in developing world-class products."*

- *Do you think security is a major concern for senior citizens in the country?*

  The talk of security for senior citizens is a very live concern today. Several organizations like the Dignity Foundation have been instrumental in contributing to their welfare. Senior citizens (particularly those who reside in remote areas) should be alert all the time. As for me, I fortunately have good neighbours; we know one another well. Moreover, I have a housekeeper who has been with me for over thirty years. So, I am hopefully safe! (*Laughs*)

- *How can women be more successful in breaking the glass ceiling and making a mark in their careers?*

  Each individual should shatter the glass ceiling in her environment. Many are now doing so, particularly in Mumbai. One must update herself in her field of work and ensure that she keeps abreast of current developments and innovations in her business turf. This is essential for long-standing success, more so in view of the changing times.

Standing Her Ground

Known to be the Manhattan of India, Mumbai presents us with numerous opportunities. Tarjani exploited every opportunity that came her way, putting it to optimum use. "In Mumbai, you're on your own," she chimes. "You aren't asked questions. Out here, you're free to go ahead and do you what you like. Mumbai is an epithet of professionalism to the core."

Tarjani enjoys an active retirement life today. She isn't content with contributing her intellectual inputs to the ladies' wing of the Indian Merchants Chambers and the Rotary Club. She is currently on the board of directors of Asian Paints India Limited, Indian Rayon and Industries Limited, Mahindra Inter-trade Limited, DSP Merrill Trustee Co Private Limited and a member of the local advisory board of ABN-AMRO Bank.

Tarjani has never ceased to experiment with different paths in her yearning to seek spiritual enlightenment. Enamoured by the divine nuances of Sanskrit, she can consume voluminous texts on Aurobindo and the Gita and Upanishads. She loves travelling and has an insatiable zest for Indian classical music, theatre and drama.

In spite of the numerous avenues Mumbai provides for fun and leisure, Tarjani's enthusiastic participation in the corporate world is only indicative of her 'never-say-die' spirit. She has an entirely different story to tell though. "I am trying not to get involved in too many activities on a full-fledged scale. That is why I consciously keep myself free half the time," she declares. "I do not want to devote all my time to work too. That is why I do not have an office at home." We understand that life has much more to offer. And she continues to live her life to the fullest.

Her family and city gave her the freedom to make life's choices. She never faced any obstacles on the home front. When her parents were alive, they gave her tremendous strength to accomplish all the feats she can boast of today. Her brothers have extended infinite support in all her decisions. An embodiment of the entire ethos of today's contemporary Indian women, Tarjani proclaims that marriage was always an option for her. Staying unmarried wasn't a conscious decision though. "I was just so engrossed in my work that I didn't give marriage a thought," she laughs.

"To date, there is nothing I wanted that I didn't get," Tarjani admits. Yet, she was not demanding. Be it IDBI or EXIM, she has made her mark with professionalism and dedication. Tarjani has a final say: "I feel like a Sherpa clearing the way for the upward mobility of women."

> "Success isn't about being the first. An achievement of worthy goals is what success is all about. The quality of the goal is the key to success. Success is also about remaining modest and continuing to have a firm head on your shoulders in spite of all that you have achieved globally."

Zia Mody
Senior Partner, AZB & Partners

21.
A Mind of Intellect

When environmentalists took the issue of illegal construction of the high-profile Pratibha building (at Breach Candy, Mumbai) to the court, a group of young lawyers snared the decision in favour of the litigation. One of the starry-eyed lawyers decided that she would not rest on her laurels. She went right ahead to distinguish herself in the intriguing field of law, which ran in her blood, establishing one of the largest law firms in India.

Zia Mody (Senior Partner of AZB & Partners) is a legal consultant for many investment banks and specializes in mergers and acquisitions. In 2004, she was nominated as one of the twenty-five most powerful businesswomen in India by *Business Today* and awarded the *Knowledge Professional of the Year* by *Financial Express.*

The Powerful Roots

Born and brought up in Mumbai, Zia Mody studied at Elphinstone College, Mumbai and then pursued higher studies at Cambridge and Harvard. Fresh out of college, she appeared for the New York Bar examination and qualified as a New York attorney, following which she worked for five years with Baker and McKenzie at its office in New York.

"My father (Soli Sorabjee) has always been my role model," Zia states proudly. She looked up to him for integrity and legal acumen. It was, however, the fairness he displayed in his dealings that taught her a lot. "Being a member of a family which had a background in law did help of course," she adds. "We used to have a lot of debates and arguments during family dinners. So, I naturally grew familiar with legal discussions."

The style and manner in which Zia argued her cases even during the early phase of her career were indicative of her indefatigable wit and charm. The subtlety of her arguments may be traced back to her work experience abroad. She returned to India while her career was at its peak. Settling in India was not solely her decision.

"On that score, I accepted my husband's decision without any regrets," she admits. She wasn't satisfied with what she did. Her impatience to put her strong business acumen to constructive use led her to bring forth a structured expansion of what we know as *AZB & Partners* today.

Meteoric Advance

Zia began a small proprietorship called 'Chambers of Zia Mody'. She named the concern CZB when one of her partners Bairam Vakil joined her in business later. After a while, Akshay Chudasama from *Lex Lude* merged his practice with them too. At this juncture, Zia had established her practice in Mumbai and Bangalore. She was not yet satisfied and desired to create a presence in Delhi as well. When she ran into a very well respected Delhi-based firm, *Ajay Bahl & Company* (which was exploring avenues for expansion too), she struck a final merger with its promoters in April and the resultant firm *AZB & Partners* emerged.

"Corporate M&A, securities law, private equity and project finance are our core strengths," Zia informs. AZB & Partners has also started working on the area of intellectual property. While Zia shares a special affinity with intellectual property law, copyrights and trademarks, she enjoys plunging into areas of securities law, foreign convertible offerings and domestic offerings too.

> *"What drives our practice is our genuine concern for clients. If someone is ready to give up the case, we take it up, although 60% of the revenues come from our work in M&A."*

The Enlightener

Success hasn't in the least corroded Zia's modesty and dignity. And the ease with which students like us could meet her only speaks volumes about her humility. As we engage in an enlightening dialogue with her, she reveals a stream of ideas, strategies and business plans she intends to implement for her firm. *Excerpts from an exclusive interview…*

- ❑ *How common is it for law firms to merge with one another and expand?*

  It is certainly not very common. We did a novel job on that front. People usually avoid such expansions because they are worried about issues of cultural differences and problems in mergers. My partner Ajay and I embarked on this idea. We saw that our idea made good strategic sense. Our idea was obviously healthy in the sense that several other people began to think along such lines only after we did what we did.

- ❑ *Is your firm a professional set-up or a family-based one?*

  It is entirely professional. We have no obligation to admit any family member. Unearthing intelligent and diligent people with fine skills is our prime area of focus. Such persons are the ones who are valuable assets to an organization if they join and choose to stay.

- ❑ *What is the most challenging factor about entrepreneurship in law?*

  Every entrepreneur requires money. If you have adequate finances that help you grow, politics should not divide you. The organization should clearly communicate to the employees the message that those who indulge in politics will be penalized. To have a flat organization, where the hierarchy doesn't take over substance, people should be able to find the need for a clear discussion. Coming together and forming a team is easier. What is difficult is sticking together. That is really where the challenge lies.

- ❑ *Where would you say your forte lies in your sphere of work?*
  Well, I'm still learning. Perhaps, I would say I manage people pretty well. Being straight and honest with people is the best way to handle them. If they know that the person they are interacting with is honest, they will definitely trust him. It is important to be fair and honest and to be perceived as being fair too.

- ❑ *How do Indian law firms compare with their foreign counterparts?*
  Lack of institutional support remains a prime cause of concern for Indian firms. Foreign firms typically run into roughly 5000 people across the globe. It means that offices spring up in 20 countries. Here, we are perfectly happy with offices in merely three cities. While some UK firms are a hundred years old, a couple of firms in the USA have existed for fifty to sixty years. It will probably take years of building up to be on a par with international standards.

The 'Super' Syndrome

Many a time, lady executives are effective in handling dicey gender issues. "While women are more sensitive to such issues, men can deliver them more firmly," Zia concurs. "A few women may have a problem of getting across clearly." However, Zia has always delivered firmly and has had no trouble on that score.

> *"Parents are beginning to display a greater willingness to provide holistic education to their daughters. There is a slight change in perception, today. A woman who gets married does not necessarily abandon her career. With the few women who have carved a niche for themselves under the sun in various fields, the world has begun to accept women more graciously than it did twenty years ago."*

She offers her solution to prevailing gender inequalities: "We can achieve gender equality if we don't talk about the superiority or inferiority of women. Every woman has some issues. The degree of societal acceptance of these issues will tell us a lot about the state of affairs in the country. While female lawyers were viewed sceptically in the past, they are welcomed with open arms today. If women are to become level-players, they are required to work extremely hard (if not harder than the menfolk), invariably making a lot of sacrifices on the personal front too."

Working women also hanker after a host of supers – the super mom, the super wife, the super manager, the super boss... the gamut is endless. According to Zia, multi-disciplining tasks can enable women to carry on with effective role juggling and perform equally well in all dimensions. "It is essential to prioritise one's tasks," she advises. She has generated a simple solution, which she applies to every problem that comes her way – she requests her mother-in-law to do whatever she cannot do. "And whatever my mother-in-law cannot do doesn't get done," she laughs.

Zia's family has been her anchor at all times. "In the field of law, no woman can achieve without the support of her family," Zia avers. Her husband is well acquainted with the backbreaking hours of study and commitment one invests in a profession like his wife's. "My father-in-law, who was earlier a judge, had passed away. My husband and mother-in-law were extremely supportive of my career as a lawyer," she recalls with gratitude.

Reconciling to the fact that they would not have enough of their celebrity mom, Zia's children have stood by her resolutely too. If Zia has any constraint, it is usually the limited time at her disposal. She works twelve to fourteen hours a day and sets aside the remainder of the time for her family.

The Instinct

Many have the will and drive to establish a firm. But few have the staying power to remain and sustain themselves in business. "One has to listen and learn well, be patient and have a milder temperament," Zia opines.

Zia Mody's enterprise is not solely a business venture, which lived passively with its promoters. The lady has played an integral role in creating an institution, an enduring entity. Today, *AZB & Partners* has evolved into a law firm of high prestige and repute – one that people talk about often and love to turn to.

Zia has always been spiritual at heart. She works for the Baha'i religion and is a member of the Local Spiritual Assembly of the Baha'i of Bombay. "I have drawn a lot of inspiration from the life, which the late Ruhiya Khanum led," she discloses.

Besides serving as a director on the board of the Advertising Standards Council, she is also a trustee of the New Era High School (a charitable Baha'i institution for young boys and girls in Panchgani) and some NGOs, which work for the empowerment of rural women.

She is keen to see her partners grow and take on responsibilities of a much larger magnitude. She intends to involve herself at a lesser level in day-to-day business activities, focusing instead on further developing certain areas of practice.

As we bid goodbye and left her office, she appeared to be all set to sink wholeheartedly into her work, escalating to a higher intellectual plane – a world of her own.

Appendices

APPENDIX I

Is Business Your Lifeblood?

There are no rules for success. One form of reasoning or application in a particular area may not hold good for all cases. Nevertheless, we bring you a unique quiz on decision-making in business. The questions have not been designed by experts, but have rather been taken from real-life instances of the people in the book.

There are no right answers to the questions. However, we will tell you how the person who went through it overcame the challenge. This will enable you to draw a comparison.

If you have a message for your favourite business leader, please feel free to mail it to us and we would arrange to forward it to her. Happy quizzing!

1. You are the chairman of a self-started company which has hired unskilled and semi-skilled workers. The workers suddenly decide to form a union for reasons best known to them. You don't allow this. The union leader threatens to throw acid on you if you don't give in. What would you do?

   a) Give in to their demand, as worker-management disputes can cast an adverse impact on the company's business.
   b) Challenge the workers to fight on an equal footing, shut down the factory's operations and automate your company.
   c) Call the police and initiate legal procedures.

2. Your male colleagues are provided greater training opportunities than you are, although you are equally competent. Finding this unfair, you have complained about it to your immediate supervisor. Alas, no action has been taken. Can you modify this?

   a) You will improve your knowledge through books and continue to learn from your colleagues.
   b) Kick up a fuss and walk out on your job.
   c) Apply for leave of absence.

3. Your husband is a rich and highly reputed industrialist. You are a qualified engineer equipped with an MBA degree and you had given up your job for raising a family. You have proven your mettle as an efficient homemaker. Soon, you discover that there is a suitable position vacant in your husband's organization. What would you do?

   a) Recommend a relative to fill the vacuum as you are impressed with his/her credentials and therefore feel that he/she will be most competent to take up the job.
   b) Take the challenge yourself.
   c) Leave it to your husband to decide what is to be done. His work is his own business. You'd rather start your own!

4. Your father has founded a small company in India. The company is not faring well. You have currently graduated in Management studies from a university abroad and you receive an offer for a very high-paying job in the USA. You are caught in a momentum of two worlds. After much thought and debate, you would:

   a) Jump into the family business and chart out unconventional strategies to expand its scale of operations.
   b) Continue to work abroad. Why should you struggle in India, when you will be holding a high position in a prestigious company in the USA?
   c) You will return to India in due course of time. However, you would like to work abroad for a while to acquire some experience before you join the family business.

5. Taking a trip abroad is very critical for the growth and success of the organization you work for. Just a day before you leave, your son comes down with high fever.

   a) You cancel the tour and explain the reason thereof.
   b) You go ahead anyway and entrust the responsibility of taking care of your child to a trustworthy friend/relative.
   c) Stay behind and arrange another person who can represent the company instead of you.

6. Your father is a legend in his domain. You are highly inspired by him and his beliefs and work ethics. You would:

   a) Follow in your father's footsteps. You want to be just like him.

   b) Explore the opportunities in the career world and take up a job, which provides ample scope for promotions and recognition. You can apply your father's principles in any field you choose.
   c) Chase your dreams and build your own enterprise.

7. You are growing at a very quick pace as an employee of a company you are working for abroad. In the meanwhile, you obtain an offer to work in a company in India in your chosen field of excellence. However, the pay is relatively lower. What would you do?

   a) You would politely decline the offer. You are revelling in luxury and you are happy just where you are. Why else did you invest backbreaking hours of study?
   b) You will return to India on the insistence of your spouse/family/friends.
   c) You will assume the higher post in India. Nothing can be more important than recognition for one's achievements.

8. You have graduated in Fine Arts. However, you feel your strength lies in spotting and promoting talent. Would you prefer to be an artist or venture into the booming art business?

   a) You would hone your skills to establish yourself as an artist.
   b) The high degree of commercialisation of art has disgruntled you. The hardnosed arena of business has eroded its aesthetic appeal. Meanwhile, you do not find a career as an artist monetarily rewarding either. You would rather raise a family and spend time with your children.
   c) You would conduct an elaborate market research and set up an Art business house. Make hay while the sun shines!

9. Your father is a highly distinguished lawyer. You have chosen to study law too. However, you are yet to establish your credibility. Would you set up a new law firm and expand your practice countrywide or be happy working in your father's company?

   a) I am open to new initiatives. But I deem it better not to take any initiative myself.
   b) If opportunities exist, I would build my own turf and expand.
   c) I find it wiser to stick to the basics and work under my father.

10. You hold a very responsible position in your present organization, where you have played an integral role in restructuring the management. You are however transferred to a company which is a non-viable and sick unit. What would your reaction be?

    a) You would request the highest authority to intervene.
    b) You would resign from the job, as you believe that better opportunities await you.
    c) You believe it is only a matter of months before you can turn the sick company around. You incorporate new systems and procedures and carve a niche for yourself in the new job.

11. You are not highly qualified. Yet, you believe that you can put your skills to constructive use to make something of yourself. Do you think you could head an organization one day?

    a) If I perform well and generate new ideas, I can definitely head an organization.
    b) 'Being an organizational head' is only wishful thinking. A good academic portfolio is the core criterion for a leader and good credentials will equip him/her to take effective decisions and circumvent new challenges. So, heading a business is not my cup of tea.
    c) If I meet the right people in the right place at the right time and develop the right contacts, I can rise to the top.

12. As the holder of an MBA degree, you have topped your batch and joined a bank as a trainee. Many other bright young people join the organization along with you, each of whom is highly efficient and talented. Where would you rank your chance of heading the same organization?

    a) United we stand, divided we fall. Team spirit is crucial for the success of any organization. I will achieve success if I work in a team.
    b) It is a zero-sum game and largely a question of luck too.
    c) Many others are better than me and hence more deserving of the post. Each person's capabilities are different. I don't believe in comparing myself with others.

13. You are an engineering graduate. You have consistently been a rank-holder in academics and you receive a scholarship to pursue a PhD in Textile Technology from a university in the USA. You are excited about the prospect of doing a PhD abroad. However, your forte lies in marketing and finance. You are in two minds.

    a) You follow your passion and travel abroad to acquire a PhD.
    b) You enrol in a management institute and foray into the corporate world soon after.
    c) You choose neither. Perhaps, you would rather take a break, dabble in music/dance for a few months and then bounce back with renewed vigour.

14. You belong to a full-fledged business family. Your desire to follow your academic passions remains unheeded and you are married to a corporate tycoon soon after you turn eighteen. A few years later, your father passes away unexpectedly. Suddenly, the responsibility of managing the family empire falls on your shoulders. Your family and folks eye you critically as they are not confident you will run the show up to expectations.

    a) You are hurt, you will prove them right to teach them a lesson.
    b) Withstand the blows and criticisms, occupy the chairman's seat, work your hardest to push the company's annual turnover and set up new factories to expand further.
    c) You hold a discussion with your family members and work out an alternative arrangement to run the organization.

15. You invest large sums in a television serial production company. When you begin production, your stories are rejected. You incur losses and do not receive any returns for your investments; you only succeed in running up a huge bill. You:

    a) Start afresh, introduce cost-effective concepts and recover your losses.
    b) Set up a business in any other field, which you believe can get you huge profits because of its boom in the economy.
    c) Seek employment elsewhere. You are not cut out for TV serial production. You'd rather be a TV star, model or actor.

Keys

Give yourself the corresponding points against each option

Question	*The Leader's Choice*	*a)*	*b)*	*c)*
1	b)	1	3	2
2	a)	3	2	1
3	b)	1	3	2
4	c)	1	2	3
5	b)	1	2	3
6	c)	1	2	3
7	c)	1	1	3
8	c)	1	2	3
9	b)	2	3	1
10	c)	1	2	3
11	a)	3	1	2
12	a)	3	2	1
13	b)	2	3	1
14	b)	1	3	2
15	a)	3	2	1
Total				

You have just benchmarked yourself against some of the top leaders in the industry. If your score is 30 or more, you have solid business acumen and a high level of motivation to succeed in your career. You are well on your way to the topmost cadre in your field.

APPENDIX II

Join the Bandwagon of Corporate Highfliers

There is always ample room for improvement. The best of women career contenders require greater exposure in certain areas as against others. You don't need to be an intellectually gifted person to be spotted! A charming personality, professional values that spell integrity, fine corporate etiquette, good impression management skills and efficient communication practices can do the trick in getting you that coveted post. However, your conduct and demeanour can unconsciously cast a positive/negative social perception among people around you. It is therefore imperative that you wear a pleasant countenance at all times and consciously develop certain techniques of voice modulation and intonation, body language, effective modes of communication and an arresting appearance. For more information on the lives of business celebrities and corporate culture, please write to us or log on to www.v2e.net.

On the basis of research (which is by no means comprehensive, though it is certainly representative), we have presented a few criteria that you will normally be judged on in the real-life corporate scenario.

The ABCs

There are many instances of managers who do not return calls, put callers on hold for a long time, greet people curtly and snap at virtually anyone who comes in their way! The belief that one can get a task done only by driving people around is a myth. Give politeness a chance. Thoughtfulness in your gestures and genuineness in endeavours will reflect your earnestness to treat people respectfully. Extending courtesies like *Good morning, Please* and *Thank you* can do wonders in helping you forge an impeccable reputation. Avoid stepping on another person's toes. This action is not only perceived as annoying but also an indication of how clumsy and socially inept you are.

Do not let emotion-laden beliefs affect your reasoning. When your emotions confront a logical argument face-to-face, address the conflict at hand and refrain from personal attacks.

If you want to hold everyone's attention, lowering your voice to a calm, huskier tone is often a better strategy than raising it.

In short, all that you learnt during your blithe kindergarten days can be applied to your boardroom too.

Gracious e-Manners

The responsiveness and efficiency of the business you handle are often judged by your emails. Even if you are hooked on to your customers, following e-manners would help in clinching that semi-finished deal. Use words economically when you draft a proposal. Make the subject line specific and use the CC and BCC fields judiciously.

Avoid forwarding emails in chains unnecessarily. Sign the email with your name and remember to provide your contact email ID/number(s)/address. Most importantly, avoid typing in CAPITAL letters! Doing so is considered highly unprofessional.

Phone Etiquette

Be sure to introduce yourself and personalize your communication. Identify the purpose of the call quickly. Do not waste much time in the conversation if the purpose of the call is not relevant to your goals and objective or the other party does not display any interest in what you have to offer.

The Big Boss

Take it that your boss is a person who doesn't like surprises. Do take him in confidence, no matter what you plan to do. Of course, there are always exceptions to the rule. Nonetheless, this small act on your part can make you move mountains in the organization!

Who's the Real Boss?

Strangely, a competitor can be a co-worker while a subordinate assumes the role of the big bad boss. What's more, this transformation can sometimes take place overnight! If you maintain consistency in your interactions instead of either expressing your displeasure or showering respect on their "corporate standing", you would gain in the long run.

No Gripe!

Avoid making interruptions. Instead, apologize if you need to. Perhaps, you could use written chits or comments if you wish to intervene in a discussion/ conversation and express your idea. Decide what complaints are worth filing and arrange them in the right format and style. Remember – the objective is not to accuse a person but to get your job done.

The Best Employee

Be as attentive to your best employee as you would be to your best customer. If you don't have your best employee you will soon lose your best customer.

Effective Employee Understanding

Managers and executives who communicate their ideas clearly are those who are sensitive to human needs, open to true dialogue with employees and efficient in imparting information with warmth and candour. A positive communication attitude and meticulous planning before embarking on any course of action will go a long way in increasing your adaptability to different channels of employee information. Overload of data must be dispensed with. Providing your employees more communication input than they can process will result in a decline in turnover and employee productivity.

Good performance feedback mechanisms, strong social support systems, suggestion systems, employee meetings, job satisfaction surveys and, above all, participative leadership are essential to improve the flow of upward communication (communication from lower levels of authority to higher levels) in an organization.

International Business Practices

In Rome, do as the Romans do! If you are taking off on a business tour in an unfamiliar city/country, try to grasp some knowledge and awareness of the language, time zone and food habits of the business location you are in. To err is human. So, if in doubt, err in a conservative fashion. Adhering to a conventional style is often much safer on such occasions.

Dress Code and Make-up

Nothing is more insulting to your co-workers than expressing lack of enthusiasm in the manner in which you dress and conduct yourself. When you select a particular outfit, cast your favourites aside and dress according to the occasion. For women, business suits have begun to serve as better substitutes for saris, today.

For women: Heavy makeup can be very off-putting. But don't opt for the plain Jane look either. Downplay that shade of blusher. Light, pleasing makeup can make your facial features more definite and symmetrical. Perhaps eyeliner would make your eyes more communicative. If you prefer a more western style, you can contour your eyelids with light eye shadow.

A common note: Avoid cloying perfumes/colognes/deodorants. Furthermore, being judgmental about other people's appearances won't augur well for your image either.

Cocktails and Business Parties

Few corporate executives guzzle and gorge at dinner parties. Please understand that a business party is an occasion for closing deals, presenting new business proposals and acquiring new clients. You can taste your favourites later!

While at the dinner table however, you must be mindful of using the correct hand to operate your fork and knife! You could add a little zing with your own manner and style. Also, it is important to be adaptive to every culture and tradition.

Invitations

Personalize your invitations and facilitate an easy response, if necessary. You could resort to RSVP tactics. If you are incurring your own expenses to conduct a particular event, please ensure that your invitation projects the right message.

Gifts and Presents

Many factors are to be kept in view while offering a gift, of which the purpose, occasion, receiver and manner of presentation are the most important ones. Gifting should be a mutual feel-good process. A present extended as an obligation or a return gift is not a gift at all.

APPENDIX III

Flex Your Management Muscles

Here is a set of unusual management exercises that will determine the degree of your career-mindedness as well as your managerial abilities and team-building skills. If you want an appropriate analysis of your answers, do please reply truthfully to the following questions. Good luck!

1. You desire to dive into a career which does not agree with the mindset of your husband and/or your family of origin. However, it definitely tallies with your talents and inner thirsts. Now, you find a perfect opportunity to make a foray into your dream career. A job in a company that you've been craving for knocks at your doorstep. Your family discourages you from accepting it for various reasons. You would:

   a) Take it up at all costs, providing no explanations to your folks.
   b) Take it up after giving your family a broad-based account of the job at hand and explaining to them how you could make a difference to yourself and to others, as it enables you to give expression to your talents and elicits the best from you.
   c) Say 'No' to the offer and do what you feel will please your folks because you dread facing opposition from them.

2. You have a quarrel with your mother/spouse before you leave for work, one morning. As you travel to your office, you are not really in the best of spirits. On reaching your cubicle, you detect a trivial disturbing factor: either a missing pen-stand or an overflowing trashcan.

   a) You take deep breaths and count to ten till the storm inside you subsides. Then you plan your agenda for the day and begin your work.
   b) The emotions are too much for you to handle. You blow your fuse and give a good piece of your mind to the nearest subordinate.
   c) You try your level best to engage yourself in work, which would require you to stay back at your office for longer hours to delay confrontations with your mother/spouse.

3. For many days on end, you have been planning that much-awaited weekend escapade for a perfect, romantic holiday with your family. A sudden 'Now or never' meeting with a very promising client crops up at the last minute.

a) You make alternate arrangements to see that the meeting takes place as scheduled, while you take off on your holiday – perhaps by having a teleconference or a live session with your client over the Net.

b) You won't let work eat into your personal life too. You'd rather let this opportunity skip by without much ado. There will be many more next time!

c) You would rather forgo the holiday and attend the meeting. You can't abandon your colleagues who need you. Moreover, your presence is crucial for clinching the deal.

4. As a senior executive of a prestigious automobile company, you rise early each morning and dash off to work, returning home only in time for dinner. Your spouse works night shifts in a highly reputed international BPO conglomerate. You barely get more than an hour to talk to him/her before you have to dash off. Your job is going great guns. But you begin to realize that the discordant job timings are putting a strain on the relationship. You would:

   a) Turn a deaf ear to the increasing gap between you and your spouse. No sweat. That's how all DINK (Double Income, No Kids) couples are.

   b) Relinquish your responsibilities in the company. The stress levels are too high for you to manage. You prefer staying home and salvaging your relationship.

   c) Look for another job, which would give you ample time to put the relationship back on track. Myriad opportunities are lying in store for you. So, why should you worry?

5. You are a fresh MBA graduate and it is your first day in a private insurance company. You are hired as a management trainee and promised that you will be confirmed in the management cadre within a year. The management is however reorganized to streamline workflow and combine and upgrade clerical jobs. As a result, you are made to take charge of a six-person unit within a month.

   a) You will arrange a meeting with the persons in your team and seek their support and cooperation to accomplish the task.

   b) You goad your team to work longer hours and threaten to cut their salaries if they do not participate actively in performing the assigned tasks.

c) You will confront the management and tell them that you are right now not capable of taking up this assignment.

6. You are hired as a software trainer in a computer corporation started nine months ago. After a few weeks, you observe a wide discrepancy between the values expressed in the company's corporate culture document statements and the actual management practices within the organization. You:

   a) Blow the whistle on the management and walk out of the company in a huff.

   b) Challenge the inconsistencies between the company's values and managerial behaviour.

   c) Become disillusioned. This company isn't different from any other. Why will executives change traditional values that govern an organization? You feel you should accept things the way they are.

7. A twin offer is placed before you – a posting in another city/country as well as a promotion. Your husband and children are not going to be very happy if you stay away from them for many months. You would:

   a) Decline the offer and remain right where you are. You have neither the verve nor the inclination to explore alternative options.

   b) Accept the promotion right away. This opportunity is too good to miss!

   c) Look for other jobs which offer similar positions within the city or hunt for better posts even within the company that you presently work for.

8. You are a high-ranking female corporate executive in a bank. A potential male rival (who is older than you by five-ten years) is vying for the post of Deputy CEO, which you are also entitled to. You believe the post is rightfully yours. What is your line of thought?

   a) You deserve the promotion because you can take on newer and more challenging responsibilities with better finesse than your competitor. After all, you are the person who introduced team-based ethos in the bank and established strong mentoring systems.

   b) You have a pressing financial problem at home and a raise is definitely what you have your eyes peeled for.

c) You can't wait to rout your rival and show him that women can be better corporate heads and more efficient managers than men. Why should men receive more opportunities than women?

9. You are chosen to clinch a deal with a man only because you are a young woman and a very attractive one, at that. You would:

   a) Wear your most attractive outfit to strike a successful deal with your client, thereby expressing your loyalty to the organization.
   b) Impress upon the management that you are capable of closing deals on the basis of intellectual capabilities. You politely refuse to take up this assignment because you feel it has not been given to you for the right reason.
   c) Explicitly state that you refuse to deal with a man for such an absurd reason.

10. As an employee, you are aware that one of your colleagues (who is close to the top management) is leaking out confidential financial information to a rival company. You would:

   a) Keep quiet and mind your own business. The subsequent decrease in the company's profits is solely the management's problem.
   b) Discuss the matter with him and remind him of the consequences if he does not mend his ways.
   c) Report the matter to the management after ensuring that your identity would be kept confidential.

11. A new sales manager is hired for a company. He is very resourceful, dynamic and participative. Overnight, he establishes his competence and becomes the company's passport to higher levels of profitability. You are a man who is over 40 years of age and the Executive Director of the company. One morning, a conscientious young female employee reports that the sales manager has been discriminating and harassing her sexually for many weeks. The news is unbelievable but true. What action would you take?

   a) You believe that the young lady is using her gender to slander the poor sales manager. You take her to task, pointing out to her how upset you are of her display of professional jealousy.
   b) You summon the sales manager to your chambers and tell him how much an asset his presence is to the organization and impress

upon him the need to treat all his colleagues with respect, which can also earn him a promotion in the near future.

c) Fire the sales manager. Sexual harassment finds no place in the organization, no matter how brilliant the predator is.

12. You are a young marketing manager of an FMCG company. Your career takes you through hosts of business tours across the country. In recent times, your husband and in-laws have been exerting pressure on you to have a baby. (With the progress of each day, you are not getting any younger!) You would:

    a) Discuss the matter with your husband and in-laws and find out in what manner everyone can pitch in to support you. You look for external sources of support to take care of your child. After making such arrangements you can consider raising children.

    b) Abandon the rigours of your career and throw yourself into the web of family affairs.

    c) Give up the idea of having children. You have no intentions of jeopardizing a promising future.

13. As a first-line manager, you conduct strong performance appraisals and practice guidelines for effective feedback to your employees. Over time, you discover that some of your employees become overtly angry, hostile, morose and verbally abusive, on hearing that their actual performance is not as good as they had perceived it to be. You are caught in a maelstrom of conflicting pressures without a 'perfect' solution.

    a) You accept the need to provide performance feedback to all your employees and deem it essential to maintain fair relationships within groups and encourage them to comply with regulations.

    b) As people would venture to say very often, the poor performance of an employee is to be blamed largely on the boss. So, you refrain from sharing your honest perceptions of the performance of your employees at the risk of hurting their morale.

    c) You call them for a meeting and explain to them the importance of a performance appraisal. You introduce positive reinforcements and assure them of better reward systems and your confidence in their abilities.

14. You are the head of the HR department of a prominent MNC. One of the corporate executives has a heart attack and undergoes a bypass surgery. This incident is an urgent indication of the high levels of stress generated by work overload, time deadlines, lesser leisure time and constant jetlags which arise from frequent travel. You would:

    a) Implement comprehensive intervention programmes, strengthen the social support systems within the organization, introduce flexi-time work options and incorporate relaxation techniques like yoga etc.

    b) Send overworked employees out on a sabbatical.

    c) Recruit employees more selectively, keeping in view the Person-Environment (P-E) fit factor, certain that some people are simply not cut out for executing certain tasks because of their physical and psychological frailties.

15. You are a first-generation entrepreneur, who has established a steel factory, whose turnover touches nearly Rs.3000 crore today. You are planning to retire in a few days, confident that your only son will take the baton from you. One day, your son announces that he aspires to forge a career in advertising and makes it very clear that he is not interested in managing the business. Now, this is devastating news for you.

    a) You proclaim that advertising is a facade and compel him to join the business, which you very painstakingly built over the years and brought to its current status.

    b) Your son hasn't understood your wish. What should the company live for? You decide to go public.

    c) You provide your son the freedom to make his own choices. However, you are always there to provide him guidance and be his sounding board.

Messages

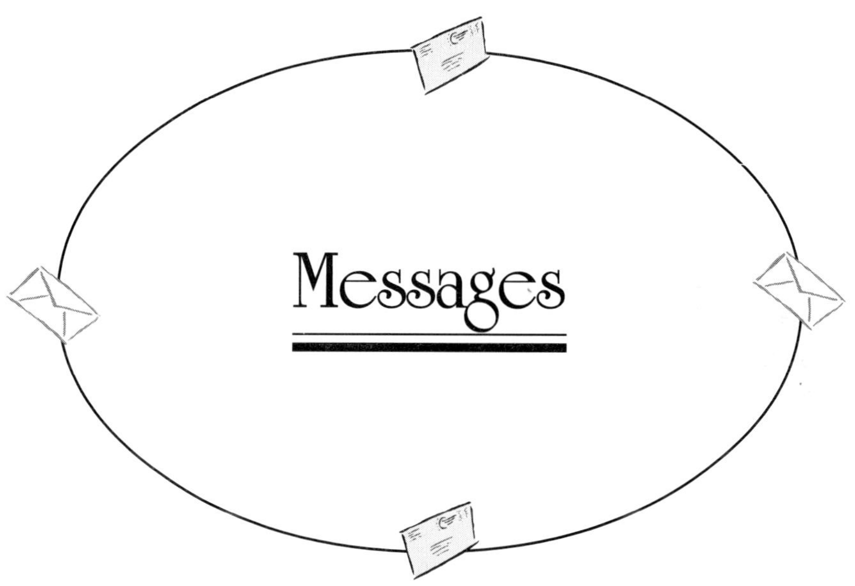

MESSAGES

The Voyage to Excellence could not be more aptly named. I am amazed at the passion with which Debashish Ghosh and Nischinta Amarnath have undertaken the project. It reflects an enormous desire to learn, to grow and to evolve, qualities that I admire and which I wish I had seen more often in my days as a college lecturer. The struggle that the two have gone through, juggling academic requirements with the demands of travelling and meeting some of the country's finest business brains has set me thinking. If all our youngsters showed as much enthusiasm in their work – whatever it be – our academic system would be forced to change in response. Rote learning would give way to celebrating the spirit of inquiry and superficial information would give way to deep understanding.

I couldn't agree more with their choice of subject. Businesswomen in India have never had it easy and this book is an excellent indicator of exactly what are the problems that plague their careers. Some of those profiled have battled personal crises, others have fought against the invisible glass ceiling, still others have leaned on the support of family and friends to balance home and office.

I have always believed the future belongs to women. This is one more reason for me to reaffirm my view.

–Prabhu Chawla

Editor, India Today

This book is not just about women in business. It is a celebration of what it takes to succeed in the face of high social and cultural odds. There is no innate reason why business success should be gender-specific. Nevertheless, it is a hard reality that progress on the corporate ladder is still largely male dominated. It is inspiring therefore to delve into the stories of women who have shattered the shibboleths and, in the process, emerged as icons of corporate folklore. Their stories are stories of passion, courage, and outstanding performance.

I have had the privilege of meeting and interacting with many of the women entrepreneurs included in this book. I am delighted that their lives and successes are being celebrated. I am even more delighted that one of the

A good beginning, the book could be a genesis of who's who of Indian women who have made their mark in business and enterprise. A laudable and fledgling effort.

–Satya Saran
Editor, Femina

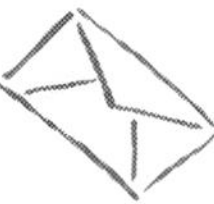

They boldly go where few Indian youth have gone before and chronicle the lives of 21 extraordinary women. A superlative attempt.

www.sify.com

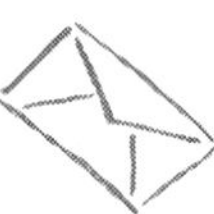

The Voyage to Excellence is an extremely timely enterprising venture of two young authors. Their zeal and perseverance is truly contagious. The book would make for very interesting reading. The exciting journeys of great achievements of 21 of India's top women business leaders is a pioneering venture that will, I am sure, serve as a beacon for thousands of young girls and boys who are on the threshold of their careers.

–Dr. Shekhar Chaudhuri
Director, IIM, Kolkata

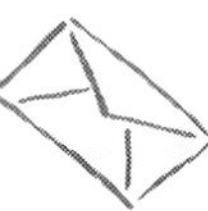